Pro Node.js for Developers

Colin J. Ihrig

Apress·

Pro Node.js for Developers

ISBN-13 (pbk): 978-1-4302-5860-5

ISBN-13 (electronic): 978-1-4302-5861-2

President and Publisher: Paul Manning
Lead Editor: Ewan Buckingham
Technical Reviewer: Andy Olsen
Editorial Board: Steve Anglin, Mark Beckner, Ewan Buckingham, Gary Cornell, Louise Corrigan, Jim DeWolf, Jonathan Gennick, Jonathan Hassell, Robert Hutchinson, Michelle Lowman, James Markham, Matthew Moodie, Jeff Olson, Jeffrey Pepper, Douglas Pundick, Ben Renow-Clarke, Dominic Shakeshaft, Gwenan Spearing, Matt Wade, Steve Weiss, Tom Welsh
Coordinating Editor: Mark Powers
Copy Editors: Thomas McCarthy and Kezia Endsley
Compositor: SPi Global
Indexer: SPi Global
Artist: SPi Global
Cover Designer: Anna Ishchenko

Distributed to the book trade worldwide by Springer Science+Business Media New York, 233 Spring Street, 6th Floor, New York, NY 10013. Phone 1-800-SPRINGER, fax (201) 348-4505, e-mail orders-ny@springer-sbm.com, or visit www.springeronline.com. Apress Media, LLC is a California LLC and the sole member (owner) is Springer Science + Business Media Finance Inc (SSBM Finance Inc). SSBM Finance Inc is a Delaware corporation.

For information on translations, please e-mail rights@apress.com, or visit www.apress.com.

Apress and friends of ED books may be purchased in bulk for academic, corporate, or promotional use. eBook versions and licenses are also available for most titles. For more information, reference our Special Bulk Sales–eBook Licensing web page at www.apress.com/bulk-sales.

Any source code or other supplementary material referenced by the author in this text is available to readers at www.apress.com/9781430258605. For detailed information about how to locate your book's source code, go to www.apress.com/source-code/.

This book is dedicated to my son, CJ. I love you so much!

This book is also dedicated to the entire Node.js community.

Contents at a Glance

Contents

About the Author

Colin Ihrig has been experimenting with JavaScript for fun and profit for over 15 years. He is currently a full-time Node.js engineer, as well as a JavaScript writer and evangelist in his spare time. Colin received his Bachelor of Science in Engineering and Master of Science in Computer Engineering from the University of Pittsburgh in 2005 and 2008, respectively. Colin can be reached via his personal web page at http://www.cjihrig.com.

About the Technical Reviewer

Andy Olsen is a freelance consultant/trainer based in the UK, and has been working in distributed systems for 20 years. Andy started working in C in the mid 1980s, but it might as well have been the mid 1880s, it seems so long ago. Andy migrated into C++, Java, and .NET as times and fashions changed, and is currently kept (too?) busy in web-based systems, both client-side and server-side. Andy lives by the seaside in Swansea and enjoys running, coffee shops, and watching the Swans.

Acknowledgments

I would like to thank everyone who helped make this book possible. Special thanks to Mark Powers and Ewan Buckingham of the Apress editorial team. I would also like to thank the technical reviewer, Andy Olsen, for his valuable feedback. Of course, many thanks go out to my friends and family.

Introduction

Since its creation in 2009, Node.js has grown into a powerful and increasingly popular asynchronous development framework, used for creating highly scalable JavaScript applications. Respected companies such as Dow Jones, LinkedIn, and Walmart are among the many organizations to have seen Node's potential and adopted it into their businesses.

Pro Node.js for Developers provides a comprehensive guide to this exciting young technology. You will be introduced to Node at a high level before diving deeply into the key concepts and APIs that underpin its operation. Building upon your existing JavaScript skills, you'll be shown how to use Node.js to build both web- and network-based applications, to deal with various data sources, capture and generate events, spawn and control child processes, and much more.

Once you've mastered these skills, you'll learn more advanced software engineering skills that will give your code a professional edge. You'll learn how to create easily reusable code modules, debug and test your applications quickly and effectively, and scale your code from a single thread to the cloud as demand for your application increases.

CHAPTER 1

■ ■ ■

Getting Started

JavaScript was initially named Mocha when it was developed at Netscape in 1995 by Brendan Eich. In September 1995, beta releases of Netscape Navigator 2.0 were shipped with Mocha, which had been renamed LiveScript. By December 1995 LiveScript, after another renaming, had become JavaScript, the current name. Around that time Netscape was working closely with Sun, the company responsible for creating the Java programming language. The choice of the name JavaScript caused a lot of speculation. Many people thought that Netscape was trying to piggyback on the hot name Java, a buzzword at the time. Unfortunately, the naming choice caused a lot of confusion, as many automatically assumed that the two languages were related somehow. In reality they have very little in common.

Despite the confusion, JavaScript became a very successful client-side scripting language. In response to JavaScript's success, Microsoft created its own implementation, named JScript, and released it with Internet Explorer 3.0 in August 1996. In November 1996 Netscape submitted JavaScript for standardization to Ecma International, an international standards organization. In June 1997 JavaScript became the standard ECMA-262.

Over the years, JavaScript has remained the de facto standard for client-side development. However, the server space was a completely different story. For the most part, the server realm has belonged to languages such as PHP and Java. A number of projects have implemented JavaScript as a server language, but none of them were particularly successful. Two major hurdles blocked JavaScript's widespread adoption on the server. The first was its reputation. JavaScript has long been viewed as a toy language, suitable only for amateurs. The second hurdle was JavaScript's poor performance compared with that of some other languages.

However, JavaScript had one big thing going for it. The Web was undergoing unprecedented growth, and the browser wars were raging. As the only language supported by every major browser, JavaScript engines began receiving attention from Google, Apple, and other companies. All of that attention led to huge improvements in JavaScript performance. Suddenly JavaScript wasn't lagging anymore.

The development community took note of JavaScript's newfound power and began creating interesting applications. In 2009 Ryan Dahl created Node.js, a framework primarily used to create highly scalable servers for web applications. Node.js, or simply Node, is written in C++ and JavaScript. To drive Node, Dahl tapped into the power of Google's V8 JavaScript engine (V8 is the engine inside Google Chrome, the most popular browser in existence). Using V8, developers can write full-blown applications in JavaScript - applications that would normally be written in a language like C or Java. Thus, with the invention of Node, JavaScript finally became a bona fide server-side language.

The Node Execution Model

In addition to speed, Node brought an unconventional execution model to the table. To understand how Node is different, we should compare it with Apache, the popular web server in the Linux, Apache, MySQL, and PHP (LAMP) software stack. First, Apache processes only HTTP requests, leaving application logic to be implemented in a language such as PHP or Java. Node removes a layer of complexity by combining server and application logic in one place. Some developers have criticized this model for eliminating the traditional separation of concerns employed in the LAMP stack. However, this approach also gives Node unprecedented flexibility as a server.

Node also differs from many other servers in its use of concurrency. A server like Apache maintains a pool of threads for handling client connections. This approach lacks scalability because threads are fairly resource-intensive. Additionally, a busy server quickly consumes all of the available threads; as a result, more threads, which are expensive to create and tear down, are spawned. Node, on the other hand, executes within a single thread. While this may seem like a bad idea, in practice it works well because of the way most server applications work. Normally, a server receives a client request, then performs some high-latency I/O operation such as a file read or database query. During this time the server blocks, waiting for the I/O operation to complete. Instead of sitting idle, the server could be handling more requests or doing other useful work.

In traditional servers, it's acceptable for a thread to do nothing while blocking on an I/O operation. However, Node has only one thread, and blocking it causes the entire server to hang. To mitigate this problem, Node uses nonblocking I/O almost exclusively. For example, if Node needs to perform a database query, it simply issues the query and then processes something else. When the query finally returns, it triggers an asynchronous callback function that is responsible for processing the query's results. A pseudocode example of this process is shown in Listing 1-1.

Listing 1-1. Pseudocode Example of a Nonblocking Database Query

```
var sql = "SELECT * FROM table";

database.query(sql, function(results) {
  // process the results
});
// do something else instead of waiting
```

Node's nonblocking, asynchronous execution model provides extremely scalable server solutions with minimal overhead. Many high-profile companies, including Microsoft, LinkedIn, Yahoo!, and the retail giant Walmart have taken notice of Node and begun implementing projects with it. For example, LinkedIn migrated its entire mobile stack to Node and "went from running 15 servers with 15 instances (virtual servers) on each physical machine, to just four instances that can handle double the traffic." Node has also received significant media recognition, such as winning the 2012 InfoWorld Technology of the Year Award.

Installing Node

The first step to getting started with Node is installation. This section will help you get Node up and running on your Ubuntu, OS X, or Windows machine. The simplest way to install Node is via the Install button on the Node home page, http://nodejs.org, shown in Figure 1-1. This will download the binaries or installer appropriate for your operating system.

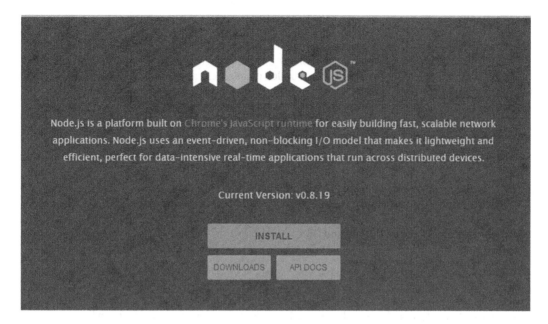

Figure 1-1. *Installing Node from the project home page*

You can also browse all of the platforms' binaries, installers, and source code at http://nodejs.org/download. Windows users will most likely want to download the Windows Installer (.msi file), while Mac users should opt for the Mac OS X Installer (.pkg file). Linux and SunOS users can download binaries, but it is probably simpler to install using a package manager.

Installing via Package Managers

For instructions on installing Node via your operating system's package manager, go to https://github.com/joyent/node/wiki/Installing-Node.js-via-package-manager. This page contains instructions for Windows, OS X, and Linux. Again, Windows and Mac users should use the previously discussed installers. As far as Linux is concerned, instructions are available for Gentoo, Debian, Linux Mint, Ubuntu, openSUSE, SLE, Red Hat, Fedora, Arch Linux, FreeBSD, and OpenBSD.

Ubuntu users can install Node and all requisite software using the Advanced Packaging Tool (APT) commands shown in Listing 1-2. These steps also install npm, Node's package management software (covered in Chapter 2).

Listing 1-2. Installing Node Using Ubuntu's Package Manager

```
$ sudo apt-get install python-software-properties python g++ make
$ sudo add-apt-repository ppa:chris-lea/node.js
$ sudo apt-get update
$ sudo apt-get install nodejs npm
```

If the add-apt-repository command fails, install the software-properties-common package using the command shown in Listing 1-3.

Listing 1-3. Installing the Software-Properties-Common Package

```
$ sudo apt-get install software-properties-common
```

Building from Source

If you want to contribute to Node's C++ core, or simply experiment with its functionality, you will need to compile the project's source code. You can obtain the source code from the download page, or from the project's GitHub repository, https://github.com/joyent/node. Once the code is downloaded, extract it from the archive if applicable. Prior to building Node, Ubuntu users need to install Python and other build tools; use the command shown in Listing 1-4. When installing Python, be sure to install version 2.7, not the newer Python 3.

Listing 1-4. Installing Prerequisite Software Packages on Ubuntu

```
$ sudo apt-get install python-software-properties python g++ make
```

Ubuntu and OS X users can build Node by issuing the commands shown in Listing 1-5 from within the source code directory. Note that the full path to the source code directory should not contain any spaces.

Listing 1-5. Installing Node from Source on Ubuntu and OS X

```
./configure
make
sudo make install
```

On Windows, you need to install Visual C++ and Python 2.7 in order to build Node. Visual C++ can be downloaded for free from Microsoft with Visual Studio Express. Python is also available free of charge at www.python.org/. To compile Node, issue the command shown in Listing 1-6.

Listing 1-6. Installing Node from Source on Windows

```
> vcbuild.bat release
```

Final Installation Steps

No matter which installation route you decided on, by this point Node should be ready to use. To verify that everything is set up correctly, open a new terminal window, and run the node executable (see Listing 1-7). The -v flag causes Node to print the installed version and then exit. In this example, version 0.10.18 of Node is installed.

Listing 1-7. Checking the Version of Node from the Command Line

```
$ node -v
v0.10.18
```

You should also verify that npm is installed (see Listing 1-8).

Listing 1-8. Checking the Version of npm from the Command Line

```
$ npm -v
1.3.8
```

A final installation note: it's likely that you'll need to install Python and a C++ compiler on your machine even if you didn't install Node from source. Doing this ensures that native modules written in C++ can be compiled and run with your Node installation. On Windows, this involves installing Microsoft's Visual C++ compiler (see the previous section, "Building from Source"). For any other operating system, the build essentials should include the necessary compiler.

The Read-Eval-Print-Loop

Node provides an interactive shell, known as the *Read-Eval-Print-Loop*, or REPL. The REPL reads input from the user, evaluates the input as JavaScript code, prints the result, and then waits for more input. The REPL is useful for debugging and for experimenting with small snippets of JavaScript code. To start the REPL, launch Node with no command line arguments. You then see the REPL command prompt, the > character. From the prompt, begin entering arbitrary JavaScript code.

Listing 1-9 shows how to start the REPL and input code. In this example, a variable, named foo, is created with the string value "Hello World!". On the third line, the REPL prints "undefined" because the variable declaration statement returns no value. Next, the statement foo; causes the value of foo to be inspected. As expected, the REPL returns the string "Hello World!". Finally, the value of foo is printed to the terminal using the console.log() function. After foo is printed, the REPL displays "undefined" again, because console.log() returns no value.

Listing 1-9. Starting the REPL and Inputting JavaScript Code

```
$ node
> var foo = "Hello World!";
undefined
> foo;
'Hello World!'
> console.log(foo);
Hello World!
undefined
```

You can also enter multiline expressions in the REPL. For example, a for loop has been entered into the REPL in Listing 1-10. The ... is used by the REPL to indicate a multiline expression in progress. Note that ... is displayed by the REPL, not typed by the user.

Listing 1-10. An Example of Executing a Multiline Expression in the REPL

```
> for (var i = 0; i < 3; i++) {
... console.log(i);
... }
0
1
2
undefined
```

REPL Features

The REPL has a number of features that increase usability, the most useful of which is the ability to browse previously issued commands using the up and down arrow keys. To terminate any command and return to a blank prompt, type Control+C. Pressing Control+C twice from a blank line causes the REPL to terminate. You can quit the REPL at any time by pressing Control+D. You can use the Tab key to see a list of possible completions to the current command. If there is only one possible option, Node automatically inserts it. The list includes keywords, functions, and variables. For example, Listing 1-11 shows the completion options when t is entered at the prompt.

5

Listing 1-11. Autocomplete Options Shown by Typing t Followed by Tab

```
> t
this          throw        true         try
typeof        tls          tty          toLocaleString
toString
```

The REPL also provides a special variable, _ (underscore), that always contains the result of the last expression. Listing 1-12 shows several example uses of _. First, an array of strings is created, causing _ to reference the array. The pop() method is then used to remove the last element of the array, baz. Finally, the length of baz is accessed, causing _ to become 3.

Listing 1-12. Example Uses of the _ Variable

```
> ["foo", "bar", "baz"]
[ 'foo', 'bar', 'baz' ]
> _.pop();
'baz'
> _.length
3
> _
3
```

REPL Commands
.help

The .help command displays all of the available REPL commands. Listing 1-13 shows the output of running the .help command.

Listing 1-13. Output of the .help REPL Command

```
> .help
.break Sometimes you get stuck, this gets you out
.clear Alias for .break
.exit Exit the repl
.help Show repl options
.load Load JS from a file into the REPL session
.save Save all evaluated commands in this REPL session to a file
```

.exit

The .exit command terminates the REPL. This command is equivalent to pressing Control+D.

.break

The .break command, used to bail out of a multiline expression, is useful if you make a mistake or simply choose not to complete the expression. Listing 1-14 shows an example of using the .break command to terminate a for loop prior to completion. Notice that the normal > prompt is shown after the .break command.

Listing 1-14. Terminating a Multiline Expression Using the .break Command

```
> for (var i = 0; i < 10; i++) {
... .break
>
```

.save filename

The .save command saves the current REPL session to the file specified in filename. If the file does not exist, it is created. If the file does exist, the existing file is overwritten. REPL commands and output are not saved. Listing 1-15 shows an example use of the .save command. In this example, the current session is saved to the file repl-test.js. The resulting contents of repl-test.js are shown in Listing 1-16. Notice that the file does not contain the REPL prompt or output or the .save command.

Listing 1-15. Saving the Current REPL Session Using the .save Command

```
> var foo = [1, 2, 3];
undefined
> foo.forEach(function(value) {
... console.log(value);
... });
1
2
3
undefined
> .save repl-test.js
Session saved to:repl-test.js
```

Listing 1-16. The Contents of repl-test.js Generated by the .save Command

```
var foo = [1, 2, 3];
foo.forEach(function(value) {
console.log(value);
});
```

.load filename

The .load command executes the JavaScript file specified in filename. The file is executed as if each line were typed directly into the REPL. Listing 1-17 shows the output of loading the file repl-test.js from Listing 1-16.

Listing 1-17. The result of executing repl-test.js, using the .load command

```
> .load repl-test.js
> var foo = [1, 2, 3];
undefined
> foo.forEach(function(value) {
... console.log(value);
... });
1
2
3
undefined
```

.clear

Similar to .break, .clear can be used to terminate multiline expressions. .clear is also used to reset the REPL's context object. At this point, you don't need to understand the details, but Listing 1-18 shows a Node program that embeds a REPL. In other words, running this program actually invokes an instance of the REPL. Additionally, you can define a custom execution environment for the REPL. In this case, the embedded REPL has a defined variable, foo, that holds the string "Hello REPL". Calling .clear from within the embedded REPL resets the context and deletes foo.

Listing 1-18. Embedding a REPL Within Another Node Program

```
var repl = require("repl");

repl.start({}).context.foo = "Hello REPL";
```

Executing Node Programs

Although the REPL environment is useful, it is seldom used in production systems. Instead, programs are written as one or more JavaScript files and then interpreted by Node. The simplest Node program is shown in Listing 1-19. The example simply prints the string "Hello World!" to the console.

Listing 1-19. Source Code for the Node Hello World! Program

```
console.log("Hello World!");
```

Copy the code in Listing 1-19 into a new file, and save it as hello.js. Next, open a terminal window, and execute hello.js (see Listing 1-20). Note that Node does not require you to specify the .js file extension. If the input file is not found and no file extension is provided, Node will try adding the extensions .js, .json, and .node. Node interprets .js files as JavaScript source code and files with a .json extension as *JavaScript Object Notation* (JSON) files. Files with a .node extension are treated as compiled add-on modules.

Listing 1-20. Executing a Node Program from the Command Line

```
$ node hello.js
```

■ **Note**   JSON is a plain text standard for data interchange. This book assumes that the reader is already familiar with JSON. However, if you need an introduction or refresher, JSON is covered in Appendix A.

Summary

Congratulations! You have officially taken the first steps toward developing Node applications. This chapter has given you a high-level introduction to Node and guided you through the installation process. You have even written some Node code using the REPL. The remainder of this book builds on this chapter, covering the most important aspects of Node development. Node is best known for creating scalable web servers, so of course that feature is covered. However, you'll also learn much more, including file system programming, streaming data, application scaling, and Node's module system.

CHAPTER 2

■ ■ ■

The Node Module System

As a developer, you can solve many complex problems using the core Node functionality. However, one of Node's true strengths is its developer community and abundance of third-party modules. Keeping track of all of these modules is Node's package manager, npm. The npm FAQ page jokingly states that npm is not an acronym for "Node package manager" and instead is a recursive backronym abbreviation for "npm is not an acronym." Regardless of its meaning, npm is a command line tool that, since Node version 0.6.3, comes bundled with the Node environment.

What npm does—and does very well—is manage Node modules and their dependencies. At the time of writing, there were over 47,000 packages in the official registry. You can browse all of the available packages at the registry's site, https://npmjs.org/. In addition to each individual module, the site shows various rankings, including which modules are the most popular and which are depended upon the most. If you'd rather get your hands dirty on the command line, you can search the registry using the npm search command, which lets you search for packages based on one or more keywords. For example, npm search can be used to locate all the modules containing the word database in the name or description (see Listing 2-1). The first time you run this command, expect to experience a short delay as npm builds a local index.

Listing 2-1. Using npm search to Locate Modules in the npm Registry

```
$ npm search database
```

Installing Packages

In order to use a module, you must install it on your machine. This is normally as simple as downloading a few JavaScript source files (some modules require downloading or compiling binaries as well). To install a package, type npm install, followed by the package name. For example, the commander module provides methods for implementing command line interfaces. To install the latest version of commander, issue the command shown in Listing 2-2.

Listing 2-2. Installing the Latest Version of the commander Package Using npm

```
$ npm install commander
```

If you're not interested in installing the latest version of a package, you can specify a version number. Node modules follow a *major.minor.patch* versioning scheme. For example, to install commander version 1.0.0, use the command shown in Listing 2-3. The @ character is used to separate the package name from the version.

Listing 2-3. Installing Version 1.0.0 of commander

```
$ npm install commander@1.0.0
```

Changes to the major version number can indicate that a module has changed in a non-backwards-compatible way (known as a breaking change). Even changes to the minor version can accidentally introduce breaking changes. Therefore, you'll typically want to install the latest patch of a certain release—a scenario that npm supports with the x wildcard. The command shown in Listing 2-4 installs the latest patch of version 1.0 of commander. (Note that the x wildcard can also be used in place of the major and minor revisions.)

Listing 2-4. Installing the Latest Patch of commander 1.0

```
$ npm install commander@1.0.x
```

You can also select versions using relational version range descriptors. Relational version range descriptors select the most recent version that matches a given set of criteria. The various relational version range descriptors supported by npm are listed in Table 2-1.

Table 2-1. *Relational Version Range Descriptors*

Relational Version Range Descriptor	Version Criteria
=version	Exactly matches version.
>version	Greater than version.
>=version	Greater than or equal to version.
<version	Less than version.
<=version	Less than or equal to version.
~version	Greater than or equal to version, but less than the next major version.
*	Newest version available.
""	Newest version available.
$version_1$ - $version_2$	Greater than or equal to $version_1$, and less than or equal to $version_2$.
$range_1$ || $range_2$	Matches versions specified by either $range_1$ and $range_2$.

Based on Table 2-1, all of the commands in Listing 2-5 are valid npm commands.

Listing 2-5. Various npm install Commands Using Relational Version Range Descriptors

```
$ npm install commander@"=1.1.0"
$ npm install commander@">1.0.0"
$ npm install commander@"~1.1.0"
$ npm install commander@"*"
$ npm install commander@""
$ npm install commander@">=1.0.0 <1.1.0"
$ npm install commander@"1.0.0 - 1.1.0"
$ npm install commander@"<=1.0.0 || >=1.1.0"
```

Installing from URLs

In addition, npm allows packages to be installed directly from git URLs. These URLs must take on one of the forms shown in Listing 2-6. In the listing, commit-ish represents a tag, SHA, or branch that can be supplied as an argument to git checkout. Note that the links in the example do not point to any specific git projects.

> ■ **Note** You do not need to understand `git` and GitHub to use Node. However, most Node modules use the GitHub ecosystem for source control and bug tracking. Although GitHub and its use are well outside the scope of this book, it is highly advisable to become familiar with it.

Listing 2-6. git URL Formats Supported by npm

```
git://github.com/user/project.git#commit-ish
git+ssh://user@hostname:project.git#commit-ish
git+ssh://user@hostname/project.git#commit-ish
git+http://user@hostname/project/blah.git#commit-ish
git+https://user@hostname/project/blah.git#commit-ish
```

Packages can also be installed from tarball URLs. For example, to install the master branch of a GitHub repository, use the syntax shown in Listing 2-7. Though this URL does not point to an actual repository, you can experiment by downloading the commander module: `https://github.com/visionmedia/commander.js/tarball/master`.

Listing 2-7. Installing a Tarball from a GitHub Repository

```
$ npm install https://github.com/user/project/tarball/master
```

Package Locations

When packages are installed, they are saved somewhere on your local machine. Typically, this location is a subdirectory named node_modules within your current directory. To determine the location, use the command npm root. You can also view all the installed modules using the npm ls command. After installing the commander module, you can verify that it exists using npm ls. For the purposes of this example, install version 1.3.2. Listing 2-8 shows that commander version 1.3.2 is installed. Also, notice that a module named keypress is installed. The tree structure indicates that commander depends on the keypress module. Since npm is able to recognize this dependency, it automatically installs any required modules.

Listing 2-8. Listing All of the Currently Installed Packages Using npm ls

```
$ npm ls
/home/colin/npm-test
└─┬ commander@1.3.2
  └── keypress@0.1.0
```

You can also see the installed modules by browsing the node_modules subdirectory. In this example, commander is installed in node_modules/commander, and keypress is installed in node_modules/commander/node_modules/keypress. If keypress had any dependencies, they would be installed in yet another node_modules subdirectory under the keypress directory.

Global Packages

Packages, as described thus far, are libraries that are included in your program. Referred to as local packages, these must be installed in every project using them. Another type of package, known as a global package, needs to be installed in only one location. Although global packages typically do not include code libraries, they can. As a rule of thumb, global packages normally contain command line tools, which should be included in the PATH environment variable.

To install a package globally, simply issue npm install with the -g or --global option. In fact, you can process global packages by adding the -g option to most npm commands. For example, you can view the installed global packages by issuing the command npm ls -g. You can also locate the global node_modules folder using the npm root -g command.

Linking Packages

Using npm, you can create links to local packages. When you link to a package, it can be referenced as if it were a global package. This is especially useful if you are developing a module and want another project to reference your local copy of the module. Linking is also useful if you want to deploy your module without publishing it to the public npm registry.

Package linking is a two-step process. The first step, creating the link, is done by changing to the directory of the project you want to make linkable. Listing 2-9 shows how to create a link to your module, assuming that your module is located in foo-module. After executing the npm link command, verify that the link was created using npm ls -g.

Listing 2-9. Creating a Link Using npm link

```
$ cd foo-module
$ npm link
```

The second step in module linking, actually referencing the link, is very similar to a package installation. First, change to the directory of the project that will import the linked module. Next, issue another npm link command. However, this time you must also specify the linked module's name. An example of this procedure is shown in Listing 2-10. In the example, the foo-module link from Listing 2-9 is referenced from a second module, bar-module.

Listing 2-10. Referencing an Existing Link Using npm link

```
$ cd bar-module
$ npm link foo-module
```

Unlinking Packages

The process for removing linked modules is very similar to the process for creating them. To remove a linked module from an application, use the npm unlink command, followed by the name. Listing 2-11 shows the command for removing the linked foo-module from bar-module.

Listing 2-11. Removing a Reference to a Link Using npm unlink

```
$ cd bar-module
$ npm unlink foo-module
```

Similarly, to remove a link from your system, change to the linked module's directory, and issue the npm unlink command. Listing 2-12 shows how to remove the foo-module link.

Listing 2-12. Removing a Linked Module Using npm unlink

```
$ cd foo-module
$ npm unlink
```

Updating Packages

Since any package that is actively developed eventually releases a new version, your copy will become outdated. To determine if your copy is out of date, run npm outdated in your project directory (see Listing 2-13). In the example, which assumes that an outdated version 1.0.0 of commander is installed, npm indicates that the latest version is 2.0.0 but that your copy is only 1.0.0. Listing 2-13 checks all of the local packages. You can check individual packages by specifying their names, and you can process global packages by specifying the -g option.

Listing 2-13. Displaying Outdated Packages Using npm outdated

```
$ npm outdated
npm http GET https://registry.npmjs.org/commander
npm http 304 https://registry.npmjs.org/commander
commander@2.0.0 node_modules/commander current=1.0.0
```

To update any outdated local packages, use the npm update command. Much like outdated, update works on all local packages by default. Again, you can target individual modules by specifying their names. You can also update global packages using the -g option. In Listing 2-14, npm updates itself using the -g option.

Listing 2-14. Updating npm Using npm update

```
$ npm update npm -g
```

Uninstalling Packages

To remove a package, use either the npm uninstall or npm rm command (the two commands can be used interchangeably), and specify one or more packages to be removed. You can also remove global packages by providing the -g option. Listing 2-15 shows how to remove the commander module using npm rm.

Listing 2-15. Uninstalling commander Using npm rm

```
$ npm rm commander
```

The `require()` Function

As shown in the previous section, Node packages are managed using npm. However, to import modules into your programs, the require() function is used. require() accepts a single argument, a string specifying the module to load. If the specified module path exists, require() returns an object that can be used to interface with the module. If the module cannot be located an exception is thrown. Listing 2-16 shows how the commander module is imported into a program using the require() function.

Listing 2-16. Using the require() Function

```
var commander = require("commander")
```

Core Modules

Core modules are modules compiled into the Node binary. They are given the highest precedence by require(), meaning that in the event of a module-naming conflict, the core module is loaded. For example, Node contains a core module named http, which, as the name implies, provides features for working with the Hypertext Transfer Protocol (HTTP). No matter what, a call to require("http") will always load the core http module. As a side note, the core modules are located in the lib directory of the Node source code.

File Modules

File modules are non-core modules loaded from the file system. They can be specified using absolute paths, relative paths, or from the node_modules directory. Module names that begin with a slash (/) are treated as absolute paths. For example, in Listing 2-17, a file module, foo, is loaded using an absolute path.

Listing 2-17. A File Module Import Using an Absolute Path

```
require("/some/path/foo");
```

■ **Caution**   Some operating systems such as Windows use a case-insensitive file system. This allows you to write require("commander"), require("COMMANDER"), or require("CoMmAnDeR"). However, on a case-sensitive file system such as Linux, the last two calls would fail. Therefore, you should assume case sensitivity, no matter what operating system you're using.

Node also supports Windows-style file paths. On Windows, Node allows the slash and backslash characters (/ and \) to be used interchangeably. For the sake of consistency, and to avoid escaping the backslash character, this book primarily uses Unix-style paths. However, be aware that all the paths shown in Listing 2-18 are valid on Windows.

Listing 2-18. Example Module Paths Valid on Windows

```
require("/some/path/foo");
require("C:/some/path/foo");
require("C:\\some\\path\\foo");
require("\\some/path\\foo");
```

Module paths that begin with one or two dots (. or ..) are interpreted as relative paths—that is, they are considered relative to the file that called require(). Listing 2-19 shows three examples of relative module paths. In the first example, foo is loaded from the same directory as the calling script. In the second, foo is located in the calling script's parent directory. In the third, foo is located in a subdirectory, sub, of the calling script's directory.

Listing 2-19. Example Module Imports Using Relative Paths

```
require("./foo");
require("../foo");
require("./sub/foo");
```

If a module path does not correspond to a core module, an absolute path, or a relative path, then Node begins searching in node_modules folders. Node begins with the calling script's parent directory and appends /node_modules. If the module is not found, Node moves one level up the directory tree, appends /node_modules, and searches again. This pattern is repeated until the module is located or the root of the directory structure is reached. The example in Listing 2-20 assumes that a project is located in /some/path and shows the various node_modules directories that would be searched, in order.

Listing 2-20. Example of the Search Order of node_modules Directories

```
/some/path/node_modules
/some/node_modules
/node_modules
```

File Extension Processing

If require() does not find an exact match, it attempts to add .js, .json, and .node file extensions. As mentioned in Chapter 1, .js files are interpreted as JavaScript source code, .json files are parsed as JSON source, and .node files are treated as compiled add-on modules. If Node is still unable to find a match, an error is thrown.

It is also possible to programmatically add support for additional file extensions using the built-in require.extensions object. Initially, this object contains three keys, .js, .json, and .node. Each key maps to a function that defines how require() imports files of that type. By extending require.extensions, you can customize the behavior of require(). For example, Listing 2-21 extends require.extensions such that .javascript files are treated as .js files.

Listing 2-21. Extending the require.extensions Object to Support Additional File Types

```
require.extensions[".javascript"] = require.extensions[".js"];
```

You can even add custom handlers. In Listing 2-22, .javascript files cause require() to print data about the imported file to the console.

Listing 2-22. Adding a Custom Handler to the require.extensions Object

```
require.extensions[".javascript"] = function() {
 console.log(arguments);
};
```

■ **Caution**   Though this feature has recently been deprecated, the module system API is locked, so require.extensions is unlikely to ever disappear completely. The official documentation recommends wrapping non-JavaScript modules in another Node program or compiling them to JavaScript a priori.

Resolving a Module Location

If you are interested only in learning where a package is located, use the require.resolve() function, which uses the same mechanism as require() to locate modules. However, instead of actually loading the module, resolve() only returns the path to the module. If the module name passed to resolve() is a core module, the module's name is returned. If the module is a file module, resolve() returns the module's file name. If the Node cannot locate the specified module, an error is thrown. The example in Listing 2-23 shows usage of resolve() in the REPL environment.

Listing 2-23. Locating the http Module Using require.resolve()

```
> require.resolve("http");
'http'
```

Module Caching

A file module that is loaded successfully is cached in the require.cache object. Subsequent imports of the same module return the cached object. One caveat is that the resolved module path must be exactly the same. This is so because a module is cached by its resolved path. Therefore, caching becomes a function of both the imported module and the calling script. Let's say your program depends on two modules, foo and bar. The first module, foo, has no dependencies, but bar depends on foo. The resulting dependency hierarchy is shown in Listing 2-24. Assuming that foo resides in the node_modules directory, it is loaded twice. The first load occurs when foo is resolved to the your-project/node_modules/foo directory. The second load occurs when foo is referenced from bar and resolves to your-project/node_modules/foo/node_modules.

Listing 2-24. A Dependence Hierarchy Where foo Is Referenced Multiple Times

```
your-project
├── foo@1.0.0
└─┬ bar@2.0.0
  └── foo@1.0.0
```

The `package.json` File

In an earlier section you saw that npm recognizes dependencies between packages and installs modules accordingly. But how does npm understand the concept of module dependencies? As it turns out, all of the relevant information is stored in a configuration file named package.json, which must be located in your project's root directory. As the file extension implies, the file must contain valid JSON data. Technically, you do not need to provide a package.json, but your code will essentially be inaccessible to npm without one.

The JSON data in package.json is expected to adhere to a certain schema. Minimally, you *must* specify a name and version for your package. Without these fields, npm will be unable to process your package. The simplest package.json file possible is shown in Listing 2-25. The package's name is specified by the name field. The name should uniquely identify your package in the npm registry. By using npm, the name becomes part of a URL, a command line argument, and a directory name. Therefore, names cannot begin with a dot or an underscore and cannot include spaces or any other non-URL-safe characters. Best practice also dictates that names be short and descriptive and not contain "js" or "node", as these are implied. Also, if you plan to release your package to the general public, verify that the name is available in the npm registry.

Listing 2-25. A Minimal package.json File

```
{
  "name": "package-name",
  "version": "0.0.0"
}
```

A package's version is specified in the version field. The version, when combined with the name, provides a truly unique identifier for a package. The version number specifies the major release, minor release, and patch number, separated by dots (npm allows versions to begin with a v character). You can also specify a build number by appending a tag to the patch number. There are two types of tags, prerelease and postrelease. Postrelease tags increase the version number, while prerelease tags decrease it. A postrelease tag is a hyphen followed by a number. All other tags are prerelease tags. The example in Listing 2-26 shows version tagging in action. Several tagged versions and an untagged version (0.1.2) are listed in descending order.

Listing 2-26. Several Tagged Versions and One Untagged Version Listed in Descending Order

```
0.1.2-7
0.1.2-7-beta
0.1.2-6
0.1.2
0.1.2beta
```

Description and Keywords

The description field is used to provide a textual description of your package. Similarly, use the keywords field to provide an array of keywords to further describe your package. Keywords and a description help people discover your package because they are searched by the npm search command. Listing 2-27 shows a package.json excerpt containing description and keywords fields.

Listing 2-27. Specifying a Description and Keywords in the package.json File

```
"description": "This is a description of the module",
"keywords": [
  "foo",
  "bar",
  "baz"
]
```

Author and Contributors

The primary author of a project is specified in the author field. This field can contain only one entry. However, a second field, contributors, can contain an array of people who contributed to the project. There are two ways to specify a person. The first is as an object containing name, email, and url fields. An example of this syntax is shown in Listing 2-28. The example specifies a single primary author and two additional contributors.

Listing 2-28. Specifying an Author and Contributors in the package.json File

```
"author": {
  "name": "Colin Ihrig",
  "email": "colin@domain.com",
  "url": "http://www.cjihrig.com"
},
"contributors": [
  {
    "name": "Jim Contributor",
    "email": "jim@domain.com",
    "url": "http://www.domain.com"
  },
  {
    "name": "Sue Contributor",
    "email": "sue@domain.com",
    "url": "http://www.domain.com"
  }
]
```

Alternatively, the objects representing people can be written as strings. In a string, a person is specified by name, then by an email address inside angle brackets, followed by a URL inside parentheses. The objects syntax shown in Listing 2-28 has been rewritten in Listing 2-29 using strings.

Listing 2-29. Specifying an Author and Contributors as Strings Instead of Objects

```
"author": "Colin Ihrig <colin@domain.com> (http://www.cjihrig.com)",
"contributors": [
  "Jim Contributor <jim@domain.com> (http://www.domain.com)",
  "Sue Contributor <sue@domain.com> (http://www.domain.com)"
]
```

The Main Entry Point

Since packages can consist of many files, Node needs some way of identifying its main entry point. Like most other configuration options, this is handled in the package.json file. In the main field you can tell Node which file to load when your module is imported using require(). Let's assume that your module is named foo, but its main entry point is located in a file named bar.js, which is located in the src subdirectory. Your package.json file should contain the main field shown in Listing 2-30.

Listing 2-30. Specifying the Package's Main Entry Point

```
"main": "./src/bar.js"
```

The preferGlobal Setting

Some packages are meant to be installed globally, but there is no way to actually enforce this intention. However, you can at least generate a warning if the user installs your module locally by including the preferGlobal field and setting it to true. Again, this will **not** actually prevent the user from performing a local install.

Dependencies

Package dependencies are specified in the dependencies field of the package.json file. This field is an object that maps package names to version strings. The version string can be any version expression understood by npm, including git and tarball URLs. Listing 2-31 shows an example of a dependencies field for a package depending only on commander.

Listing 2-31. A Simple dependencies Field

```
"dependencies": {
  "commander": "1.1.x"
}
```

Notice that commander's version string uses the x wildcard in Listing 2-31. It is generally considered best practice to use this syntax when specifying module dependencies because major and minor version updates can signify incompatible changes, while patch changes normally just represent bug fixes. It is good to keep up with package updates, but do so only after thorough testing. For example, if the version string used in Listing 2-31 were >=1.1.0, then bugs could mysteriously appear in your program after updating to version 1.2.0. To automatically update the dependencies field as you install new packages, append the --save flag to the npm install command. So, to add commander to the package.json file during installation, issue the command npm install commander --save.

Developmental Dependencies

Many packages have dependencies that are used only for testing and development. These packages should not be included in the dependencies field. Instead, place them in the separate devDependencies field. For example, the mocha package is a popular testing framework commonly used in the Node community. Packages using mocha for testing should list it in the devDependencies field, as shown in Listing 2-32.

Listing 2-32. Listing mocha as a Developmental Dependency

```
"devDependencies": {
  "mocha": "~1.8.1"
}
```

Developmental dependencies can also be automatically added to the package.json file. To do so, append the --save-dev flag to the npm install command. An example of this is the command npm install mocha --save-dev.

Optional Dependencies

Optional dependencies are packages you want to use but can live without—for example, a module that improves cryptography performance. If it's available, by all means use it. If for whatever reason it's not available, your application can fall back on a slower alternative. Normally, npm will fail if a dependency is not available. With optional dependencies, npm will proceed despite their absence. Much as with devDependencies, optional dependencies are listed in a separate optionalDependencies field. Optional dependencies can also be automatically added to the package.json file during installation by specifying the --save-optional flag to npm install.

If you choose to use optional dependencies, your program must still account for the case where the package is not present. This is done by wrapping references to the module inside try...catch and if statements. In the example in Listing 2-33, commander is assumed to be an optional dependency. Since the require() function throws an exception if commander is not present, it is wrapped in a try...catch statement. Later in the program, check that commander has a defined value before using it.

Listing 2-33. Using Defensive Programming when Referencing an Optional Dependency

```
var commander;

try {
  commander = require("commander");
} catch (exception) {
  commander = null;
}

if (commander) {
  // do something with commander
}
```

Engines

The engines field is used to specify the versions of node and npm that your module works with. Engine versioning is similar to the scheme used for dependencies. Best practices differ, however, depending on whether you are developing a stand-alone application or a reusable module. Applications should use conservative versioning to ensure that new releases of dependencies do not introduce errors. Reusable modules, on the other hand, should use aggressive versioning to ensure that, whenever possible, they work with the latest versions of Node. The example in Listing 2-34 includes an engines field. In the example, the node field uses aggressive versioning, always opting for the latest version. Meanwhile, the npm version string is conservative, allowing only patch updates.

19

Listing 2-34. Defining Supported Engine Versions in the package.json File

```
"engines": {
  "node": ">=0.10.12",
  "npm": "1.2.x"
}
```

Scripts

The scripts field, when present, contains a mapping of npm commands to script commands. The script commands, which can be any executable commands, are run in an external shell process. Two of the most common commands are start and test. The start command launches your application, and test runs one or more of your application's test scripts. In the example in Listing 2-35, the start command causes node to execute the file server.js. The test command echoes that no tests are specified. In a real application, test would likely invoke mocha or some other testing framework.

Listing 2-35. Specifying a scripts Field in the package.json File

```
"scripts": {
  "start": "node server.js",
  "test": "echo \"Error: no test specified\" && exit 1"
}
```

■ **Caution**   Do your best to avoid using platform specific commands whenever possible. For example, using a Makefile is common practice on Unix systems, but Windows has no make command.

To execute the start and test commands, simply pass the command name to npm. Listing 2-36, based on the scripts field in Listing 2-35, shows the output of the test command. You can see from the output that npm treats an exit code other than zero as an error and aborts the command.

Listing 2-36. Launching the npm test Command

```
$ npm test

> example@0.0.0 test /home/node/example
> echo "Error: no test specified" && exit 1

\"Error: no test specified\"
npm ERR! Test failed.  See above for more details.
npm ERR! not ok code 0
```

Note that you cannot simply add arbitrary commands and call them from npm. For example, issuing the command npm foo will not work, even if you have defined foo in the scripts field. There are also commands that act as *hooks* and are executed when certain events occur. For example, the install and postinstall commands are executed after your package is installed using npm install. The scripts field (see Listing 2-37) uses these commands to display messages after package installation. For a complete listing of available script commands, issue the command npm help scripts.

Listing 2-37. Some npm Hooks

```
"scripts": {
  "install": "echo \"Thank you for installing!\"",
  "postinstall": "echo \"You're welcome!\""
}
```

Additional Fields

A number of other fields are commonly found in the package.json file. For example, you can list your project's home page in the homepage field, the software license type in the license field, and the repository where your project's source code lives in the repository field. The repository field is especially useful if you plan to publish you module to the npm registry, as your module's npm page will contain a link to your repository. Additionally, by including a repository field, users can quickly navigate to the repository using the command npm repo module-name (where module-name is the npm name of your module).

You can even add your own application-specific fields as long as there are no naming conflicts. For more information on the package.json file, issue the command npm help json.

Generating a package.json File

While the syntax of a package.json file is not terribly complex, it can be tedious and error prone. The hardest part can be remembering your package's dependencies and their versions. To help mitigate this problem, Node provides npm init, a command line wizard that prompts you for the values of key fields and automatically generates a package.json file. If you already have a package.json file, npm init maintains all of its information, adding only new information.

As an example, assume that you have a project directory named foo-module. Inside that directory is foo.js, the main entry point of your module. Your module has only one dependency, commander, that has been installed during the course of development. Additionally, you have a test script, test.js, which exercises your module. Now comes the time to create the package.json file. Issue the command npm init, and step through the wizard shown in Listing 2-38.

Listing 2-38. Using npm init to Generate a package.json File

```
$ npm init
This utility will walk you through creating a package.json file.
It only covers the most common items, and tries to guess sane defaults.

See `npm help json` for definitive documentation on these fields
and exactly what they do.

Use `npm install <pkg> --save` afterwards to install a package and
save it as a dependency in the package.json file.

Press ^C at any time to quit.
name: (foo-module)
version: (0.0.0) 1.0.0
description: An awesome new Node module.
entry point: (foo.js)
test command: test.js
git repository:
keywords: node, awesome, foo
author: Colin Ihrig <cjihrig@domain.com>
license: (BSD)
About to write to /home/colin/foo-module/package.json:
```

```
{
  "name": "foo-module",
  "version": "1.0.0",
  "description": "An awesome new Node module.",
  "main": "foo.js",
  "dependencies": {
    "commander": "~1.1.1"
  },
  "devDependencies": {},
  "scripts": {
    "test": "test.js"
  },
  "repository": "",
  "keywords": [
    "node",
    "awesome",
    "foo"
  ],
  "author": "Colin Ihrig <cjihrig@domain.com>",
  "license": "BSD"
}

Is this ok? (yes)
npm WARN package.json foo-module@1.0.0 No README.md file found!
```

Notice that some values, including the name, foo-module, are parenthesized. These values are npm guesses. You can accept them by pressing the Enter key. If you want to use your own values, simply type them in before pressing Enter. For some fields, such as description, npm will not offer a guess. In these cases, you can either provide a value or leave the field blank, as shown in the git repository field. At the end of the wizard, npm displays the generated JSON data. At this point either accept the proposed data and generate the package.json file, or abort the entire process.

Finally, npm provides a warning message that no README.md file was found. README.md is an optional, yet recommended, file providing documentation on your module. The .md file extension indicates that the file contains *Markdown* data. Markdown, a type of markup language that is easily converted to HTML yet easier to read than HTML, is a natural fit for Node documentation because GitHub is capable of displaying Markdown and most Node projects are hosted on GitHub. It is good general practice to always include a README.md file in your project's root directory. If present, the file name is specified in the package.json file using the readmeFilename field. The example in Listing 2-39 shows a Markdown file. The same Markdown, as rendered on GitHub, is shown in Figure 2-1. Additional information on Markdown syntax is widely available online.

Listing 2-39. Using Markdown Syntax

```
#Level One Heading
This test is *italicized*, while this text is **bold**.

##Level Two Heading
By combining the two, this text is ***bold and italicized***.
```

Figure 2-1. *The Markdown from Listing 2-39 rendered on GitHub*

A Complete Example

This is probably a good time to look at a complete example of a Node program that includes a dependency. In this example, we'll create a Hello World style program that prints colored text to the console. In order to create colored text, the program will import a third party module named `colors`. The source code for the example program is shown in Listing 2-40. Add the source code to a file named `colors-test.js` and save it. The first line of code imports the `colors` module using the `require()` function. The second line prints the message `"Hello Node!"` to the console. The `.rainbow` appended to the console message causes the characters in the string to print in a variety of colors.

Listing 2-40. Using the `colors` Module to Print Rainbow Text

```
var colors = require("colors");

console.log("Hello Node!".rainbow);
```

Since `colors` is not a core module, you need to install it before running the program. To do so, issue the command `npm install colors`. After the installation completes, execute the program by issuing the command `node colors-test`. You should see a colorful message printed to the console. If you're part of a team, other people will need to run your code. For a program this small, only having one dependency, your teammates could simply check your code out of source control and install `colors`. However, this approach isn't really feasible for large programs with tens or even hundreds of dependencies. If you ever want anyone else to run your nontrivial programs, you're going to have to provide a `package.json` file. To generate `package.json`, run `npm init`. Execute the wizard step by step, entering values as needed. (An example `package.json` file for this project is shown in Listing 2-41.) Your program can now be installed with only your source code, the `package.json` file, and npm.

Listing 2-41. The package.json file for the Rainbow Text Program

```
{
  "name": "colors-test",
  "version": "1.0.0",
  "description": "An example program using the colors module.",
  "main": "colors-test.js",
  "dependencies": {
    "colors": "~0.6.0-1"
  },
  "devDependencies": {},
  "scripts": {
    "test": "echo \"Error: no test specified\" && exit 1"
  },
  "repository": "",
  "keywords": [
    "colors",
    "example"
  ],
  "author": "Colin Ihrig <cjihrig@domain.com>",
  "license": "BSD"
}
```

■ **Note**   Many developers do not check the node_modules folder into source control. As this folder can be regenerated using npm, excluding it can save space in source control. However, application developers should consider committing their node_modules folder to avoid mysterious bugs that can arise if dependencies introduce incompatible changes. Unfortunately, this can introduce problems when the application is loaded on a different machine or operating system. An alternative is to use the npm shrinkwrap utility to lock down exact module versions which are known to work. shrinkwrap not only locks down the versions for top level dependencies, but also for all of their dependencies (which can't be accomplished via the package.json file). Instead of checking node_modules into source control, simply run npm shrinkwrap, and check in the resulting npm-shrinkwrap.json file (in the same directory as package.json). Module developers, on the other hand, should not commit their dependencies or use shrinkwrap. Instead, they should work to ensure that their code is as compatible as possible across versions.

Module Authoring

So far, this chapter has focused on working with existing modules. This section explains how modules actually come into existence. In Node, modules and files have a one to one correspondence. That means that a file is a module that can be imported into other files using require(). To demonstrate this concept create two files, foo.js and bar.js, in the same directory. The contents of foo.js are shown in Listing 2-42. This file imports the second file, bar.js, whose contents are shown in Listing 2-43. Inside of foo.js, the return value from require() is saved in the variable bar, which is printed to the console.

Listing 2-42. The Contents of foo.js, which Imports the File bar.js

```
var bar = require("./bar");

console.log(bar);
```

Inside of bar.js, a function named bar() is defined. The module contains two print statements, one at the module level, and another in the bar() function.

Listing 2-43. The Contents of bar.js, which is Imported in Listing 2-42

```
function bar() {
  console.log("Inside of bar() function");
}

console.log("Inside of bar module");
```

To run the example, issue the command node foo.js. The resulting output is shown in Listing 2-44. The call to require() in foo.js imports bar.js, which causes the first message to be printed. Next, the bar variable is printed, displaying an empty object. Based on this example, there are two questions that need to be answered. First, what exactly is the empty object? Second, how can the bar() function be invoked from outside of bar.js.

Listing 2-44. The Output from Running the Code in Listing 2-42

```
$ node foo.js
Inside of bar module
{}
```

The module Object

Node provides a free variable, module, in every file which represents the current module. module is an object which contains a property named exports, that defaults to an empty object. The value of exports is returned by the require() function, and defines a module's public interface. Since exports was never modified in Listing 2-43, this explains the empty object seen in Listing 2-44.

To make the bar() function available outside of bar.js, we have two choices. First, bar could be assigned to module.exports inside of bar.js (as shown in Listing 2-45). Notice that the exports object has been overwritten with a function.

Listing 2-45. Rewriting bar.js to Export bar()

```
module.exports = function bar() {
  console.log("Inside of bar() function");
}

console.log("Inside of bar module");
```

foo.js can then access the bar() function as shown in Listing 2-46. Since the bar variable now points to a function, it can be invoked directly.

Listing 2-46. Rewriting foo.js to Access bar() from Listing 2-45

```
var bar = require("./bar");

console.log(bar);
bar();
```

The drawback to this approach is that the bar module cannot export anything but the bar() function. The second option is to simply attach the bar() function to the existing exports object, as shown in Listing 2-47. This technique allows the module to export an arbitrary number of methods and properties. To accommodate this change, foo.js would access the bar() function as bar.bar().

Listing 2-47. Exporting bar() by Augmenting the Existing exports Object

```
module.exports.bar = function bar() {
  console.log("Inside of bar() function");
}

console.log("Inside of bar module");
```

The module object provides several other properties which are less commonly used. These properties are summarized in Table 2-2.

Table 2-2. *Additional Properties of the module Object*

Property	Description
id	An identifier for the module. Typically this is the fully resolved filename of the module.
filename	The fully resolved filename of the module.
loaded	A Boolean value representing the module's state. If the module has finished loading, this will be true. Otherwise, it will be false.
parent	An object representing the module that loaded the current module.
children	An array of objects representing the modules imported by the current module.

Publishing to npm

In order to publish your modules to npm, you must first create a npm user account. Listing 2-48 illustrates the commands required to set up a npm account. The first three commands are used to associate your personal information. The last command, npm adduser, will prompt you for a username and create a npm account (assuming the username is available). Once an account is created, the user's published modules can be viewed at https://npmjs.org/~username.

Listing 2-48. Creating a npm User Account

```
npm set init.author.name "John Doe"
npm set init.author.email "john@domain.com"
npm set init.author.url "http://www.johnspage.com"
npm adduser
```

After setting up an npm account, you must create a `package.json` file for your module. The process for doing this has already been covered in this chapter. Finally, issue the command `npm publish` to create a npm entry based on the `package.json` file.

Summary

This chapter has covered a lot of material—and it needed to. A big part of developing Node applications is working with npm and third-party packages. From this chapter you should have gotten a good grasp on npm, the `require()` function, the `package.json` file, and module authoring. Although the entire package system cannot be covered comprehensively in a single chapter, you now should know enough to work through the rest of this book. Fill in any gaps in your knowledge by reading the documentation online.

CHAPTER 3

■ ■ ■

The Node Programming Model

Before trying to write any meaningful Node applications, it's important to understand what's going on under the hood. Probably the most important thing to understand is that JavaScript—and Node by extension—is single threaded. This means that Node applications can do exactly one thing at a time. However, JavaScript can give the illusion of being multithreaded through the use of an *event loop*. The event loop is used to schedule tasks in Node's event-driven programming model. Each time an event occurs, it is placed in Node's event queue. In each iteration of the event loop, a single event is dequeued and processed. If, during processing, this event creates any additional events, they are simply added to the end of the queue. When the event is completely handled, control is returned to the event loop, and another event is processed.

The example in Listing 3-1 illustrates how the event loop allows multiple tasks to appear to execute in parallel. In this example, setInterval() is used to create two periodic tasks which each run once per second. The first task is a function displaying the string foo, while the second task displays bar. When the application is run, setInterval() causes each function to run approximately once every 1,000 milliseconds. The result is that foo and bar are printed once per second. Remember, to execute a Node program, just type "node", followed by the program's file name.

Listing 3-1. An Example Application Giving the Illusion of Multithreaded Execution

```
setInterval(function() {
  console.log("foo");
}, 1000);

setInterval(function() {
  console.log("bar");
}, 1000);
```

Based on the code in Listing 3-1, JavaScript appears to be doing multiple things at once. Unfortunately, it is all too easy to verify its true single-threaded nature. In Listing 3-2, an infinite loop has been introduced into one of the repeating functions. The infinite loop prevents the first function from ever returning. Therefore, control is never passed back to the event loop, preventing anything else from executing. If the code were truly multithreaded, bar would continue to be printed to the console even though the other function was stuck in an infinite loop.

Listing 3-2. Exploiting Node's Single-Threaded Nature by Introducing an Infinite Loop

```
setInterval(function() {
  console.log("foo");

  while (true) {
  }
}, 1000);
```

```
setInterval(function() {
  console.log("bar");
}, 1000);
```

Asynchronous Programming

Another important aspect of the Node programming model is the fact that almost everything is done asynchronously. Asynchronicity is so common that many synchronous functions contain the string sync in their name to avoid confusion. Under Node's paradigm, sometimes referred to as *continuation-passing style* (CPS) programming, asynchronous functions take an extra argument, a function that is called after the asynchronous code has finished executing. This additional argument is referred to as a *continuation* or, more commonly, a *callback function.*

An example of an asynchronous function call is shown in Listing 3-3. This code reads a file from the file system and prints the contents to the screen. Accessing the file system will be revisited later in the book, but for now, this example should be simple enough to understand. The core fs module, imported on the first line, is used for working with the file system. The readFile() method works asynchronously, reading in the file foo.txt using UTF-8 encoding. Once the file is read, the anonymous callback function is invoked. The callback function takes two parameters, error and data, which represent any error conditions and the contents of the file, respectively.

Listing 3-3. An Example of Asynchronous File Reading

```
var fs = require("fs");

fs.readFile("foo.txt", "utf8", function(error, data) {
  if (error) {
    throw error;
  }

  console.log(data);
});

console.log("Reading file...");
```

This short example illustrates two important conventions for Node developers. First, if a method takes a callback function as an argument, it should be the final argument. Second, if a method takes an error as an argument, it should be the first argument. These are not rules of the language but generally agreed upon calling conventions in the Node developer community.

When this program is executed, it demonstrates another important aspect of asynchronous programming. To test the example program, save the source code in a file named file-reader.js. Next, create a second file, foo.txt, in the same directory as the Node script. For simplicity, just add the word "foo" to the file, and save it. Listing 3-4 shows the output of running the example program. Notice that the message Reading file... is displayed before the contents of the file, despite the fact that the message is not printed until the last line of code.

Listing 3-4. Console Output of the File Reader Example Program

```
$ node file-reader.js
Reading file...
foo
```

When readFile() is invoked, it makes a *nonblocking* I/O call to the file system. The fact that the I/O is nonblocking means that Node does not wait for the file system to return the data. Instead, Node continues to the next statement, which happens to be a console.log() call. Eventually, the file system returns with the contents of foo.txt.

When this happens, the readFile() callback function is invoked, and the file contents are displayed. This behavior appears to contradict the fact that Node programs are single threaded, but you must keep in mind that the file system is not a part of Node.

Callback Hell

The CPS syntax used in Node can easily lead to a situation known as *callback hell*. Callback hell occurs when callbacks are nested within other callbacks several levels deep. This can lead to code that is confusing and difficult to read and maintain. Callback hell is sometimes referred to as the Pyramid of Doom, its name coming from the pyramidal structure the code takes on.

As an example, let's revisit the file reader program from Listing 3-3. If we were to access a file that didn't exist, an exception would be thrown, and the program would crash. To make the program sturdier, first check that the file exists and that it is actually a file (not a directory or some other structure). The modified program is shown in Listing 3-5. Notice that the program now contains calls to fs.exists() and fs.stat(), as well as the original call to readFile(). With all of these utilizing callback functions, the level of code indentation increases. Couple this with the indentation from structures like if statements, and you see how callback hell can become a problem in complex Node applications.

Listing 3-5. A File Reader Program with Callback Hell Beginning to Creep In

```
var fs = require("fs");
var fileName = "foo.txt";

fs.exists(fileName, function(exists) {
  if (exists) {
    fs.stat(fileName, function(error, stats) {
      if (error) {
        throw error;
      }

      if (stats.isFile()) {
        fs.readFile(fileName, "utf8", function(error, data) {
          if (error) {
            throw error;
          }

          console.log(data);
        });
      }
    });
  }
});
```

Later in this chapter, you'll learn about async, a module that can help prevent callback hell. However, you can also avoid the problem by using small named functions as callbacks, instead of nested anonymous functions. For example, Listing 3-6 refactors Listing 3-5 to use named functions. Notice that references to the named functions cbExists(), cbStat(), cbReadFile() have replaced the anonymous callback functions. The downside is that the code is slightly longer and might be harder to follow. For such a small application, this is probably overkill, but for large applications it can be essential to the overall software architecture.

Listing 3-6. The File Reader Example Refactored to Prevent Callback Hell

```
var fs = require("fs");
var fileName = "foo.txt";

function cbReadFile(error, data) {
  if (error) {
    throw error;
  }

  console.log(data);
}

function cbStat(error, stats) {
  if (error) {
    throw error;
  }

  if (stats.isFile()) {
    fs.readFile(fileName, "utf8", cbReadFile);
  }
}

function cbExists(exists) {
  if (exists) {
    fs.stat(fileName, cbStat);
  }
}

fs.exists(fileName, cbExists);
```

Exception Handling

Asynchronous code also has major implications for exception handling. In synchronous JavaScript code,
try ... catch ... finally statements are used to handle errors. However, Node's callback-driven nature
allows functions to execute outside the error-handling code in which they are defined. For example, Listing 3-7 adds
traditional error handling to the file reader example from Listing 3-3. Additionally, the name of the file to read has
been hard-coded to the empty string. Therefore, when readFile() is called, it is unable to read the file and populates
the error argument of the callback function. The callback function then throws the error. Intuitively, one assumes
that the catch clause will handle the thrown error. However, by the time the callback function is executed,
the try ... catch statement is no longer a part of the call stack, and the exception is left uncaught.

Listing 3-7. An Incorrect Attempt at Asynchronous Error Handling

```
var fs = require("fs");

try {
  fs.readFile("", "utf8", function(error, data) {
    if (error) {
      throw error;
    }
```

```
    console.log(data);
  });
} catch (exception) {
  console.log("The exception was caught!")
}
```

Synchronous exceptions can still be handled with try...catch...finally statements, but you will find that they are relatively useless in Node. The majority of Node exceptions are of the asynchronous variety, and can be handled in a number of ways. For starters, all functions that take an error argument should be sure to check it—at least the example in Listing 3-7 does that right. In the example, the exception has been detected, but is then immediately thrown again. Of course, in a real application, you would want to handle the error, not throw it.

The second way to process asynchronous exceptions is to set up a global event handler for the process's uncaughtException event. Node provides a global object, named process, that interacts with the Node process. When an unhandled exception bubbles all the way back to the event loop, an uncaughtException error is created. This exception can be handled using the process object's on() method. Listing 3-8 shows an example of a global exception handler.

Listing 3-8. An Example of Global Exception Handler

```
var fs = require("fs");

fs.readFile("", "utf8", function(error, data) {
  if (error) {
    throw error;
  }

  console.log(data);
});

process.on("uncaughtException", function(error) {
  console.log("The exception was caught!")
});
```

While global exception handlers are useful for preventing crashes, they should not be used to recover from errors. When not properly handled, an exception leaves your application in an indeterminate state. Attempting to move on from such a state can bring additional errors. If your program does include a global exception handler, use it only to gracefully terminate the program.

Domains

A domain is the preferred mechanism for handling asynchronous errors in Node. Domains, a relatively new feature (introduced in version 0.8), allow multiple I/O operations to be grouped into a single unit. When a timer, event emitter (covered in Chapter 4), or callback function registered with a domain creates an error, the domain is notified so the error can be handled appropriately.

The example in Listing 3-9 shows how domains are used to handle exceptions. On the second line of the example, the domain module is imported, and a new domain is created. The domain's run() method is then used to execute the supplied function. Within the context of run(), all *new* timers, event emitters, and callback methods are implicitly registered with the domain. When an error is thrown, it triggers the domain's error handler. Of course, if the handler function is not defined, the exception proceeds to crash the program. Finally, when the domain is no longer needed, its dispose() method is called.

Listing 3-9. Exception Handling Using Domains

```
var fs = require("fs");
var domain = require("domain").create();

domain.run(function() {
  fs.readFile("", "utf8", function(error, data) {
    if (error) {
      throw error;
    }

    console.log(data);
    domain.dispose();
  });
});

domain.on("error", function(error) {
  console.log("The exception was caught!")
});
```

Explicit Binding

As previously mentioned, timers, event emitters, and callback functions created in the context of run() are implicitly registered with the corresponding domain. However, if you create multiple domains, you can explicitly bind to another domain, even in the context of run(). For example, Listing 3-10 creates two domains, d1 and d2. Within d1's run() method, an asynchronous timer that throws an error is created. Because the exception occurs in d1's run() callback, the exception is normally handled by d1. However, the timer is explicitly registered with d2 using its add() method. Therefore, when the exception is thrown, d2's error handler is triggered.

Listing 3-10. An Example of a Bound Callback Function Using Domains

```
var domain = require("domain");
var d1 = domain.create();
var d2 = domain.create();

d1.run(function() {
  d2.add(setTimeout(function() {
    throw new Error("test error");
  }, 1));
});

d2.on("error", function(error) {
  console.log("Caught by d2");
});

d1.on("error", function(error) {
  console.log("Caught by d1")
});
```

As we've just seen, add() is used to explicitly bind timers to a domain. This also works for event emitters. A similar method, remove(), removes a timer or event emitter from a domain. Listing 3-11 shows how remove() is used to unbind a timer. One very important thing to note is that removing the timer variable from d2 does not automatically bind it to d1. Instead, the exception thrown by the timer's callback function does not get caught, and the program crashes.

Listing 3-11. Using remove() to Unbind a Timer from a Domain

```
var domain = require("domain");
var d1 = domain.create();
var d2 = domain.create();

d1.run(function() {
  var timer = setTimeout(function() {
    throw new Error("test error");
  }, 1);

  d2.add(timer);
  d2.remove(timer);
});

d2.on("error", function(error) {
  console.log("Caught by d2");
});

d1.on("error", function(error) {
  console.log("Caught by d1")
});
```

■ **Note**   Each domain has an array property, members, that contains all the timers and event emitters explicitly added to the domain.

Domains also provide a bind() method that can be used to explicitly register a callback function with the domain. This is useful because it allows a function to be bound to a domain without immediately executing the function, as run() would. The bind() method takes a callback function as its only argument. The function returned is a registered wrapper around the original callback. As with the run() method, exceptions are handled through the domain's error handler. Listing 3-12 revisits the file reader example using the domain bind() method to handle errors associated with the readFile() callback function.

Listing 3-12. An Example of a Bound Callback Function Using Domains

```
var fs = require("fs");
var domain = require("domain").create();

fs.readFile("", "utf8", domain.bind(function(error, data) {
  if (error) {
    throw error;
  }

  console.log(data);
  domain.dispose();
}));
```

```
domain.on("error", function(error) {
  console.log("The exception was caught!")
});
```

There is another method, intercept(), that is nearly identical to bind(). In addition to catching any thrown exceptions, intercept() also detects any Error objects passed as the first argument of the callback function. This eliminates the need to check for any errors passed to the callback function. For example, Listing 3-13 rewrites Listing 3-12 using the intercept() method. The two examples behave identically, but notice that in 3-13 the callback no longer has an error argument. We've also eliminated the if statement used to detect the error argument.

Listing 3-13. Error Handling Using the Domain intercept() Method

```
var fs = require("fs");
var domain = require("domain").create();

fs.readFile("", "utf8", domain.intercept(function(data) {
  console.log(data);
  domain.dispose();
}));

domain.on("error", function(error) {
  console.log("The exception was caught!")
});
```

The async Module

async is a third party, open source module which is extremely useful for managing asynchronous control flow. At the time of writing, async was the second-most-depended-upon module in the npm registry. Although it was originally developed for Node applications, async can also be used on the client side, as the module is supported by many popular browsers, including Chrome, Firefox, and Internet Explorer. Developers can provide one or more functions, and using the async module, define how they will be executed—whether in series or with a specified degree of parallelism. Given the module's popularity, flexibility, and power, async is the first third party module thoroughly explored in this book.

Executing in Series

One of the most challenging aspects of asynchronous development is enforcing the order in which functions execute while maintaining readable code. However, with async, enforcing serial execution is simply a matter of using the series() method. As its first argument, series() takes an array or object containing functions that are to be executed in order. Each function takes a callback as an argument. Following Node conventions, the first argument to each callback function is an error object, or null, if there is no error. The callback functions also accept an optional second argument representing the return value. Invoking the callback function causes series() to move on to the next function. However, if any functions pass an error to their callback, then none of the remaining functions are executed.

The series() method also accepts an optional second argument, a callback that is invoked after all of the functions have completed. This final callback accepts two arguments, an error and an array or object containing the results from the functions. If any functions pass an error to their callback, control is immediately passed to the final callback function.

Listing 3-14 contains three timer tasks, each of which populates an element of the results array. In this example, task 1 takes 300 milliseconds to complete, task 2 takes 200 milliseconds, and task 3 takes 100 milliseconds. Assuming that we would like the tasks to run in order, the code would need to be restructured so that task 3 is invoked from task 2, which in turn is invoked from task 1. Additionally, we have no way of knowing when all of the tasks are completed and the results are ready.

Listing 3-14. An Example of Timer Tasks Executing with No Established Control Flow

```
var results = [];

setTimeout(function() {
  console.log("Task 1");
  results[0] = 1;
}, 300);

setTimeout(function() {
  console.log("Task 2");
  results[1] = 2;
}, 200);

setTimeout(function() {
  console.log("Task 3");
  results[2] = 3;
}, 100);
```

Listing 3-15 shows the results of running the previous example. Notice that the tasks do not execute in the proper order and there is no way to verify the results returned from the tasks.

Listing 3-15. Console Output Verifying That the Tasks Execute Out of Order

```
$ node timer-tasks
Task 3
Task 2
Task 1
```

Listing 3-16 shows how we can use async's series() method to solve all of the problems associated with control flow without significantly complicating the code. The first line imports the async module, which, as you learned in Chapter 2, can be installed using the command npm install async. Next, a call to series() is made, with an array of functions containing the original timer tasks wrapped inside anonymous functions. Inside each task the desired return value is passed as the second argument of the callback function. The call to series() also includes a final callback function, which solves the problem of not knowing when all of the results are ready.

Listing 3-16. An Example of Executing Functions in Series Using Async

```
var async = require("async");

async.series([
  function(callback) {
    setTimeout(function() {
      console.log("Task 1");
      callback(null, 1);
    }, 300);
  },
```

```
  function(callback) {
    setTimeout(function() {
      console.log("Task 2");
      callback(null, 2);
    }, 200);
  },
  function(callback) {
    setTimeout(function() {
      console.log("Task 3");
      callback(null, 3);
    }, 100);
  }
], function(error, results) {
  console.log(results);
});
```

Listing 3-17 shows the console output of Listing 3-16, which verifies that the three tasks are executed in the designated order. Additionally, the final callback provides a mechanism for inspecting the results. In this case, the results are formatted as an array, because the task functions were passed in an array. Had the tasks been passed using an object, the results would also be formatted as an object.

Listing 3-17. Console Output of Code in Listing 3-16

```
$ node async-series
Task 1
Task 2
Task 3
[ 1, 2, 3 ]
```

Handling Errors

As previously mentioned, if any functions pass an error to their callback function, execution is immediately short-circuited to the final callback function. In Listing 3-18, an error has been intentionally introduced in the first task. Also, the third task has been removed for brevity, and the final callback now checks for errors.

Listing 3-18. The Series Example Has Been Modified to Include an Error

```
var async = require("async");

async.series([
  function(callback) {
    setTimeout(function() {
      console.log("Task 1");
      callback(new Error("Problem in Task 1"), 1);
    }, 200);
  },
  function(callback) {
    setTimeout(function() {
      console.log("Task 2");
      callback(null, 2);
    }, 100);
  }
```

```
], function(error, results) {
  if (error) {
    console.log(error.toString());
  } else {
    console.log(results);
  }
});
```

The resulting output after introducing an error is shown in Listing 3-19. Notice that the error in the first task prevents the second task from ever executing at all.

Listing 3-19. Console Output in the Presence of an Error

```
$ node async-series-error
Task 1
Error: Problem in Task 1
```

Executing in Parallel

The async module can also execute multiple functions in parallel using the parallel() method. Of course, JavaScript is still single threaded, so your code won't actually execute in parallel. The parallel() method behaves exactly like series(), except that async does not wait for one function to return before invoking the next, giving the illusion of parallelism. Listing 3-20 shows an example of executing the same three tasks using parallel(). This example also passes the tasks in using an object, since you've already seen the array syntax in the previous examples.

Listing 3-20. Executing Three Tasks in Parallel Using Async

```
var async = require("async");

async.parallel({
  one: function(callback) {
    setTimeout(function() {
      console.log("Task 1");
      callback(null, 1);
    }, 300);
  },
  two: function(callback) {
    setTimeout(function() {
      console.log("Task 2");
      callback(null, 2);
    }, 200);
  },
  three: function(callback) {
    setTimeout(function() {
      console.log("Task 3");
      callback(null, 3);
    }, 100);
  }
}, function(error, results) {
  console.log(results);
});
```

Listing 3-21 shows the output from Listing 3-20. In this case, the tasks executed out of program order. Also, notice that the final line of output, which displays the task results, is an object, not an array.

Listing 3-21. Console Output from Executing Tasks in Parallel

```
$ node async-parallel
Task 3
Task 2
Task 1
{ three: 3, two: 2, one: 1 }
```

Limiting Parallelism

The parallel() method attempts to execute all of the functions passed to it as soon as possible. A similar method, parallelLimit(), behaves exactly like parallel(), except that you can place an upper bound on the number of tasks executed in parallel. Listing 3-22 shows an example use of the parallelLimit() method. In this case, the parallelism limit is set to two, using an additional argument before the final callback. It should be noted that parallelLimit() does not execute functions in discrete batches of *n*. Instead, the function simply ensures that there are never more than *n* functions executing at once.

Listing 3-22. Executing Three Tasks in Parallel, with a Maximum Parallelism of Two

```
var async = require("async");

async.parallelLimit({
  one: function(callback) {
    setTimeout(function() {
      console.log("Task 1");
      callback(null, 1);
    }, 300);
  },
  two: function(callback) {
    setTimeout(function() {
      console.log("Task 2");
      callback(null, 2);
    }, 200);
  },
  three: function(callback) {
    setTimeout(function() {
      console.log("Task 3");
      callback(null, 3);
    }, 100);
  }
}, 2, function(error, results) {
  console.log(results);
});
```

Listing 3-23 shows the resulting output from Listing 3-22. Notice that tasks 1 and 2 are completed before the third task, even though its timer has the smallest delay. This indicates that task 3 does not begin executing until one of the first two tasks completes.

Listing 3-23. The Output from Running the Code in Listing 3-22

```
$ node parallel-limit.js
Task 2
Task 1
Task 3
{ two: 2, one: 1, three: 3 }
```

The Waterfall Model

The waterfall model is a serial model that is useful when the tasks are dependent on the results of previously completed tasks. Waterfalls can also be thought of as assembly lines, where each task performs some part of a larger task. Waterfalls are created using the async method waterfall(). Setting up a waterfall is very similar to using series() or parallel(). However, there are a few key differences. First, the list of functions constituting the waterfall can only be stored in an array (object notation is not supported). The second key difference is that only the results of the last task are passed to the final callback function. The third difference is that the task functions can take additional arguments provided by the previous task.

Listing 3-24 shows an example of a waterfall. It uses the Pythagorean theorem to compute the length of a triangle's hypotenuse. The Pythagorean theorem states that for right triangles, the squared length of the hypotenuse is equal to the sum of the squares of the other two sides. The theorem is commonly written as $a^2 + b^2 = c^2$, where c is the length of the hypotenuse. In Listing 3-24, the problem has been broken down into three tasks using the waterfall() method. The first task creates two random numbers to act as the values a and b. These values are passed to the task's callback function, which in turn makes them the first two arguments to the second task. The second task computes the sum of the squares of a and b and passes this value to the third task. The third task computes the square root of the value passed to it. This value, the length of the hypotenuse, is passed to the final callback function, where it is printed to the console.

Listing 3-24. A Waterfall That Computes the Length of a Right Triangle's Hypotenuse

```
var async = require("async");

async.waterfall([
  function(callback) {
    callback(null, Math.random(), Math.random());
  },
  function(a, b, callback) {
    callback(null, a * a + b * b);
  },
  function(cc, callback) {
    callback(null, Math.sqrt(cc));
  }
], function(error, c) {
  console.log(c);
});
```

The Queue Model

async also supports task queues using the queue() method. Unlike the previous execution models, which execute a number of functions passed in as arguments, the queue model allows you to dynamically add tasks at any point during execution. Queues are useful for solving producer-consumer type problems. Because JavaScript is single threaded, you can safely ignore the potential concurrency problems that normally arise with producer-consumer problems.

Listing 3-25 shows the basic initialization of an async queue. The queue object is created using the queue() method, which takes a task-handling function as an input argument. The task handler takes two arguments, a user-defined task and a callback function that should be called with an error argument once the task is processed. In this example, no error has occurred, so the callback function is invoked, with null as its argument. The queue() method also takes an argument specifying the queue's level of parallelism, similar to the parallelLimit() method. The queue shown in Listing 3-25 can process up to four tasks at once.

Listing 3-25. Initialization of an async Queue

```
var async = require("async");
var queue = async.queue(function(task, callback) {
  // process the task argument
  console.log(task);
  callback(null);
}, 4);
```

Once the queue is set up, begin adding tasks to it using its push() and unshift() methods. Like the array methods of the same names, unshift() and push() add tasks to the beginning and end of the queue, respectively. Both methods can add a single task to the queue or, by passing in an array, multiple tasks. Both methods also accept an optional callback function; if present, it is invoked with an error argument after each task is completed.

In Listing 3-26, an interval is used to add a new task to the end of the queue from the previous example every 200 milliseconds. In this example, each task is just an object with a numeric id field. However, a task can actually be any data, as dictated by your application. The optional callback argument has been included in this example. In this case, the callback function simply prints a message stating that a task has been completed.

Listing 3-26. An Example of Adding Tasks to an async Queue

```
var i = 0;

setInterval(function() {
  queue.push({
    id: i
  }, function(error) {
    console.log("Finished a task");
  });
  i++;
}, 200);
```

Additional Queue Methods and Properties

At any point, you can determine the number of elements in the queue by using the length() method. You can also control the queue's level of parallelism using the concurrency property. For example, if the queue length exceeds a threshold, you can increase the number of concurrent tasks using the code shown in Listing 3-27.

Listing 3-27. Updating a Queue's Concurrency Based on Its Load

```
if (queue.length() > threshold) {
  queue.concurrency = 8;
}
```

Queues also support a number of callback functions, which are triggered on certain events. These callback functions are saturated(), empty(), and drain(). The saturated() function is triggered any time the queue's length becomes equal to its concurrency, empty() is called any time the last task is removed from the queue, and drain() is called when the last task has been completely processed. An example of each function is shown in Listing 3-28.

Listing 3-28. Example of Use of saturated(), empty(), and drain()

```
queue.saturated = function() {
  console.log("Queue is saturated");
};

queue.empty = function() {
  console.log("Queue is empty");
};

queue.drain = function() {
  console.log("Queue is drained");
};
```

Repeating Methods

The async module also provides other methods that repeatedly call a function until some condition is met. The most basic of these is whilst(), whose behavior resembles that of a while loop. Listing 3-29 demonstrates how whilst() is used to implement an asynchronous while loop. The whilst() method takes three functions as arguments. The first is a *synchronous* truth test, which takes no arguments, and is checked before each iteration. The second function passed to whilst() is executed each time the truth test returns true. This function takes a callback as its only argument and can be thought of as the loop body. The loop body's callback function takes an optional error as its only argument, which has been set to null in this example. The third argument of whilst() is executed once the truth test returns false, and acts as a final callback function. This function also takes an optional error as its only argument.

Listing 3-29. A Simple Loop Implementation Using whilst()

```
var async = require("async");
var i = 0;

async.whilst(function() {
  return i < 5;
}, function(callback) {
  setTimeout(function() {
    console.log("i = " + i);
    i++;
    callback(null);
  }, 1000);
}, function(error) {
  console.log("Done!");
});
```

Repeating Variations

The async module provides three additional methods for implementing asynchronous loop-like structures. These methods are doWhilst(), until(), and doUntil(), and they behave almost exactly like whilst(). The first, doWhilst(), is the asynchronous equivalent of a do-while loop, and until() is the inverse of whilst(), executing until the truth test returns true. Similarly, doUntil() is the inverse of doWhilst(), executing as long as the truth test returns false. The signatures for these methods are shown in Listing 3-30. Notice that the body argument comes before the test for doWhilst() and doUntil().

Listing 3-30. Method Signatures of doWhilst(), until(), and doUntil()

```
async.doWhilst(body, test, callback)
async.until(test, body, callback)
async.doUntil(body, test, callback)
```

Additional async Functionality

async provides a number of other utility functions in addition to the ones already covered. For example, async provides memoize() and unmemoize() methods for implementing memoization. The module also provides series and parallel versions of many common methods used for dealing with collections. Some of these methods are each(), map(), filter(), reduce(), some(), and every(). A complete listing of the methods provided by async, as well as reference code, is available on the module's GitHub page: https://github.com/caolan/async.

■ **Note** Memoization is a programming technique that attempts to increase performance by caching a function's previously computed results. When a memoized function is called, its input arguments are mapped to the output in a software cache. The next time the function is called with the same inputs, the cached value is returned instead of the function executing again.

Summary

This chapter has begun the exploration of the Node programming model. Reading the chapter should have left you with a better understanding of the concepts of asynchronous programming and nonblocking I/O. If you are still unsure, go back and read the chapter again. If you plan to do any serious Node development, understanding these concepts is absolutely essential. Exception handling, also covered here, could have probably been put off until later, but as asynchronous error handling can be a tricky subject, it's best to get it on the table as soon as possible.

This chapter has also introduced async, one of the most popular Node modules in existence. An extremely powerful tool in any Node developer's toolbox, async also works in the browser, making it an asset to front-end developers as well. Just about any execution pattern can be abstracted using the models provided by async. Additionally, models can be nested inside others. For example, you can create a set of functions that execute in parallel, with each function containing a nested waterfall.

CHAPTER 4

■ ■ ■

Events and Timers

The previous chapter introduced Node's event-driven programming model. This chapter takes a more in-depth look at events and event handling. A solid understanding of event handling will allow you to create sophisticated, event-driven applications, such as web servers. This chapter introduces event emitters—objects used to create new events. After learning how to create events, the chapter turns to event handling. Finally, the chapter wraps up with a discussion of timers and function scheduling in Node.

Event Emitters

In Node, objects that generate events are called event emitters. Creating an event emitter is as simple as importing the events core module and instantiating an EventEmitter object. The EventEmitter instance can then create new events using its emit() method. An example which creates an event emitter is shown in Listing 4-1. In this example, the event emitter creates a foo event.

Listing 4-1. An Example of a Simple Event Emitter

```
var events = require("events");
var emitter = new events.EventEmitter();

emitter.emit("foo");
```

Event names can be any valid string, but camelCase naming is used by convention. For example, an event created to indicate that a new user was added to the system would likely be named userAdded or something similar.

Often, events need to provide additional information beyond the event name. For example, when a key is pressed, the event also specifies which key is typed. To support this functionality, the emit() method can accept an arbitrary number of optional arguments after the event name. Returning to the example of creating a new user, Listing 4-2 shows how additional arguments are passed to emit(). This example assumes that some I/O (likely a database transaction) operation is performed, which creates a new user. Once the I/O operation is complete, the event emitter, emitter, creates a new userAdded event and passes in the user's username and password.

Listing 4-2. An Example of Passing Arguments to an Emitted Event

```
var events = require("events");
var emitter = new events.EventEmitter();
var username = "colin";
var password = "password";

// add the user
// then emit an event
emitter.emit("userAdded", username, password);
```

Listening for Events

In the example in Listing 4-2, an event emitter was used to create an event. Unfortunately, an event is rather pointless if no one is listening for it. In Node, event listeners are attached to event emitters using the on() and addListener() methods. The two methods can be used interchangeably. Both methods take an event name and handler function as arguments. When an event of the specified type is emitted, the corresponding handler functions are invoked. For example, in Listing 4-3, a userAdded event handler is attached to emitter using the on() method. Next, emitter emits a userAdded event, causing the handler to be invoked. The output from this example is shown in Listing 4-4.

Listing 4-3. Setting Up an Event Listener Using on()

```
var events = require("events");
var emitter = new events.EventEmitter();

var username = "colin";
var password = "password";

// an event listener
emitter.on("userAdded", function(username, password) {
  console.log("Added user " + username);
});

// add the user
// then emit an event
emitter.emit("userAdded", username, password);
```

▦ **Note** An event listener can detect only those events that occur after the listener is attached. That is, a listener is not capable of detecting past events. Therefore, as Listing 4-3 shows, be sure to attach a listener before emitting events.

Listing 4-4. The Output from Running the Code in Listing 4-3

```
$ node user-event-emitter.js
Added user colin
```

One-Time Event Listeners

Sometimes you may be interested in reacting to an event only the first time it occurs. In these situations you can use the once() method. once() is used exactly like on() and addListener(). However, the listener attached using once() is executed a maximum of one time and then removed. Listing 4-5 shows an example use of the once() method. In this example, once() is used to listen for foo events. The emit() method is then used to create two foo events. However, because the event listener was registered using once(), only the first foo event is handled. Had the event listener been registered using on() or addListener(), both foo events would have been handled. The output of running the example is shown in Listing 4-6.

Listing 4-5. An Example of a One-Time Event Listener Using once()

```
var events = require("events");
var emitter = new events.EventEmitter();

emitter.once("foo", function() {
  console.log("In foo handler");
});
```

```
emitter.emit("foo");
emitter.emit("foo");
```

Listing 4-6. The Output from Running the Code in Listing 4-5

```
$ node once-test.js
In foo handler
```

Inspecting Event Listeners

At any point in its lifetime, an event emitter can have zero or more listeners attached to it. The listeners for each event type can be inspected in several ways. If you are interested in only determining the number of attached listeners, then look no further than the EventEmitter.listenerCount() method. This method takes an EventEmitter instance and an event name as arguments and returns the number of attached listeners. For example, in Listing 4-7 an event emitter is created, and two uninteresting foo event handlers are attached. The last line of the example displays the number of foo handlers attached to the emitter by calling EventEmitter.listenerCount(). In this case, the example outputs the number 2. Notice that the listenerCount() call is attached to the EventEmitter class, and not a specific instance. Many languages refer to this as a static method. However, the Node documentation identifies listenerCount() as a class method, and so this book follows suit.

Listing 4-7. Determining the Number of Listeners Using EventEmitter.listenerCount()

```
var events = require("events");
var EventEmitter = events.EventEmitter;
// get the EventEmitter constructor from the events module
var emitter = new EventEmitter();

emitter.on("foo", function() {});
emitter.on("foo", function() {});
console.log(EventEmitter.listenerCount(emitter, "foo"));
```

If getting the number of handlers attached to an event emitter is not enough, the listeners() method can be used to retrieve an array of event handler functions. This array provides the number of handlers via the length property, as well as the actual functions invoked when an event occurs. With that said, modifying the array returned by listeners() does not affect the handlers maintained by the event emitter object.

Listing 4-8 provides an example use of the listeners() method. In this example, a foo event handler is added to an event emitter. listeners() is then used to retrieve the array of event handlers. The array forEach() method is then used to iterate over the event handlers, invoking each one along the way. Since the event handler in this example does not take any arguments and does not alter the program state, the call to forEach() essentially replicates the functionality of emitter.emit("foo").

Listing 4-8. An Example That Iterates Over Event Handlers via the listeners() Method

```
var events = require("events");
var EventEmitter = events.EventEmitter;
var emitter = new EventEmitter();

emitter.on("foo", function() { console.log("In foo handler"); });
emitter.listeners("foo").forEach(function(handler) {
  handler();
});
```

The newListener Event

Each time a new event handler is registered, the event emitter emits a newListener event. This event is used to detect new event handlers. You typically use newListener when you need to allocate resources or perform some action for each new event handler. A newListener event is handled just like any other. The handler expects two arguments: the event name as a string and the handler function. For example, in Listing 4-9 a foo event handler is attached to an event emitter. Behind the scenes, the emitter emits a newListener event, causing the newListener event handler to be invoked.

Listing 4-9. Adding a newListener Event Handler

```
var events = require("events");
var emitter = new events.EventEmitter();

emitter.on("newListener", function(eventName, listener) {
  console.log("Added listener for " + eventName + " events");
});

emitter.on("foo", function() {});
```

It is important to remember that the newListener event exists when creating your own events. Listing 4-10 shows what can happen if you forget. In this example, the developer has created a custom newListener event handler that expects to be passed a Date object. When a newListener event is emitted, everything works as expected. However, when a seemingly unrelated foo event handler is created, an exception is thrown because the built-in newListener event is emitted with the string foo as its first argument. Since Date objects have a getTime() method but strings do not, a TypeError is thrown.

Listing 4-10. An Invalid Handler for newListener Events

```
var events = require("events");
var emitter = new events.EventEmitter();

emitter.on("newListener", function(date) {
  console.log(date.getTime());
});

emitter.emit("newListener", new Date());
emitter.on("foo", function() {});
```

Removing Event Listeners

An event listener can be removed after it's been attached to an event emitter. For example, to reset an event emitter to some initial state in which it has no listeners, the simplest approach is to use the removeAllListeners() method. This method can be called with no arguments, in which case all event listeners are removed. Alternatively, passing in an event name causes the handlers for the named event to be removed. The syntax of removeAllListeners() is shown in Listing 4-11.

Listing 4-11. Syntax of the removeAllListeners() Method

```
emitter.removeAllListeners([eventName])
```

If removeAllListeners() is too coarse-grained for your needs, turn to the removeListener() method. This method is used to remove individual event listeners, and takes two arguments—the name of the event and the handler function to remove. Listing 4-12 shows an example use of removeListener(). In this case, a foo event listener is added to an event emitter, then immediately removed. When the event is emitted, nothing happens because there are no attached listeners. Notice that the removeListener() usage is identical to that of the on() and addListener() methods, although they perform inverse operations.

Listing 4-12. Removing an Event Handler Using removeListener()

```
var events = require("events");
var emitter = new events.EventEmitter();

function handler() {
  console.log("In foo handler");
}

emitter.on("foo", handler);
emitter.removeListener("foo", handler);
emitter.emit("foo");
```

If you plan to use removeListener(), avoid anonymous handler functions. By their very nature, anonymous functions are not bound to a named reference. If an anonymous event handler is created, a second identical anonymous function will not successfully remove the handler. This is so because two distinct Function objects are not considered equivalent unless they point to the same location in memory. Therefore, the example shown in Listing 4-13 will **not** remove an event listener.

Listing 4-13. An Incorrect Use of removeListener() with Anonymous Functions

```
var events = require("events");
var emitter = new events.EventEmitter();

emitter.on("foo", function() {
  console.log("foo handler");
});
emitter.removeListener("foo", function() {
  console.log("foo handler");
});
emitter.emit("foo");
```

Detecting Potential Memory Leaks

Typically, a single event emitter will require just a handful of event listeners. So, if an application programmatically adds event listeners to an event emitter, and suddenly that emitter has a few hundred event listeners, that could indicate some type of logic error, which could result in a memory leak. An example of this would be a loop that adds event listeners. If the loop contained a logic error, a large number of event handlers could be created, consuming unnecessary memory. By default, Node prints a warning message if more than ten listeners are added for any single event. This threshold can be controlled using the setMaxListeners() method. This method takes an integer as its only argument. By setting this value to 0, the event emitter will accept unlimited listeners without printing a warning message. Note that program semantics are not affected by setMaxListeners() (it only causes a warning message to be printed). Instead, it simply provides a useful debugging mechanism. The usage for setMaxListeners() is shown in Listing 4-14.

Listing 4-14. Syntax of the setMaxListeners() Method

```
emitter.setMaxListeners(n)
```

Inheriting from Event Emitters

All of the examples thus far have explicitly concerned the managing of EventEmitter instances. As an alternative, you can create custom objects that inherit from EventEmitter and include additional application-specific logic. Listing 4-15 shows how this is done. The first line imports the familiar EventEmitter constructor. The second line imports the util core module. As the name implies, util provides a number of useful utility functions. The inherits() method, which is of particular interest in this example, takes two arguments, both of which are constructor functions. inherits() causes the first constructor to inherit the prototype methods from the second. In this example, the custom User constructor inherits from EventEmitter. Inside the User constructor, the EventEmitter constructor is called. Additionally, a single method, addUser(), is defined which emits userAdded events.

Listing 4-15. Creating an Object That Extends EventEmitter

```
var EventEmitter = require("events").EventEmitter;
var util = require("util");

function UserEventEmitter() {
  EventEmitter.call(this);

  this.addUser = function(username, password) {
    // add the user
    // then emit an event
    this.emit("userAdded", username, password);
  };
};

util.inherits(UserEventEmitter, EventEmitter);
```

▪ **Note**   JavaScript employs a type of inheritance known as prototypal inheritance, which differs from classical inheritance—the sort used in a language such as Java. In prototypal inheritance, there are no classes. Instead, objects act as prototypes for other objects.

Listing 4-16 shows how the custom User event emitter is used. For the purposes of this example, assume that the User constructor is defined in the same file—although theoretically it could be defined elsewhere and imported using the require() function. In this example, a new User is instantiated. Next, a userAdded event listener is added. Then the addUser() method is called to simulate the creation of a new user. Since addUser() emits a userAdded event, the event handler gets invoked. Also, notice the print statement on the final line of the example. This statement checks whether the user variable is an instance of EventEmitter. Since User inherits from EventEmitter, this will evaluate to true.

Listing 4-16. Using a Custom Event Emitter

```
var user = new UserEventEmitter();
var username = "colin";
var password = "password";

user.on("userAdded", function(username, password) {
  console.log("Added user " + username);
});

user.addUser(username, password)
console.log(user instanceof EventEmitter);
```

Using Events to Avoid Callback Hell

Chapter 3 explored a number of ways to avoid callback hell, one of which is using the async module. Event emitters offer another elegant method for avoiding the Pyramid of Doom. As an example, let's use Listing 4-17 to revisit the file reader application from Listing 3-5.

Listing 4-17. A File Reader Program with Callback Hell Beginning to Creep In

```
var fs = require("fs");
var fileName = "foo.txt";

fs.exists(fileName, function(exists) {
 if (exists) {
   fs.stat(fileName, function(error, stats) {
     if (error) {
       throw error;
     }

     if (stats.isFile()) {
       fs.readFile(fileName, "utf8", function(error, data) {
         if (error) {
           throw error;
         }

         console.log(data);
       });
     }
   });
 }
});
```

Listing 4-18 shows how to rewrite the file reader application using event emitters. In this example, a FileReader object that encapsulates all of the file reading functionality is created. The EventEmitter constructor and the util module are required to set up the event emitter inheritance. Additionally, the fs module is needed to get access to the file system.

Inside the FileReader constructor, the first thing you'll notice is that this is aliased to the private _self variable. This is done to maintain a reference to the FileReader object inside the asynchronous file system callback functions. Inside these callbacks, the this variable does not refer to the FileReader. This means that the emit() method is not accessible via the this keyword in these callbacks.

Other than the _self variable, the code is fairly straightforward. The exists() method is used to check whether the file exists. If it does, a stats event is emitted. The stats listener is then triggered, calling the stat() method. If the file is a normal file and no errors occur, then a read event is emitted. The read event triggers the read listener, which attempts to read and print the contents of the file.

Listing 4-18. Refactoring the File Reader Application Using Event Emitters

```
var EventEmitter = require("events").EventEmitter;
var util = require("util");
var fs = require("fs");
```

```
function FileReader(fileName) {
  var _self = this;

  EventEmitter.call(_self);

  _self.on("stats", function() {
    fs.stat(fileName, function(error, stats) {
      if (!error && stats.isFile()) {
        _self.emit("read");
      }
    });
  });

  _self.on("read", function() {
    fs.readFile(fileName, "utf8", function(error, data) {
      if (!error && data) {
        console.log(data);
      }
    });
  });

  fs.exists(fileName, function(exists) {
    if (exists) {
      _self.emit("stats");
    }
  });
};

util.inherits(FileReader, EventEmitter);

var reader = new FileReader("foo.txt");
```

Timers and Scheduling

As all of the familiar JavaScript functions for handling timers and intervals are available in Node as globals, you don't need to import them using require(). The setTimeout() function is used to schedule a one-time callback function to execute at some time in the future. The arguments to setTimeout() are the callback function to execute, the amount of time (in milliseconds) to wait before executing it, and zero or more arguments to pass to the callback function. Listing 4-19 shows how setTimeout() is used to schedule a callback function to execute after a one second delay. In this example, the callback function takes two arguments, foo and bar, which are populated by the final two arguments to setTimeout().

■ **Note**   Remember that JavaScript time (computer time in general, actually) is not 100% accurate, and so callback functions are highly unlikely to execute exactly when specified. And because JavaScript is single threaded, a long-running task can completely throw off timing.

Listing 4-19. Creating a Timer That Executes After a Delay of One Second

```
setTimeout(function(foo, bar) {
  console.log(foo + " " + bar);
}, 1000, "foo", "bar");
```

The `setTimeout()` function also returns a timeout identifier that can be used to cancel the timer before the callback function is executed. Timers are canceled by passing the timeout identifier to the `clearTimeout()` function. Listing 4-20 shows a timer being canceled prior to execution. In this example the timer is canceled immediately after it is created. However, in a real application, a timer is typically canceled based on some event occurring.

Listing 4-20. Canceling a Timer Using the `clearTimeout()` Function

```
var timeoutId = setTimeout(function() {
  console.log("In timeout function");
}, 1000);

clearTimeout(timeoutId);
```

Intervals

In essence, an interval is a timer that repeats periodically. The respective functions for creating and canceling an interval are `setInterval()` and `clearInterval()`. Like `setTimeout()`, `setInterval()` accepts a callback function, a delay, and optional callback arguments. It also returns an interval identifier that can be passed to `clearInterval()` in order to cancel the interval. Listing 4-21 demonstrates how intervals are created and canceled using `setInterval()` and `clearInterval()`.

Listing 4-21. An example of Creating and Canceling an Interval

```
var intervalId = setInterval(function() {
  console.log("In interval function");
}, 1000);

clearInterval(intervalId);
```

The `ref()` and `unref()` Methods

A timer or interval that is the only item remaining in the event loop will prevent the program from terminating. However, this behavior can be programmatically altered using the `ref()` and `unref()` methods of a timer or interval identifier. Calling the `unref()` method allows the program to exit if the timer/interval is the only item left in the event loop. For example, in Listing 4-22 an interval is the only item scheduled in the event loop following the call to `setInterval()`. However, because `unref()` is called on the interval, the program terminates.

Listing 4-22. An example of an Interval That Does Not Keep the Program Alive

```
var intervalId = setInterval(function() {
  console.log("In interval function");
}, 1000);

intervalId.unref();
```

If `unref()` has been called on a timer or interval but you wish to revert to the default behavior, the `ref()` method can be called. The usage of `ref()` is shown in Listing 4-23.

Listing 4-23. Usage of the `ref()` Method

```
timer.ref()
```

Immediates

Immediates are used to schedule a callback function for immediate execution. This allows a function to be scheduled after the currently executing function. Immediates are created using the `setImmediate()` function, which takes a callback and optional callback arguments as its arguments. Unlike `setTimeout()` and `setInterval()`, `setImmediate()` does not accept a `delay` argument, as the delay is assumed to be zero. Immediates can also be cancelled using the `clearImmediate()` function. An example of creating and canceling an immediate is shown in Listing 4-24.

Listing 4-24. An Example of Creating and Canceling an Immediate

```
var immediateId = setImmediate(function() {
  console.log("In immediate function");
});

clearImmediate(immediateId);
```

Splitting Up Long-Running Tasks

Anyone familiar with JavaScript development in the browser has no doubt encountered a situation where a long-running piece of code makes the user interface unresponsive. This behavior is an artifact of JavaScript's single-threaded nature. For example, the `compute()` function in Listing 4-25 contains a long-running loop simulating computationally intensive code that, even with an empty loop body, will cause a noticeable lag in an application's response time.

Listing 4-25. A Synthetic Computationally Intensive Function

```
function compute() {
 for (var i = 0; i < 1000000000; i++) {
   // perform some computation
 }
}

compute();
console.log("Finished compute()");
```

   In the browser world, a common solution to this problem is to split up computationally expensive code into smaller chunks using `setTimeout()`. The same technique works in Node as well, however, the preferred solution is `setImmediate()`. Listing 4-26 shows how the computationally intensive code can be broken into smaller pieces using `setImmediate()`. In this example, one iteration is processed each time `compute()` is invoked. This process allows other code to run while still adding iterations of `compute()` to the event loop. Note, however, that execution will be significantly slower than with the original code, because each function invocation handles only one loop iteration. A better balance of performance and responsiveness can be achieved by performing more work per function call. For example, `setImmediate()` could be called after every 10,000 iterations. The best approach will be dependent on your application's needs.

Listing 4-26. Breaking Up Computationally Intensive Code Using `setImmediate()`

```
var i = 0;

function compute() {
 if (i < 1000000000) {
```

```
    // perform some computation
    i++;
    setImmediate(compute);
  }
}

compute();
console.log("compute() still working...");
```

Scheduling with `process.nextTick()`

Node's process object contains a method named `nextTick()` which provides an efficient scheduling mechanism which is similar to an immediate. `nextTick()` takes a callback function as its only argument, and invokes the callback on the next iteration of the event loop, referred to as a *tick*. Since the callback function is scheduled for the next tick, `nextTick()`does not require a `delay` argument. According to the official Node documentation, `nextTick()` is also more efficient than, and thus preferred over, a similar call to `setTimeout(fn, 0)`. Listing 4-27 shows an example of function scheduling using `nextTick()`.

Listing 4-27. Scheduling a Function Using `process.nextTick()`

```
process.nextTick(function() {
  console.log("Executing tick n+1");
});

console.log("Executing nth tick");
```

■ **Caution**   In older versions of Node, `process.nextTick()` was the preferred tool for breaking up computationally intensive code. However, recursive calls to `nextTick()` are now discouraged; `setImmediate()` should be used instead.

Unfortunately, there is no way to pass arguments to the callback function. Luckily, this limitation can easily be overcome by creating a function that binds any desired arguments. For example, the code in Listing 4-28 will not work as expected, because there is no way to pass arguments to the callback function. However, the code in Listing 4-29 will work, because the function's arguments are bound before being passed to `nextTick()`.

Listing 4-28. An Incorrect Attempt at Passing Arguments to `process.nextTick()`

```
process.nextTick(function(f, b) {
  console.log(f + " " + b);
});
// prints "undefined undefined"
```

Listing 4-29. Passing a Function with Bound Arguments to `process.nextTick()`

```
function getFunction(f, b) {
  return function myNextTick() {
    console.log(f + " " + b);
  };
}

process.nextTick(getFunction("foo", "bar"));
// prints "foo bar"
```

Implementing Asynchronous Callback Functions

process.nextTick() is often used to create functions that accept an asynchronous callback function as the final argument. Without using nextTick(), a callback function is not truly asynchronous, and it behaves like a normal (synchronous) function call. Synchronous callback functions can lead to starvation by preventing other tasks in the event loop from executing. They can also cause confusion for those using your code if they are expecting asynchronous behavior.

Listing 4-30 shows a simple function that adds two numbers and then passes their sum to a callback function. Node's calling conventions dictate that the callback function should execute asynchronously. Therefore, one would expect the code to print The sum is: followed by the actual sum, 5. However, the callback function is not called asynchronously using nextTick(). Therefore, the sum is actually printed *first*, as Listing 4-31 shows. To avoid confusion, the function might more appropriately be named addSync().

Listing 4-30. An example of a Synchronous Callback Function

```
function add(x, y, cb) {
  cb(x + y);
}

add(2, 3, console.log);
console.log("The sum is:");
```

Listing 4-31. Output of Running the Code in Listing 4-30

```
$ node sync-callback.js
5
The sum is:
```

Luckily, transforming a synchronous callback function into an asynchronous one is fairly straightforward, as shown in Listing 4-32. In this example, the callback function is passed to nextTick(). Also, notice that having the callback function wrapped inside an anonymous function allows the values of x and y to pass through nextTick(). These simple changes cause the program to behave as originally expected. Listing 4-33 shows the resulting correct output.

Listing 4-32. A Proper Asynchronous Callback Function Using process.nextTick()

```
function add(x, y, cb) {
  process.nextTick(function() {
    cb(x + y);
  });
}

add(2, 3, console.log);
console.log("The sum is:");
```

Listing 4-33. Output of Running the Asynchronous Code in Listing 4-32

```
$ node async-callback.js
The sum is:
5
```

Maintaining Consistent Behavior

Any nontrivial function is likely to have multiple control flow paths. It is important that all of these paths be uniformly asynchronous or uniformly synchronous. In other words, a function should not behave asynchronously for one set of inputs, but synchronously for another. Additionally, you must ensure that the callback function is invoked only once. This is a common source of problems, as many developers assume that invoking a callback function causes the current function to return. In reality, the function continues to execute once the callback function returns. An extremely simple fix for this problem is to return every time nextTick() is called.

Consider the function in Listing 4-34, which determines whether a number is negative or not. If the n argument is less than 0, true is passed to the callback function. Otherwise, false is passed. Unfortunately, this example suffers from two major problems. The first is that the true callback behaves asynchronously, while the false callback is synchronous. The second is that when n is negative, the callback function is executed twice, once at the end of isNegative() and a second time when the nextTick() callback is executed.

Listing 4-34. An Inconsistent Implementation of a Callback Function

```
function isNegative(n, cb) {
  if (n < 0) {
    process.nextTick(function() {
      cb(true);
    });
  }

  cb(false);
}
```

Listing 4-35 shows a correct implementation of the same function (notice that both invocations of the callback function are now asynchronous). Additionally, both calls to nextTick() cause isNegative() to return, ensuring that the callback function can be invoked only once.

Listing 4-35. A Consistent Implementation of the Callback Function from Listing 4-34

```
function isNegative(n, cb) {
  if (n < 0) {
    return process.nextTick(function() {
      cb(true);
    });
  }

  return process.nextTick(function() {
    cb(false);
  });
}
```

Of course, this is a contrived example. The code can be greatly simplified, as Listing 4-36 shows.

Listing 4-36. A Simplified Version of the Code in Listing 4-35

```
function isNegative(n, cb) {
  process.nextTick(function() {
    cb(n < 0);
  });
}
```

Summary

This chapter has explored events, timers, and scheduling control in the Node.js world. Together, this chapter and the previous one should give you a solid grasp of Node fundamentals. Taking this understanding as a base, the remainder of this book focuses on exploring the various Node APIs and creating exciting applications with them. The next chapter shows you how to create command line interfaces—the first step toward building real-world Node applications.

CHAPTER 5

■ ■ ■

The Command Line Interface

The first four chapters showed you the fundamentals of Node development. Starting with this chapter, the book shifts directions and begins focusing on the various APIs and modules used to create Node applications. This chapter focuses specifically on creating command line interfaces (CLI) for interacting with users. First, you will learn command line basics with Node's built-in APIs. From there, you can expand upon the basics using the commander module, which you may remember from several npm examples in Chapter 2.

Command Line Arguments

Command line arguments constitute one of the most fundamental ways of providing input to computer programs. In Node applications, command line arguments are made accessible via the argv array property of the global process object. Listing 5-1 shows how argv, like any other array, can be iterated over using the forEach() method.

Listing 5-1. An Example of Iterating over the argv Array

```
process.argv.forEach(function(arg, index) {
  console.log("argv[" + index + "] = " + arg);
});
```

To inspect the actual values held in argv, save the code from Listing 5-1 in a new JavaScript source file named argv-test.js. Next, run the code, and observe the output (see Listing 5-2). Notice that four arguments are passed to our Node program: -foo, 3, --bar=4, and -baz. However, based on the program's output, there are six elements in argv. No matter what combination of command line arguments you provide, argv always contains an additional two elements at the beginning of the array. This is because the first two elements of argv are always node (the name of the executable) and the path to the JavaScript source file. The remainder of the argv array is composed of the actual command line arguments.

Listing 5-2. Output from Running the Code in Listing 5-1

```
$ node argv-test.js -foo 3 --bar=4 -baz
argv[0] = node
argv[1] = /home/colin/argv-test.js
argv[2] = -foo
argv[3] = 3
argv[4] = --bar=4
argv[5] = -baz
```

Parsing Argument Values

Based on the command line in Listing 5-2, we appear to be trying to pass in three arguments: foo, bar, and baz. However, each of the three arguments works differently. The value of foo comes from the argument that follows it (we assume it is an integer). In this case, the value of foo is 3. Unlike foo, the value of bar, 4, is encoded in the same argument, following an equal sign. Meanwhile, baz is a Boolean argument. Its value is true if the argument is provided and false otherwise. Unfortunately, by simply examining the values in argv, none of these semantics are captured.

To extract the correct command line argument values, we can develop a custom parser (see Listing 5-3). In the example, the parseArgs() function is responsible for parsing the command line, extracting values, and returning an object that maps each argument to its proper value. This function works by looping over each element in argv, checking for recognized argument names. If the argument is foo, then an integer is parsed from the following argument. The loop variable, i, is also incremented to save time, as it is unnecessary to execute the loop body for the value of foo. If the argument is determined to be baz, we simply assign the value true. To extract the value of bar, a regular expression is used. If the string --bar= is followed by a series of one or more numbers, then those numbers are parsed into an integer value. Finally, all of the arguments are returned via the args object and printed to the console.

Listing 5-3. A Command Line Parser for the Example in Listing 5-2

```
function parseArgs() {
  var argv = process.argv;
  var args = {
    baz: false
  };

  for (var i = 0, len = argv.length; i < len; i++) {
    var arg = argv[i];
    var match;

    if (arg === "-foo") {
      args.foo = parseInt(argv[++i]);
    } else if (arg === "-baz") {
      args.baz = true;
    } else if (match = arg.match(/--bar=(\d+)/)) {
      args.bar = parseInt(match[1]);
    }
  }

  return args;
}

var args = parseArgs();

console.log(args);
```

Listing 5-4 shows the output from running the code in Listing 5-3. As you see, all of the arguments have been properly extracted. But what happens when the user input is malformed? Listing 5-5 shows the output of running the same program with different arguments. In this case, baz is misspelled as az, and the user has forgotten to provide a value for foo.

Listing 5-4. The Result of Running the Code in Listing 5-3

```
$ node argv-parser.js -foo 3 --bar=4 -baz
{ foo: 3, bar: 4, baz: true }
```

Listing 5-5. The Output Resulting from Malformed User Input

```
$ node argv-parser.js -foo -az --bar=4
{ foo: NaN, bar: 4 }
```

In the output of Listing 5-5, notice that baz is completely missing and foo has a value of NaN (Not-A-Number), because the parser is attempting to convert -az to an integer. Since baz has not been passed in from the command line, ideally its value will be false. Similarly, foo and bar should have some default value in order to handle cases like this. Prepopulating the args object in parseArgs() won't prevent foo from getting set to NaN in this case.

Instead, we can post-process args using a sanitize() function (see Listing 5-6). This function checks the value of each argument and assigns it an appropriate value if it doesn't already have one. In this example, JavaScript's built-in isFinite() method is used to ensure that foo and bar are valid integers. Since baz is a Boolean, the code simply checks if it is not equal to true, and sets it to false if so. This ensures that baz is actually set to Boolean false—not left as undefined, which is a different falsy value. Note that the parseArgs() code is not included in this example as it has not changed.

Listing 5-6. A sanitize() Function That Assigns Default Values to Arguments

```
function sanitize(args) {
  if (!isFinite(args.foo)) {
    args.foo = 0;
  }

  if (!isFinite(args.bar)) {
    args.bar = 0;
  }

  if (args.baz !== true) {
    args.baz = false;
  }

  return args;
}

var args = sanitize(parseArgs());

console.log(args);
```

Command Line Arguments in commander

If the amount of work required to implement simple command line parsing seems like a bit much to you, rest assured you are not alone. Luckily, a module like commander makes command line parsing simple. A third-party module, commander is used to simplify such common CLI tasks as argument parsing and reading user input. To install commander, use the command npm install commander. To accommodate command line argument parsing, commander provides the option() and parse() methods. Each call to option() registers a valid command line argument with commander. Once all possible arguments are registered using option(), the parse() method is used to extract argument values from the command line.

It's probably simplest to use an example to show how commander's command line argument system works. In Listing 5-7, commander is configured to accept three arguments: --foo, --bar, and --baz. The --foo argument can also be specified using -f. This is considered the argument's short version. All commander arguments must have a short and long name. The short name should be a single dash followed by one letter, and the long name should have two dashes preceding the name.

Listing 5-7. An Example Command Line Parser Using commander

```
var commander = require("commander");

commander
  .option("-f, --foo <i>", "Integer value for foo", parseInt, 0)
  .option("-b, --bar [j]", "Integer value for bar", parseInt, 0)
  .option("-z, --baz", "Boolean argument baz")
  .parse(process.argv);

console.log(commander.foo);
console.log(commander.bar);
console.log(commander.baz);
```

Notice the <i> and [j] following --foo and --bar. These are values that are expected to follow the argument. When angle brackets are used, as with --foo, the additional value must be specified, or an error is thrown. The square brackets used with --bar indicate that the additional value is optional. --baz is considered a Boolean argument because it does not take any additional arguments. Following the argument string is the description string. These strings are human-readable and are used for displaying help, which is covered momentarily.

The next thing to point out is that the --foo and --bar options also refer to parseInt() and the number 0 (zero). parseInt() is passed as an optional argument that is used to parse the additional argument. In this case, the values of --foo and --bar are evaluated as integers. Finally, if no value is provided for --foo or --bar, they are set to 0.

Once all the options are registered, parse() is called to process the command line. Technically, any array can be passed to parse(), but passing in process.argv makes the most sense. After parsing, the values of the arguments are available according to their long names, as shown in the three print statements.

Automatically Generated Help

commander automatically generates a --help (or -h) argument based on the option configuration. Listing 5-8 shows the automatically generated help from the previous example.

Listing 5-8. Automatically Generated help for the Code in Listing 5-7

```
$ node commander-test.js --help

  Usage: commander-test.js [options]

  Options:

    -h, --help         output usage information
    -f, --foo <i>      Integer value for foo
    -b, --bar [j]      Integer value for bar
    -z, --baz          Boolean argument baz
```

There are also two methods that can be used to display the help: help() and outputHelp(). The only difference between them is that help() causes the program to exit, while outputHelp() does not. Normally, you call help() and then exit if invalid arguments are provided. However, you can call outputHelp() if you want to just display the help menu and continue executing for some reason. The use of these two methods is shown in Listing 5-9.

Listing 5-9. Use of the commander help Methods

```
commander.help()
commander.outputHelp()
```

The Standard Streams

By default, Node applications are connected to three data streams—stdin, stdout, and stderr—that provide input and output capabilities. If you are familiar with C/C++, Java, or any of a host of other languages, you have undoubtedly encountered these standard streams before. This section explores each one in detail.

Standard Input

The stdin stream (short for "standard input") is a readable stream providing input to programs. By default, stdin receives data from the terminal window used to launch the application, and is commonly used to accept input from the user at runtime. However, stdin can also receive its data from a file or another program.

From within a Node application, stdin is a property of the global process object. However, when an application starts, stdin is in a paused state—that is, no data can be read from it. For data to be read, the stream must be unpaused using the resume() method (see Listing 5-10), which takes no arguments and provides no return value.

Listing 5-10. Usage of stdin.resume()

```
process.stdin.resume()
```

In addition to unpausing the stdin stream, resume() prevents an application from terminating, as it will be in a state of waiting for input. However, stdin can be paused again, using the pause() method, to allow the program to exit. Listing 5-11 shows the usage of pause().

Listing 5-11. Usage of stdin.pause()

```
process.stdin.pause()
```

After calling resume(), your program can read data from stdin. However, you need to set up a data event handler to read the data yourself. The arrival of new data on stdin triggers a data event. The data event handler takes a single argument, the data received. In Listing 5-12, which shows how data is read from stdin using data events, the user is prompted for his/her name. resume() is then called in order to activate the stdin stream. Once the name is entered and the user presses Return, the data event handler—added using the once() method (covered in Chapter 4)—is called. The event handler then acknowledges the user and pauses stdin. Notice that inside the event handler, the data argument is converted to a string. This is done because data is passed in as a Buffer object. Buffers are used to handle raw binary data in Node applications. (This topic is covered in more detail in Chapter 8.)

Listing 5-12. An Example of Reading Data from stdin

```
process.stdin.once("data", function(data) {
  var response = data.toString();

  console.log("You said your name is " + response);
  process.stdin.pause();
});

console.log("What is your name?");
process.stdin.resume();
```

You can avoid having to convert the data to a string each time data is read by specifying the character encoding of the stdin stream a priori. To do so, use the setEncoding() method of stdin. As Table 5-1 shows, Node supports a number of different character encodings. When dealing with string data, it is advisable to set the encoding to utf8 (UTF-8). Listing 5-13 shows how Listing 5-12 can be rewritten using setEncoding().

Table 5-1. The Various String Encoding Types Supported by Node

Encoding Type	Description
utf8	Multibyte-encoded Unicode characters. UTF-8 encoding is used by many web pages, and is used to represent string data in Node.
ascii	Seven-bit American Standard Code for Information Interchange (ASCII) encoding.
utf16le	Little endian–encoded Unicode characters. Each character is two or four bytes.
ucs2	This is simply an alias for utf16le encoding.
base64	Base64 string encoding. Base64 is commonly used in URL encoding, e-mail, and similar applications.
binary	Allows binary data to be encoded as a string using only the first eight bits of each character. This coding is now deprecated, in favor of the Buffer object, and will be removed in future versions of Node.
hex	Encodes each byte as two hexadecimal characters.

Listing 5-13. Reading from stdin After Setting the Character Encoding Type

```
process.stdin.once("data", function(data) {
  console.log("You said your name is " + data);
  process.stdin.pause();
});

console.log("What is your name?");
process.stdin.setEncoding("utf8");
process.stdin.resume();
```

Reading From `stdin` Using `commander`

The `commander` module also provides several useful methods for reading data from `stdin`. The most basic of these is `prompt()`, which displays some message or question to the user and then reads in the response. The response is then passed as a string to a callback function for processing. Listing 5-14 shows how the example from Listing 5-13 can be rewritten using `prompt()`.

Listing 5-14. Reading from `stdin` Using `commander`'s `prompt()` Method

```
var commander = require("commander");

commander.prompt("What is your name? ", function(name) {
  console.log("You said your name is " + name);
  process.stdin.pause();
});
```

`confirm()`

The `confirm()` method is similar to `prompt()` but is used to parse a Boolean response. If the user enters y, yes, true, or ok, the callback is invoked with its argument set to `true`. Otherwise, the callback is invoked with its argument set to `false`. An example use of the `confirm()` method is shown in Listing 5-15, and Listing 5-16 shows sample output from the example.

Listing 5-15. Parsing a Boolean Response Using `commander`'s `confirm()` Method

```
var commander = require("commander");

commander.confirm("Continue? ", function(proceed) {
  console.log("Your response was " + proceed);
  process.stdin.pause();
});
```

Listing 5-16. Sample Output from Running the Code in Listing 5-15

```
$ node confirm-example.js
Continue? yes
Your response was true
```

`password()`

Another special case of `prompt()` is the `password()` method, which is used to get sensitive user input without having it displayed in the terminal window. As the method name implies, its biggest use case is prompting the user for a password. An example using `password()` is shown in Listing 5-17.

Listing 5-17. Prompting for a Password Using the `password()` Method

```
var commander = require("commander");

commander.password("Password: ", function(password) {
  console.log("I know your password!  It's " + password);
  process.stdin.pause();
});
```

By default, `password()` does not echo information back to the terminal. However, an optional mask string, which is echoed back to the user for every character entered, can be provided. Listing 5-18 shows an example. In it, the mask string is simply the asterisk character (*).

Listing 5-18. Prompting for a Password Using a Mask Character

```
var commander = require("commander");

commander.password("Password: ", "*", function(password) {
  console.log("I know your password!  It's " + password);
  process.stdin.pause();
});
```

choose()

The `choose()` function is useful for creating text-based menus. Taking an array of options as its first argument, `choose()` allows users to select an option from a list. The second argument is a callback invoked with the array index of the selected option. Listing 5-19 shows an example that uses `choose()`.

Listing 5-19. Displaying a Text Menu Using `choose()`

```
var commander = require("commander");
var list = ["foo", "bar", "baz"];

commander.choose(list, function(index) {
  console.log("You selected " + list[index]);
  process.stdin.pause();
});
```

Listing 5-20 shows sample output from running the previous example. One thing to note is that the menu item count begins at 1, while arrays are indexed from 0. Taking this into account, `choose()` passes the correct zero-based array index to the callback function.

Listing 5-20. Example Output from Listing 5-19

```
$ node choose-example.js
  1) foo
  2) bar
  3) baz
  : 2
You selected bar
```

Standard Output

Standard output, or `stdout`, is a writable stream to which programs should direct their output. By default, Node applications direct output to the terminal window that launched the application. The most direct way to write data to `stdout` is via the `process.stdout.write()` method. The usage of `write()` is shown in Listing 5-21. The first argument to `write()` is the data string to be written. The second argument is optional; it is used to specify the data's character encoding, which defaults to `utf8` (UTF-8) encoding. `write()` supports all of the encoding types specified in Table 5-1. The final argument to `write()` is an optional callback function. It is executed once the data is successfully written to `stdout`. No arguments are passed to the callback function.

Listing 5-21. Use of the stdout.write() Method

```
process.stdout.write(data, [encoding], [callback])
```

■ **Note** process.stdout.write() can also accept a Buffer as its first argument.

---

console.log()

After reading about stdout.write(), you might be curious how it relates to the already discussed console.log() method. Actually, console.log() is just a wrapper that calls stdout.write() under the hood. Listing 5-22 shows the source code for console.log(). This code is taken directly from the file https://github.com/joyent/node/blob/master/lib/console.js in Node's official GitHub repo. As you see, log() makes a call to _stdout.write(). Examining the entire source file shows that _stdout is simply a reference to stdout.

Listing 5-22. Source Code of console.log()

```
Console.prototype.log = function() { this._stdout.write(util.format.apply(this, arguments) + '\n');
};
```

Also, notice that the call to write() invokes the util.format() method. The util object is a reference to the core util module. The format() method is used for creating formatted strings based on the arguments passed to it. As its first argument, format() takes a format string containing zero or more *placeholders*. A placeholder is a character sequence in the format string that is expected to be replaced by a different value in the returned string. Following the format string, format() expects an additional argument for each placeholder. format() supports four placeholders, described in Table 5-2.

Table 5-2. *The Various Placeholders Supported by util.format().*

Placeholder	Replacement
%s	String data. An argument is consumed and passed to the String() constructor.
%d	Integer or floating-point numeric data. An argument is consumed and passed to the Number() constructor.
%j	JSON data. An argument is consumed and passed to JSON.stringify().
%%	A single percent sign (%) character. This does not consume any arguments.

Several examples of util.format() are shown in Listing 5-23, with the resulting output shown in Listing 5-24. These examples show how data are substituted using various placeholders. The first three examples substitute a string using the string, number, and JSON placeholders. Notice that the number placeholder is replaced by NaN. This is because the string held in the name variable cannot be converted to an actual number. In the fourth example, the JSON placeholder is used, but no corresponding argument is passed to format(). The result is simply that no substitution occurs, and the %j is included in the result. In the fifth example, format() is passed one more argument than it can handle. format() handles additional arguments by converting them to strings and appending them to the result string, with a space character as a separator. In the sixth example, multiple placeholders are used as expected. Finally, in the seventh example, no format string is provided at all. In this case, the arguments are converted to strings and concatenated, with a space character delimiter.

Listing 5-23. Several Examples Using `util.format()`

```javascript
var util = require("util");
var name = "Colin";
var age = 100;
var format1 = util.format("Hi, my name is %s", name);
var format2 = util.format("Hi, my name is %d", name);
var format3 = util.format("Hi, my name is %j", name);
var format4 = util.format("Hi, my name is %j");
var format5 = util.format("Hi, my name is %j", name, name);
var format6 = util.format("I'm %s, and I'm %d years old", name, age);
var format7 = util.format(name, age);

console.log(format1);
console.log(format2);
console.log(format3);
console.log(format4);
console.log(format5);
console.log(format6);
console.log(format7);
```

Listing 5-24. Output from Running the Code in Listing 5-23

```
$ node format.js
Hi, my name is Colin
Hi, my name is NaN
Hi, my name is "Colin"
Hi, my name is %j
Hi, my name is "Colin" Colin
I'm Colin, and I'm 100 years old
Colin 100
```

■ **Note** Anyone familiar with C/C++, PHP, or any of a slew of other languages will recognize the behavior of `util.format()`, as it provides formatting similar to the `printf()` function.

Other Printing Functions

Node also provides several less popular functions for printing to `stdout`. For example, the `util` module defines the `log()` method. The `log()` method accepts a single string as an argument and prints it to `stdout` with a timestamp. Listing 5-25 shows an example of `log()` in action. The resulting output is shown in Listing 5-26.

Listing 5-25. An Example of `util.log()`

```javascript
var util = require("util");

util.log("baz");
```

Listing 5-26. Output from Running the Code in Listing 5-25

```
$ node util-log-method.js
17 Mar 15:08:29 - baz
```

The console object also provides two additional printing methods, info() and dir(). The info() method is simply an alias to console.log(). console.dir() takes an object as its only argument. The object is stringified using the util.inspect() method and then printed to stdout. util.inspect() is the same method used to stringify extra arguments to util.format() without corresponding placeholders. inspect(), a powerful method for stringifying data, is covered below.

util.inspect()

util.inspect() is used to convert objects into nicely formatted strings. While its true power comes from its ability to be customized, we begin by looking at its default behavior. Listing 5-27 shows an example that uses inspect() to stringify an object, obj. The resulting string is shown in Listing 5-28.

Listing 5-27. An Example That Uses the util.inspect() Method

```
var util = require("util");
var obj = {
  foo: {
    bar: {
      baz: {
        baff: false,
        beff: "string value",
        biff: null
      },
      boff: []
    }
  }
};

console.log(util.inspect(obj));
```

Listing 5-28. The String Created by util.inspect() in Listing 5-27

```
{ foo: { bar: { baz: [Object], boff: [] } } }
```

Notice that foo and bar are completely stringified, but baz only displays the string [Object]. That's because, by default, inspect() only recurses through two levels while formatting the object. This behavior can be changed, though, by using the optional second argument to inspect(). This argument is an object that specifies configuration options to inspect(). If you're interested in increasing the depth of recursion, set the depth option. It can be set to null to force inspect() to recurse over the entire object. Examples of this and of the resulting string are shown in Listings 5-29 and 5-30.

Listing 5-29. Calling util.inspect() with Full Recursion Enabled

```
var util = require("util");
var obj = {
  foo: {
    bar: {
      baz: {
        baff: false,
        beff: "string value",
        biff: null
      },
      boff: []
    }
  }
};

console.log(util.inspect(obj, {
  depth: null
}));
```

Listing 5-30. The Output from Running the Code in Listing 5-29

```
$ node inspect-recursion.js
{ foo:
   { bar:
      { baz: { baff: false, beff: 'string value', biff: null },
        boff: [] } } }
```

The options argument supports several other options—showHidden, colors, and customInspect. showHidden and colors default to false, while customInspect defaults to true. When showHidden is set to true, inspect() prints all of an object's properties, including the non-enumerable ones. Setting colors to true causes the resulting string to be styled with ANSI color codes. When customInspect is set to true, objects can define their own inspect() methods, which are called to return a string used in the stringification process. In the example of this, shown in Listing 5-31, a custom inspect() method has been added to the top-level object. This custom method returns a string that hides all of the child objects. The resulting output is shown in Listing 5-32.

■ **Note**   Not all of a method's properties are created equal. In JavaScript, it is possible to create non-enumerable properties, which will not show up when an object is iterated over in a for...in loop. By setting the showHidden option, inspect() will include non-enumerable properties in its output.

Listing 5-31. Calling util.inspect() with a Custom inspect() Method

```
var util = require("util");
var obj = {
  foo: {
    bar: {
      baz: {
        baff: false,
```

```
      beff: "string value",
      biff: null
    },
    boff: []
  }
},
inspect: function() {
  return "{Where'd everything go?}";
}
};

console.log(util.inspect(obj));
```

Listing 5-32. The Result of the Custom `inspect()` Method in Listing 5-31

```
$ node inspect-custom.js
{Where'd everything go?}
```

Standard Error

The standard error stream, `stderr`, is an output stream similar to `stdout`. However, `stderr` is used for displaying error and warning messages. While `stderr` and `stdout` are similar, `stderr` is a separate entity, and so you cannot access it using a `stdout` function like `console.log()`. Luckily, Node provides a number of functions specifically for accessing `stderr`. The most direct access route to `stderr` is via its `write()` method. The usage of `write()`, shown in Listing 5-33, is identical to the `write()` method of `stdout`.

Listing 5-33. Use of the `stderr` `write()` Method

```
process.stderr.write(data, [encoding], [callback])
```

The `console` object also provides two methods, `error()` and `warn()`, for writing to `stderr`. `console.warn()` behaves exactly like `console.log()` and simply acts as a wrapper around `process.stderr.write()`. The `error()` method is simply an alias for `warn()`. Listing 5-34 shows the source code for `warn()` and `error()`.

Listing 5-34. Source Code of `console.warn()` and `console.error()`

```
Console.prototype.warn = function() {
  this._stderr.write(util.format.apply(this, arguments) + '\n');
};

Console.prototype.error = Console.prototype.warn;
```

console.trace()

The `console` object also provides a useful debugging method, named `trace()`, which creates and prints a stack trace to `stderr` without crashing the program. If you've ever encountered an error (I'm sure you have by now), then you've seen the stack trace printed when your program crashed. `trace()` accomplishes the same thing without the error and crash. Listing 5-35 shows an example using `trace()`, with its output shown in Listing 5-36. In the example a stack trace, named `test-trace`, is created within the function `baz()`, which is called from `bar()`, which in turn is called from `foo()`. Notice that these functions are the top three entries in the stack trace. The remaining functions in the stack trace are calls made by the Node framework.

Listing 5-35. Generating an Example Stack Trace Using `console.trace()`

```
(function foo() {
  (function bar() {
    (function baz() {
      console.trace("test-trace");
    })();
  })();
})();
```

Listing 5-36. Output from Running the Example in Listing 5-35

```
$ node stack-trace.js
Trace: test-trace
    at baz (/home/colin/stack-trace.js:4:15)
    at bar (/home/colin/stack-trace.js:5:7)
    at foo (/home/colin/stack-trace.js:6:5)
    at Object.<anonymous> (/home/colin/stack-trace.js:7:3)
    at Module._compile (module.js:456:26)
    at Object.Module._extensions..js (module.js:474:10)
    at Module.load (module.js:356:32)
    at Function.Module._load (module.js:312:12)
    at Function.Module.runMain (module.js:497:10)
    at startup (node.js:119:16)
```

■ **Note**   The arguments passed to `console.trace()` are forwarded to `util.format()`. Therefore, the stack trace name can be created using a format string.

Separating `stderr` and `stdout`

It is common but not required for `stderr` to be directed to the same destination as `stdout`. By default, Node's `stdout` and `stderr` are both directed to the terminal window in which the process is run. However, it is possible to redirect one stream or both. The code in Listing 5-37 can be used to easily demonstrate this concept. The example code prints one message to `stdout` using `console.log()` and a second message to `stderr` using `console.error()`.

Listing 5-37. An Example Application That Prints to Both `stdout` and `stderr`

```
console.log("foo");
console.error("bar");
```

When the code in Listing 5-37 is run normally, both messages are printed to the terminal window. The output is shown in Listing 5-38.

Listing 5-38. Console Output When Running the Code in Listing 5-37

```
$ node stdout-and-stderr.js
foo
bar
```

The same code is executed again in Listing 5-39. However, this time stdout is redirected to the file output.txt using the > operator. Note that redirection has no effect on the stderr stream. The result is that bar, which is sent to stderr, is printed in the terminal window, while foo is not.

Listing 5-39. Console Output from the Code in Listing 5-39 When stdout Is Redirected

```
$ node stdout-and-stderr.js > output.txt
bar
```

■ **Note** As you've probably noticed by now, the console methods are synchronous. This behavior—the default when the underlying stream's destination is a file or terminal window—avoids lost messages due to program crash or exit. There is more about streams and how they can be piped in Chapter 7, but for now, just know that the console methods behave asynchronously when the underlying stream is piped.

The TTY Interface

As you've already seen, the standard streams are configured to work with a terminal window by default. To accommodate this configuration, Node provides an API for inspecting the state of the terminal window. Because the streams can be redirected, all standard streams provide an isTTY property that is true if the stream is associated with a terminal window. Listing 5-40 shows how these properties are accessed for each of the streams. By default, isTTY is true for stdin, stdout, and stderr, as Listing 5-41 shows.

Listing 5-40. An Example That Checks Whether Each Standard Stream Is Connected to a Terminal

```
console.warn("stdin  = " + process.stdin.isTTY);
console.warn("stdout = " + process.stdout.isTTY);
console.warn("stderr = " + process.stderr.isTTY);
```

Listing 5-41. Output from Listing 5-40 Under Default Conditions

```
$ node is-tty.js
stdin  = true
stdout = true
stderr = true
```

Listing 5-42 demonstrates how these values change when stdout is redirected to a file. Notice that the source code uses console.warn() instead of console.log(). This is done intentionally, so that stdout can be redirected while still providing console output. As you would expect, the value of isTTY is no longer true for stdout. However, notice that isTTY is, not false, but simply undefined, the implication being that isTTY is not a property of all streams, just of those associated with a terminal.

Listing 5-42. Output from Listing 5-40 with a Redirected stdout Stream

```
$ node is-tty.js > output.txt
stdin  = true
stdout = undefined
stderr = true
```

Determining the Terminal Size

A terminal window's size, particularly the number of columns, can greatly affect the readability of a program's output. Therefore, some applications may need to tailor their output based on the terminal size. Assuming that stdout or stderr or both are associated with a terminal window, it is possible to determine the number of rows and columns in the terminal. This information is available via the stream's rows and columns properties, respectively. You can also retrieve the terminal dimensions as an array using the stream's getWindowSize() method. Listing 5-43 shows how the terminal dimensions are determined, and Listing 5-44 shows the resulting output.

Listing 5-43. Programmatically Determining the Size of a Terminal Window

```
var columns = process.stdout.columns;
var rows = process.stdout.rows;

console.log("Size:   " + columns + "x" + rows);
```

Listing 5-44. Output from Running the Code in Listing 5-43

```
$ node tty-size.js
Size:   80x24
```

■ **Note**   Determining the terminal size is not possible using stdin, as terminal dimensions are associated only with writable TTY streams.

If your program's output is dependent on the size of the terminal, what happens if a user resizes the window at runtime? Luckily, writable TTY streams provide a resize event that is triggered any time the terminal window is resized. The example in Listing 5-45 defines a function, size(), that prints out the current terminal dimensions. When launched, the program first checks whether stdout is connected to a terminal window. If it is not, an error message is displayed, and the program terminates with an error code by calling the process.exit() method. If the program is run in a terminal window, it displays the current size of the window by calling size(). The same function is then used as a resize event handler. Finally, process.stdin.resume() is called to prevent the program from terminating while you test it.

Listing 5-45. An Example That Monitors the Terminal Size

```
function size() {
  var columns = process.stdout.columns;
  var rows = process.stdout.rows;

  console.log("Size:   " + columns + "x" + rows);
}

if (!process.stdout.isTTY) {
  console.error("Not using a terminal window!");
  process.exit(-1);
}

size();
process.stdout.on("resize", size);
process.stdin.resume();
```

Signal Events

Signals are asynchronous event notifications sent to a specific process or thread. They are used to provide a limited form of interprocess communication on POSIX-compliant operating systems. (If you're developing for Windows, you might want to skip this section.) A full list of all signals and their meaning is beyond the scope of this book, but the information is readily available on the Internet.

As an example, if you press Ctrl+C while a terminal program is running, an interrupt signal, SIGINT, is sent to that program. In Node applications, signals are processed by a default handler unless a custom handler is provided. When the default handler receives a SIGINT signal, it causes the program to terminate. To override this behavior, add a SIGINT event handler to the process object, as shown in Listing 5-46.

Listing 5-46. Adding a SIGINT Signal Event Handler

```
process.on("SIGINT", function() {
  console.log("Got a SIGINT signal");
});
```

▪ **Note**   If you include the event handler from Listing 5-46 in your application, you will be unable to terminate the program using Ctrl+C. However, you can still stop the program using Ctrl+D.

User Environment Variables

Environment variables are operating system–level variables accessible by processes executing on the system. For example, many operating systems define a TEMP or TMP environment variable that specifies a directory used to hold temporary files. Accessing environment variables in Node is very straightforward. The process object has an object property, env, that contains the user environment. The env object can be interacted with just like any other object. Listing 5-47 shows how the env object is referenced. In this example, the PATH variable is displayed. Then an additional Unix-style directory is added to the beginning of the PATH. Finally, the freshly updated PATH is displayed. Listing 5-48 shows the output from this example. Note, however, that depending on your current system configuration, your own output may differ greatly.

Listing 5-47. An Example of Working with User Environment Variables

```
console.log("Original: " + process.env.PATH);
process.env.PATH = "/some/path:" + process.env.PATH;
console.log("Updated:   " + process.env.PATH);
```

Listing 5-48. Example Output from Running the Code in Listing 5-47

```
$ node env-example.js
Original:  /usr/local/bin:/usr/bin:/bin:/usr/sbin:/sbin
Updated:   /some/path:/usr/local/bin:/usr/bin:/bin:/usr/sbin:/sbin
```

Environment variables are commonly used to configure different modes of execution in an application. For example, a program might support two modes of execution, development and production. In development mode, debugging information might be printed to the console, while in production mode it might be logged to a file or disabled completely. To enable development mode, simply set an environment variable, which can be accessed from within the application. Listing 5-49 demonstrates how this concept works. In the example, the presence of the DEVELOPMENT environment variable is used to define the Boolean variable devMode, which then controls the condition of the if statement. Note that the !! (bang bang) notation is used to force conversion of any value to a Boolean.

Listing 5-49. An example of Implementing Development Mode Using Environment Variables

```
var devMode = !!process.env.DEVELOPMENT;

if (devMode) {
  console.log("Some useful debugging information");
}
```

Listing 5-50 shows one way to execute the previous example in development mode. Notice how defining the environment variable at the same command prompt that Node is launched from allows for quick one-off tests, free of the hassle of actually defining an environment variable. (However, that would work as well.)

Listing 5-50. Running the Example from Listing 5-51 in Development Mode

```
$ DEVELOPMENT=1 node dev-mode.js
Some useful debugging information
```

Summary

This chapter has introduced the basics of command line interface programming in Node. A few of the examples have even shown actual code from the Node core. You should now have a grasp of such fundamental concepts as command line arguments, the standard streams, signal handlers, and environment variables. These concepts bring together some material already covered (such as event handlers) and some (such as streams) to be covered later in this book.

This chapter has also exposed you to the basics of the commander module. At the time of writing, commander is the sixth most depended upon module in the npm registry. However, there are other, similar CLI modules you may be interested in exploring. The most prominent of these is the optimist module (optimist was created by James Halliday—a.k.a. substack—a prominent member of the Node community). You are encouraged to browse the npm repository and experiment with other modules to find the one that best suits your needs.

CHAPTER 6

The File System

For many JavaScript developers, access to the file system has been difficult to achieve. The reasoning has always been—rightfully so—that giving a Web script access to the file system was too much of a security risk. However, Node doesn't typically execute arbitrary scripts from dark corners of the Internet. As a full-blown server-side language, Node has all of the same rights and responsibilities that languages like PHP, Python, and Java do. Thus, for JavaScript developers, the file system is a reality that doesn't depend on vendor-specific implementations or hacks. This chapter shows how the file system can be just another tool in the Node developer's toolbox.

Relevant Paths

Every Node application contains a number of variables that provide insight as to where in the file system Node is working. The simplest of these variables are __filename and __dirname. The first variable, __filename, is the absolute path of the currently executing file. Similarly, __dirname is the absolute path to the directory containing the currently executing file. The example in Listing 6-1 shows the usage of __filename and __dirname. Notice that both can be accessed without importing any modules. When this example is executed from the directory /home/colin, the resulting output is shown in Listing 6-2.

Listing 6-1. Using the __filename and __dirname Variables

```
console.log("This file is " + __filename);
console.log("It's located in " + __dirname);
```

Listing 6-2. Output from Running the Code in Listing 6-1

```
$ node file-paths.js
This file is /home/colin/file-paths.js
It's located in /home/colin
```

■ **Note** The values of __filename and __dirname depend on the file that references them. Therefore, their values can be different even within a single Node application—as, for example, might happen when __filename is referenced from two different modules in an application.

The Current Working Directory

An application's current working directory is the file system directory that the application refers to when creating relative paths. An example of this is the pwd command, which returns a shell's current working directory. In a Node application, the current working directory is available via the cwd() method of the process object. An example using the cwd() method is shown in Listing 6-3. The resulting output is shown in Listing 6-4.

Listing 6-3. Using the process.cwd() Method

```
console.log("The current working directory is " + process.cwd());
```

Listing 6-4. Output from Running the Code in Listing 6-3

```
$ node cwd-example.js
The current working directory is /home/colin
```

Changing the Current Working Directory

During the course of execution, an application can change its current working directory. In a shell, this is accomplished with the cd command. The process object provides a method, named chdir(), that accomplishes the same task by taking a string argument representing the directory name to change to. This method executes synchronously and throws an exception if the directory change fails for any reason (say, if the target directory does not exist).

An example, shown in Listing 6-5, that uses the chdir() method displays the current working directory and then attempts to change to the root directory, /. If an error occurs, it is caught and then printed to stderr. Finally, the updated working directory is displayed.

Listing 6-5. Changing the Current Working Directory Using process.chdir()

```
console.log("The current working directory is " + process.cwd());

try {
  process.chdir("/");
} catch (exception) {
  console.error("chdir error:  " + exception.message);
}

console.log("The current working directory is now " + process.cwd());
```

Listing 6-6 shows a successful execution of the code in Listing 6-5. Next, try changing the path in chdir() to some nonexistent path, and run the example again. Listing 6-7 shows a failed example, one that tries to change chdir() to / foo. Notice how the current working directory remains unchanged after the failure.

Listing 6-6. A Successful Run of the Process in Listing 6-5

```
$ node chdir-example.js
The current working directory is /home/colin
The current working directory is now /
```

Listing 6-7. A Failed Run of the Process in Listing 6-5

```
$ node chdir-example.js
The current working directory is /home/colin
chdir error:  ENOENT, no such file or directory
The current working directory is now /home/colin
```

Locating the node Executable

The path to the node executable is also available via the process object. Specifically, the executable path is in the process.execPath property. Listing 6-8 shows an example displaying the node executable path, and the corresponding output is shown in Listing 6-9. Note that your own path may differ based on the operating system or the Node installation path you have in place.

Listing 6-8. Displaying the Value of the process.execPath

```
console.log(process.execPath);
```

Listing 6-9. The Output from Listing 6-8

```
$ node exec-path-example.js
/usr/local/bin/node
```

The path Module

The path module is a core module that provides a number of utility methods for working with file paths. While the path module works with file paths, many of its methods only perform simple string transformations without actually accessing the file system. Listing 6-10 shows how the path module is included in a Node application.

Listing 6-10. Importing the path Module into a Node Application

```
var path = require("path");
```

Cross-Platform Differences

Dealing with paths across multiple operating systems can be a bit of a pain. Much of it stems from the fact that Windows uses a backslash (\) to separate the parts of a file path, while other operating systems use a forward slash (/). Windows versions of Node can handle forward slashes effectively, but most native Windows applications cannot. Luckily, this detail can be abstracted away using the path.sep property. This property holds the file separator of the current operating system. This is \\ (remember, backslashes must be escaped) in Windows but / elsewhere. Listing 6-11 shows how path.sep, in conjunction with the array join() method, can be used to create platform-specific file paths.

Listing 6-11. Creating Cross-Platform Directories Using path.sep and join()

```
var path = require("path");
var directories = ["foo", "bar", "baz"];
var directory = directories.join(path.sep);

console.log(directory);
```

■ **Note** Windows uses a single backslash as its path separator. However, backslashes must be escaped inside of JavaScript string literals. That is why path.sep returns \\ in Windows.

The resulting output for non-Windows systems is shown in Listing 6-12. Later in this chapter how to actually perform file system operations on directories is explained, but for now we'll just display the directory path.

Listing 6-12. Output from Running the Code in Listing 6-11

```
$ node sep-join-example.js
foo/bar/baz
```

Another major difference between Windows and every other platform is the character that separates directories in the PATH environment variable. Windows uses a semicolon (;), but all other systems use a colon (:). The path module's delimiter property is used to abstract this away. Listing 6-13 uses the delimiter property to split the PATH environment variable and print each individual directory.

Listing 6-13. A Cross-Platform Example That Splits the PATH Environment Variable

```
var path = require("path");

process.env.PATH.split(path.delimiter).forEach(function(dir) {
  console.log(dir);
});
```

Extracting Path Components

The path module also provides easy access to several key path components. Specifically, path's extname(), basename(), and dirname() methods return a path's file extension, file name, and directory name, respectively. The extname() method finds the last period (.) in a path and returns it and all subsequent characters as the extension. If a path contains no periods, the empty string is returned. Listing 6-14 shows how extname() is used.

Listing 6-14. Use of the path.extname() Method

```
var path = require("path");
var fileName = "/foo/bar/baz.txt";
var extension = path.extname(fileName);

console.log(extension);
// extension is .txt
```

The basename() method returns the last nonempty part of a path. If the path corresponds to a file, basename() returns the full file name, including the extension. An example of this is shown in Listing 6-15. You can also retrieve the file name without the extension by passing the result of extname() as the second argument to basename(). Listing 6-16 shows an example of this.

Listing 6-15. Extracting the Full File Name from a Path using path.basename()

```
var path = require("path");
var fileName = "/foo/bar/baz.txt";
var file = path.basename(fileName);

console.log(file);
// file is baz.txt
```

Listing 6-16. Extracting the File Name Minus the Extension from a Path using `path.basename()`

```
var path = require("path");
var fileName = "/foo/bar/baz.txt";
var extension = path.extname(fileName);
var file = path.basename(fileName, extension);

console.log(file);
// file is baz
```

The `dirname()` method returns the directory portion of a path. Listing 6-17 shows the use of `dirname()`.

Listing 6-17. Extracting the Directory Name from a Path using `path.dirname()`

```
var path = require("path");
var fileName = "/foo/bar/baz.txt";
var dirName = path.dirname(fileName);

console.log(dirName);
// dirName is /foo/bar
```

Path Normalization

Paths can become overly complicated and confusing if "." and ".." parts are mixed in. This is likely to happen if paths are passed in as command line arguments from a user. For example, a user issuing the `cd` command to change directories often provides relative paths. In turn, the `path` module provides a `normalize()` method to simplify these paths. In the example in Listing 6-18, a fairly convoluted path is normalized. After following several parent and current directory references, the resulting path is simply `/baz`.

Listing 6-18. Achieving Path Normalization Using `path.normalize()`

```
var path = require("path");
var dirName = "/foo/bar/../../bar/../../baz";
var normalized = path.normalize(dirName);

console.log(normalized);
// normalized is /baz
```

The path module also has a `join()` method. Operating on an arbitrary number of strings, `join()` takes these strings and creates a single normalized path. In the example in Listing 6-19, which shows how `join()` can be used to normalize the path from Listing 6-18, the input path has been split into several strings. Note that `join()` would work exactly like `normalize()` if a single string were passed in.

Listing 6-19. Achieving Path Normalization Using `path.join()`

```
var path = require("path");
var normalized = path.join("/foo/bar", "../../bar", "../..", "/baz");

console.log(normalized);
// normalized is /baz
```

Resolving a Relative Path Between Directories

The `path.relative()` method, which can be used to determine the relative path from one directory to another, takes two strings as its arguments. The first argument represents the starting point of the calculation, while the second corresponds to the end point. In the example in Listing 6-20 showing the use of `relative()`, a relative path from `/foo/bar` to `/baz/biff` is calculated. Based on this directory structure, a relative path moves up two levels to the root directory before traversing `/baz/biff`.

Listing 6-20. Determining a Relative Path using `path.relative()`

```
var path = require("path");
var from = "/foo/bar";
var to = "/baz/biff";
var relative = path.relative(from, to);

console.log(relative);
// relative is ../../baz/biff
```

The `fs` Module

Node applications perform file I/O via the `fs` module, a core module whose methods provide wrappers around standard file system operations. Listing 6-21 shows how the file system module is imported into a Node application. You may recall this module from Chapter 3, where a file reader program was implemented.

Listing 6-21. Importing the `fs` Module into a Node Application

```
var fs = require("fs");
```

One thing especially noteworthy about the `fs` module is its proliferation of synchronous methods. More specifically, nearly all file system methods have asynchronous and synchronous versions. The synchronous ones can be identified by the use of the `Sync` suffix. The asynchronous version of each method takes a callback function as its final argument. In earlier versions of Node, many of the asynchronous `fs` methods allowed you to omit the callback function. However, according to the official documentation, as of Node 0.12, omitting the callback function will cause an exception.

As you have seen, asynchronous methods are at the heart of Node's programming model. Use of asynchronous programming allows Node to appear highly parallel while in fact it is single threaded. Careless use of even a single synchronous method has the potential to bring an entire application to a halt (see Chapter 3 if you need a refresher). So why are nearly half of all file system methods synchronous?

As it happens, many applications access the file system for configuration data. This is generally done during configuration at startup. In cases like this, it is often much simpler to synchronously read a configuration file without worrying about maximizing performance. Additionally, Node can be used to create simple utility programs, similar to shell scripts. These scripts can likely get away with synchronous behavior. As a general rule, code that can be called multiple times simultaneously should be asynchronous. While synchronous methods are at your disposable as a developer, use them with extreme caution.

Determining if a File Exists

The `exists()` and `existsSync()` methods are used to determine if a given path exists. Both methods take a path string as an argument. If the synchronous version is used, a Boolean value representing the path's existence is returned. If the asynchronous version is used, the same Boolean value is passed as an argument to the callback function.

Listing 6-22 checks for the existence of the root directory using both existsSync() and exists(). When the exists() callback function is invoked, the results of both methods are compared. Of course, both methods should return the same value. Assuming equivalence, the path is printed out, followed by the Boolean value representing its existence.

Listing 6-22. Checking for a File's Existence Using exists() and existsSync()

```
var fs = require("fs");
var path = "/";
var existsSync = fs.existsSync(path);

fs.exists(path, function(exists) {
  if (exists !== existsSync) {
    console.error("Something is wrong!");
  } else {
    console.log(path + " exists:  " + exists);
  }
});
```

Retrieving File Statistics

The fs module provides a collection of functions for reading file statistics. These functions are stat(), lstat(), and fstat(). Of course, these methods also have synchronous equivalents—statSync(), lstatSync(), and fstatSync(). The most basic form of these methods, stat(), takes a path string and callback function as arguments. The callback function is invoked with two arguments as well. The first represents any error that occurs. The second is an fs.Stats object that contains the actual file statistics. Before exploring the fs.Stats object, let's take a look at an example that uses the stat() method. In Listing 6-23, stat() is used to collect information on the file foo.js, which we assume to exist. If an exception occurs (say, if the file did not exist), error information is printed to stderr. Otherwise, the Stats object is printed.

Listing 6-23. The fs.stat() Method in Use

```
var fs = require("fs");
var path = "foo.js";

fs.stat(path, function(error, stats) {
  if (error) {
    console.error("stat error:  " + error.message);
  } else {
    console.log(stats);
  }
});
```

Listing 6-24 shows sample output from a successful run. Table 6-1 contains an explanation of the various fs.Stats object properties shown in that listing. Note that your output will likely be different, especially if you use Windows. In fact, in Windows, some properties will not be present at all.

Listing 6-24. Sample Output from the Code in Listing 6-23

```
$ node stat-example.js
{ dev: 16777218,
  mode: 33188,
  nlink: 1,
  uid: 501,
  gid: 20,
  rdev: 0,
  blksize: 4096,
  ino: 2935040,
  size: 75,
  blocks: 8,
  atime: Sun Apr 28 2013 12:55:17 GMT-0400 (EDT),
  mtime: Sun Apr 28 2013 12:55:17 GMT-0400 (EDT),
  ctime: Sun Apr 28 2013 12:55:17 GMT-0400 (EDT) }
```

Table 6-1. *Explanation of the Various* `fs.Stats` *Object Properties*

Property	Description
dev	ID of the device containing the file.
mode	The file's protection.
nlink	The number of hard links to the file.
uid	User ID of the file's owner.
gid	Group ID of the file's owner.
rdev	The device ID, if the file is a special file.
blksize	The block size for file system I/O.
ino	The file's inode number. An inode is a file system data structure that stores information about a file.
size	The file's total size in bytes.
blocks	The number of blocks allocated for the file.
atime	Date object representing the file's last access time.
mtime	Date object representing the file's last modification time.
ctime	Date object representing the last time the file's inode was changed.

The `fs.Stats` object also has several methods that help identify the type of file in question (see Table 6-2). These methods are synchronous, they take no arguments, and they return a Boolean value. For example, the `isFile()` method returns `true` for normal files, but `isDirectory()` returns `true` for directories.

Table 6-2. *Explanation of the Various fs.Stats Methods*

Method	Description
isFile()	Indicates whether a file is a normal file.
isDirectory()	Indicates whether a file is a directory.
isBlockDevice()	Indicates whether a file is a block device file. This includes devices like hard disks, CD-ROMs, and flash drives.
isCharacterDevice()	Indicates whether a file is a character device file. This includes devices like keyboards.
isSymbolicLink()	Indicates whether a file is a symbolic link. This is valid only when using lstat() and lstatSync().
isFIFO()	Indicates whether a file is a FIFO special file.
isSocket()	Indicates whether a file is a socket.

Other stats() Variations

The lstat() and fstat() variations behave almost identically to stat(). The only difference with lstat() is that if the path argument is a symbolic link, the fs.Stats object corresponds to the link itself, not the file it refers to. With fstat(), the only difference is that the first argument is a file descriptor instead of a string. File descriptors are used to communicate with open files (more detail follows shortly). Of course, statSync(), lstatSync(), and fstatSync() behave like their asynchronous counterparts. Since the synchronous methods do not have callback functions, the fs.Stats objects are returned directly.

Opening Files

Files are opened using the open() and openSync() methods. The first argument to both of these methods is a string representing the file name to be opened. The second is a flags string denoting how the file should be opened (for reading, writing, etc.). Table 6-3 summarizes the various ways Node lets you open files.

Table 6-3. *Breakdown of the Various Flags Available to open() and openSync()*

Flags	Description
r	Open for reading. An exception occurs if the file does not exist.
r+	Open for reading and writing. An exception occurs if the file does not exist.
rs	Open for reading in synchronous mode. This instructs the operating system to bypass the system cache. This is mostly used for opening files on NFS mounts. This does *not* make open() a synchronous method.
rs+	Open for reading and writing in synchronous mode.
w	Open for writing. If the file does not exist, it is created. If the file already exists, it is truncated.
wx	Similar to the w flag, but the file is opened in exclusive mode. Exclusive mode ensures that the file is newly created.
w+	Open for reading and writing. If the file does not exist, it is created. If the file already exists, it is truncated.
wx+	Similar to the w+ flag, but the file is opened in exclusive mode.

(continued)

Table 6-3. (*continued*)

Flags	Description
a	Open for appending. If the file does not exist, it is created.
ax	Similar to the a flag, but the file is opened in exclusive mode.
a+	Open for reading and appending. If the file does not exist, it is created.
ax+	Similar to the a+ flag, but the file is opened in exclusive mode.

The third argument, an optional one, to open() and openSync() specifies the mode. The mode defaults to "0666". The asynchronous open() method takes a callback function as its fourth argument. As an argument, the callback function takes an error and the file descriptor of the opened file. A file descriptor is a construct used to interface with open files. The file descriptor, whether passed to the callback function or returned by openSync(), can be passed to other functions to perform such file operations as reads and writes. The example in Listing 6-25, which uses open() to open the file /dev/null, was chosen because any writes to it are simply discarded. Note that this file does not exist in Windows. However, you can change the value of path on the second line to point to a different file. It is advisable to use a file path that does not currently exist, as the contents of an existing file, as in this example, are overwritten.

Listing 6-25. Opening /dev/null Using open()

```
var fs = require("fs");
var path = "/dev/null";

fs.open(path, "w+", function(error, fd) {
  if (error) {
    console.error("open error:  " + error.message);
  } else {
    console.log("Successfully opened " + path);
  }
});
```

Reading Data from Files

The read() and readSync() methods are used to read data from an open file. These methods take a number of arguments, so using an example will probably make working through them easier (see Listing 6-26). The example—which reads data from a file, foo.txt, in the application's directory (for simplicity's sake, error handling code has been omitted)—starts with a call to stat(). It must do so because the file's size is going to be needed later. Next, the file is opened using open(). This step is required to obtain a file descriptor. After the file is opened, a data buffer, one large enough to hold the entire file, is initialized.

Listing 6-26. Reading from a File Using read()

```
var fs = require("fs");
var path = __dirname + "/foo.txt";

fs.stat(path, function(error, stats) {
  fs.open(path, "r", function(error, fd) {
    var buffer = new Buffer(stats.size);
```

```
    fs.read(fd, buffer, 0, buffer.length, null, function(error, bytesRead, buffer) {
      var data = buffer.toString("utf8");

      console.log(data);
    });
  });
});
```

Next comes the actual call to read(). The first argument is the file descriptor provided by open(). The second is the buffer to be used to hold the data read from the file. The third is the offset within the buffer where the data will be placed (in this example the offset is zero, corresponding to the beginning of the buffer). The fourth argument is the number of bytes to read (in this example the entire contents of the file are read). The fifth is an integer specifying the position in the file to begin reading from. If the value is null, the read begins at the current file position, which is set to the beginning of the file when it is initially opened and updated with each read.

If this was a call to readSync(), it would return the number of bytes that were successfully read from the file. The asynchronous read() function takes as its final argument a callback function, which in turn takes an error object, the number of bytes read, and the buffer as arguments. Inside the callback function, the raw data buffer is converted to a UTF-8 string and then printed to the console.

■ **Note**　This example reads an entire file in one call to read(). If the file is significantly large, memory consumption could be a problem. In this case, your application should initialize a smaller buffer and read the file in smaller chunks using a loop.

The `readFile()` and `readFileSync()` Methods

The readFile() and readFileSync() methods offer a more concise way to read data from files. Taking a file name as an argument, they read the entire contents of a file automatically, without file descriptors, buffers, or other annoyances. Listing 6-27 shows the code from Listing 6-26 rewritten using readFile(). Notice that the second argument to readFile() specifies that the data should be returned as a UTF-8 string. If this argument is omitted or null, the raw buffer is returned.

Listing 6-27. Reading an Entire File Using readFile()

```
var fs = require("fs");
var path = __dirname + "/foo.txt";

fs.readFile(path, "utf8", function(error, data) {
  if (error) {
    console.error("read error:  " + error.message);
  } else {
    console.log(data);
  }
});
```

Writing Data to Files

Writing data to a file is similar to reading data. The methods used to write to a file are write() and writeSync(). In the example in Listing 6-28, using the write() method, a file named foo.txt is opened for writing. Also created is a buffer that holds the data to be written to file. Next, write() is used to actually write the data to file. The first argument to write() is the file descriptor provided by open(). The second is the buffer containing the data to be written. The third and fourth arguments correspond to the offset of the buffer to begin writing and the number of bytes to write. The fifth is an integer representing the position in the file where writing is to begin. If this argument is null, the data is written to the current file position, and writeFileSync() returns the number of bytes successfully written to file. On the other hand, write() takes a callback function with three arguments: an exception object, the number of bytes written, and the buffer object.

Listing 6-28. Writing Data to a File Using write()

```
var fs = require("fs");
var path = __dirname + "/foo.txt";
var data = "Lorem ipsum dolor sit amet";

fs.open(path, "w", function(error, fd) {
  var buffer = new Buffer(data);

  fs.write(fd, buffer, 0, buffer.length, null, function(error, written, buffer) {
    if (error) {
      console.error("write error:  " + error.message);
    } else {
      console.log("Successfully wrote " + written + " bytes.");
    }
  });
});
```

The writeFile() and writeFileSync() Methods

The methods writeFile() and writeFileSync() provide shortcuts for write() and writeSync(). The example in Listing 6-29 shows the use of writeFile(), which takes a file path and the data to write as its first two arguments. With an optional third argument you can specify encoding (which defaults to UTF-8) and other options. The callback function to writeFile() takes an error object as its only argument.

Listing 6-29. Writing to a File Using writeFile()

```
var fs = require("fs");
var path = __dirname + "/foo.txt";
var data = "Lorem ipsum dolor sit amet";

fs.writeFile(path, data, function(error) {
  if (error) {
    console.error("write error:  " + error.message);
  } else {
    console.log("Successfully wrote " + path);
  }
});
```

Two other methods, appendFile() and appendFileSync(), are used to append data to an existing file without overwriting existing data. If the file does not yet exist, it is created. These methods are used exactly like writeFile() and writeFileSync().

Closing Files

As a general programming rule of thumb, always close anything you open. In Node applications, files are closed using the close() and closeSync() methods. Both take a file descriptor as an argument. In the asynchronous version, a callback function is expected as the second argument. The callback function's only argument is used to indicate a possible error. In the example in Listing 6-30, a file is opened using open() and then immediately closed using close().

Listing 6-30. Opening and Then Closing a File with open() and close()

```
var fs = require("fs");
var path = "/dev/null";

fs.open(path, "w+", function(error, fd) {
  if (error) {
    console.error("open error:  " + error.message);
  } else {
    fs.close(fd, function(error) {
      if (error) {
        console.error("close error:  " + error.message);
      }
    });
  }
});
```

■ **Note** It is not necessary to close files opened using methods like readFile() and writeFile(). These methods handle everything internally. Also, they do not provide a file descriptor to pass to close().

Renaming Files

To rename a file, use the rename() or renameSync() methods. The first argument to these methods is the current name of the file to be renamed. As you might guess, the second is the desired new name for the file. The callback function for rename() takes only one argument, representing a possible exception. The example in Listing 6-31 renames a file named foo.txt as bar.txt.

Listing 6-31. Renaming a File Using rename()

```
var fs = require("fs");
var oldPath = __dirname + "/foo.txt";
var newPath = __dirname + "/bar.txt";

fs.rename(oldPath, newPath, function(error) {
  if (error) {
    console.error("rename error:  " + error.message);
  } else {
    console.log("Successfully renamed the file!");
  }
});
```

Deleting Files

Files are deleted using the unlink() and unlinkSync() methods, which take a file path as an argument. The asynchronous version also takes a callback function as an argument. The callback function takes only an argument representing a possible exception. In the example in Listing 6-32, showing use of the unlink() method, the application attempts to delete a file named foo.txt located in the same directory.

Listing 6-32. Deleting a File Using the fs.unlink() Method

```
var fs = require("fs");
var path = __dirname + "/foo.txt";

fs.unlink(path, function(error) {
  if (error) {
    console.error("unlink error:  " + error.message);
  }
});
```

Creating Directories

New directories are created with the mkdir() and mkdirSync() methods. The first argument to mkdir() is the path of the directory to create. As mkdir() creates only the final-level directory, mkdir() cannot be used to build an entire hierarchy of directories in a single call. This method also takes an optional second argument, which specifies the directory's permission and defaults to "0777". The asynchronous version also takes a callback function, one whose only argument is a possible exception. Listing 6-33 provides an example that uses mkdir() to create the directory tree foo/bar in the application's directory.

Listing 6-33. Creating Several Directories Using mkdir()

```
var fs = require("fs");
var path = __dirname + "/foo";

fs.mkdir(path, function(error) {
  if (error) {
    console.error("mkdir error:  " + error.message);
  } else {
    path += "/bar";
    fs.mkdir(path, function(error) {
      if (error) {
        console.error("mkdir error:  " + error.message);
      } else {
        console.log("Successfully built " + path);
      }
    });
  }
});
```

Reading the Contents of a Directory

The readdir() and readdirSync() methods are used to obtain the contents of a given directory. The directory path to read is passed in as an argument. The readdirSync() method returns an array of strings containing the files and subdirectories in the directory, whereas readdir() passes an error and the same array of files to a callback function. Listing 6-34 shows use of readdir() in reading the contents of the process's current working directory. Note that the array provided by readdir() and readdirSync() does not contain the directories "." and "..".

Listing 6-34. Reading the Contents of a Directory Using readdir()

```
var fs = require("fs");
var path = process.cwd();

fs.readdir(path, function(error, files) {
  files.forEach(function(file) {
    console.log(file);
  });
});
```

Removing Directories

You can also delete directories using the rmdir() and rmdirSync() methods. The directory path to remove is passed as the first argument to each method. The second argument to rmdir() is a callback function that takes a potential exception as its only argument. The example in Listing 6-35 uses rmdir().

Listing 6-35. Deleting a Directory Using rmdir()

```
var fs = require("fs");
var path = __dirname + "/foo";

fs.rmdir(path, function(error) {
  if (error) {
    console.error("rmdir error:  " + error.message);
  }
});
```

If you attempt to delete a nonempty directory, an error occurs. Removing such a directory takes a bit more work. The code in Listing 6-36 shows one way to implement an rmdir() function that works on nonempty directories. Before removing a nonempty directory, we first have to make it empty. To do so, remove all the files in the directory and recursively remove any subdirectories.

Listing 6-36. Implementing Recursive rmdir() Functionality

```
var fs = require("fs");
var path = __dirname + "/foo";

function rmdir(path) {
  if (fs.existsSync(path)) {
    fs.readdirSync(path).forEach(function(file) {
      var f = path + "/" + file;
      var stats = fs.statSync(f);
```

```
      if (stats.isDirectory()) {
        rmdir(f);
      } else {
        fs.unlinkSync(f);
      }
    });

    fs.rmdirSync(path);
  }
}

// now call the recursive rmdir() function
rmdir(path);
```

All of the function calls in Listing 6-36 being synchronous greatly simplifies the code and makes the algorithm easier to understand. However, synchronous functions are not the Node way. Listing 6-37 shows the same functionality implemented using asynchronous calls. The first thing to notice about this example is that the async module has been included. Thus, we can focus on the actual algorithm, as async takes care of taming the asynchronous function calls.

Listing 6-37. An Asynchronous Implementation of the Recursive rmdir()

```
var async = require("async");
var fs = require("fs");
var path = __dirname + "/foo";

function rmdir(path, callback) {
  // first check if the path exists
  fs.exists(path, function(exists) {
    if (!exists) {
      return callback(new Error(path + " does not exist"));
    }

    fs.readdir(path, function(error, files) {
      if (error) {
        return callback(error);
      }

      // loop over the files returned by readdir()
      async.each(files, function(file, cb) {
        var f = path + "/" + file;

        fs.stat(f, function(error, stats) {
          if (error) {
            return cb(error);
          }
```

```
        if (stats.isDirectory()) {
          // recursively call rmdir() on the directory
          rmdir(f, cb);
        } else {
          // delete the file
          fs.unlink(f, cb);
        }
      });
    }, function(error) {
      if (error) {
        return callback(error);
      }

      // the directory is now empty, so delete it
      fs.rmdir(path, callback);
    });
  });
});
}

// now call the recursive rmdir() function
rmdir(path, function(error) {
  if (error) {
    console.error("rmdir error:  " + error.message);
  } else {
    console.log("Successfully removed " + path);
  }
});
```

Watching Files

The fs module lets your applications watch specific files for modifications. This is accomplished using the watch() method. The first argument to watch() is the path to the file to watch. The optional second argument is an object. If present, this object should contain a Boolean property named persistent. If persistent is true (the default), the application continues running as long as at least one file is watched. The third argument to watch() is an optional callback function that is triggered each time the target file is modified.

If present, the callback function accepts two arguments. The first, the type of watch event, will be either change or rename. The callback function's second argument is the name of the file being watched.

In the example in Listing 6-38 showing the watch() method in action, a file named foo.txt is watched persistently. That is, the application does not terminate unless the program is killed or the watched file is deleted. Whenever foo.txt is modified, an event is fired and handled by the callback function. If the file is deleted, a rename event is fired and handled, and the program exits.

Listing 6-38. Watching a File Using the watch() Method

```
var fs = require("fs");
var path = __dirname + "/foo.txt";

fs.watch(path, {
  persistent: true
}, function(event, filename) {
  if (event === "rename") {
    console.log("The file was renamed/deleted.");
  } else if (event === "change") {
    console.log("The file was changed.");
  }
});
```

The watch() method also returns an object of type fs.FSWatcher. If the optional callback function is omitted, the FSWatcher can be used to handle events (via the familiar event-handling syntax covered in Chapter 4). Listing 6-39 shows an example that uses an FSWatcher to handle file-watching events. Also, notice the close() method, which is used to instruct the FSWatcher to stop watching the file in question. Therefore, this example handles only one file-change event.

Listing 6-39. Watching a File Using the Alternative watch() Syntax

```
var fs = require("fs");
var path = __dirname + "/foo.txt";
var watcher;

watcher = fs.watch(path);
watcher.on("change", function(event, filename) {
  if (event === "rename") {
    console.log("The file was renamed/deleted.");
  } else if (event === "change") {
    console.log("The file was changed.");
  }

  watcher.close();
});
```

■ **Note** Node's official documentation lists watch() as unstable because it depends on the underlying file system and is not implemented with 100 percent consistency across platforms. For example, the filename argument of the watch() callback function is not available in all systems.

Summary

This chapter has introduced Node's file system APIs. Working effectively with the file system is a key factor in any legitimate application. Without access to the file system, an application cannot accomplish tasks such as reading configuration files, creating output files, and writing to error logs. Many file system tasks in Node are handled using the fs module, and so the chapter has covered the most important methods that fs provides. However, there are a number of other methods this chapter has not covered, methods that allow you to accomplish such tasks as changing file ownership and permissions. Readers are referred to the full documentation (http://nodejs.org/api/fs.html) for a listing of all possible methods.

CHAPTER 7

Streams

Node makes extensive use of streams as a data transfer mechanism—for example, for reading and writing files and transmitting data over network sockets. Chapter 5 has already shown you the standard streams—stdin, stdout, and stderr. This chapter, which explores Node's streams API in greater detail, presents the different types of streams, how they work, and their various applications. But before starting, you should be aware that the streams API, while an important part of the Node core, is listed as unstable in the official documentation.

What Are Streams?

Streams are a mechanism for transferring data between two points. In terms of behavior, a simple garden hose provides a good analogy. When you need to water your lawn, you use a hose to connect a water supply to a sprinkler. When you turn the water on, it flows through the hose to the sprinkler. It is then up to the sprinkler to distribute the water.

Streams are conceptually very similar. Compare watering the lawn to a call to console.log(), for example. In this case, a Node application acts as the water supply. When console.log() is called, the water is turned on, and information flows through the standard output stream. At this point, Node is no longer concerned with what happens to the data. The stdout stream delivers the data to its destination. In this case, the destination (the sprinkler) could be almost anything—a terminal window, a file, another program.

Working with Streams

Node supports several types of streams, all of which inherit from EventEmitter. Each type of stream behaves slightly differently. To work with the various types of streams, first import the stream core module (see Listing 7-1).

Listing 7-1. Importing the stream Module

```
var Stream = require("stream");
```

Importing the stream module returns a reference to the Stream constructor. The constructor can then be used to instantiate new streams, as shown in Listing 7-2.

Listing 7-2. Creating a New Stream Using the stream Module

```
var Stream = require("stream");
var stream = new Stream();
```

Readable Streams

Readable streams are sources of data. A typical readable stream is a file that has been opened for reading. The simplest way to create a readable stream is to assign the stream's readable property to true and then emit data, end, close, and error events. The following sections explore how these events are used.

data Events

You use a data event to indicate that a new piece of stream data, referred to as a chunk, is available. For each data event emitted, the handler is passed the actual data chunk. Many applications emit the data chunk as a binary Buffer. This is what the official documentation specifies, although technically any data can be emitted. For consistency, it is recommended that data events use a Buffer. The example in Listing 7-3 emits a data event, with the chunk specified as a Buffer.

Listing 7-3. Creating a Readable Stream And Emitting a data Event

```
var Stream = require("stream");
var stream = new Stream();

stream.readable = true;
stream.emit("data", new Buffer("foo"));
```

The end Event

Once a stream sends all of its data, it should emit a single end event. Once the end event is emitted, no further data events should be emitted. The end event does not include any accompanying data. The example in Listing 7-4 creates a readable stream that sends data once a second for five seconds using an interval. Date comparisons are used to determine when five seconds have elapsed. At that point, an end event is emitted, and the interval is cleared.

Listing 7-4. A Readable Stream That Emits Several data Events Followed by an end Event

```
var Stream = require("stream");
var stream = new Stream();
var duration = 5 * 1000; // 5 seconds
var end = Date.now() + duration;
var interval;

stream.readable = true;
interval = setInterval(function() {
  var now = Date.now();

  console.log("Emitting a data event");
  stream.emit("data", new Buffer("foo"));

  if (now >= end) {
    console.log("Emitting an end event");
    stream.emit("end");
    clearInterval(interval);
  }
}, 1000);
```

■ **Note** The Date.now() method returns the current date and time specified as the number of milliseconds that have elapsed since January 1, 1970, 00:00:00 UTC.

The close Event

The close event is used to indicate that the underlying source of the stream data has been closed. For example, streams that read data from a file emit a close event when the file descriptor is closed. Not all readable streams emit a close event. Therefore, if you implement your own readable stream, you are not required to emit this event. If present, the close event contains no additional arguments. An example of a close event is shown in Listing 7-5.

Listing 7-5. Emitting a close Event

```
var Stream = require("stream");
var stream = new Stream();

stream.readable = true;
stream.emit("close");
```

error Events

error events are used to indicate that a problem occurred with the data stream. For example, streams that read from files emit an error event if the backing file does not exist. The error event handler is passed an Error object with details explaining the problem. The example in Listing 7-6 emits an error event.

Listing 7-6. Emitting an error Event

```
var Stream = require("stream");
var stream = new Stream();

stream.readable = true;
stream.emit("error", new Error("Something went wrong!"));
```

Controlling Readable Streams

To pause readable streams, use the pause() method. When in a paused state, a readable stream ceases to emit data events (Chapter 5 covered pause() in the context of stdin). An example use of pause() is shown in Listing 7-7.

Listing 7-7. Calling pause() on stdin

```
process.stdin.pause();
```

By default, stdin is in the paused state (see Chapter 5). In order to read data from stdin or any other paused stream, first unpause it using the resume() method. The example in Listing 7-8 shows the usage of resume(). After calling resume(), data arriving via stdin will cause data events to be emitted.

Listing 7-8. Calling resume() on stdin

```
process.stdin.resume();
```

Writable Streams

Just as readable streams are sources of data, writable streams are destinations for data. To create a writable stream, set a stream's writable property to true, and define methods named write() and end(). The following sections describe these methods, as well as the other features of writable streams.

The write() Method

The write() method is responsible for writing a chunk of data to the stream. The data chunk is passed to write() as a Buffer or a string. If the chunk is a string, the optional second argument can be used to specify the encoding. If no encoding is specified, UTF-8 will be used by default. As an optional final argument, write() also accepts a callback function. If present, the callback function is invoked once the chunk is successfully written.

The write() method also returns a Boolean value indicating whether the chunk was flushed to the underlying resource. If true is returned, the data has been flushed, and the stream can accept more. If false is returned, the data is still queued and waiting to be written. Returning false also notifies the data source to stop sending data until the writable stream emits a drain event.

The example in Listing 7-9 shows a call to stdout's write() method. The call to write() passes in a string. Since the text is UTF-8, the encoding argument is omitted. The callback function thus becomes the second argument.

Listing 7-9. A Call to stdout's write() Method

```
var success = process.stdout.write("foo\n", function() {
  console.log("Data was successfully written!");
});
  console.log("success = " + success);
```

In the resulting output (see Listing 7-10), notice the order in which the print statements execute. The call to write() completes, causing the callback function to be scheduled in the event loop. However, execution returns from write() and then continues on, to print out the value of success. At this point, as the callback function is the only item left in the event loop, it is executed, causing the final print statement to be run.

Listing 7-10. The Resulting Output from Running the Code in Listing 7-9

```
$ node write.js
foo
success = true
Data was successfully written!
```

The end() Method

The end() method, used to signal the end of the data stream, can be called without any arguments. However, it can also be called with the same arguments as write(). This is a convenient shortcut for situations where write() needs to be called only once, followed by end().

The drain Event

When write() returns false, the stream's data source should send no more data. The drain event is used to alert the source that the writable stream, having processed all its data, can begin receiving data again. The drain event does not include any accompanying data.

The finish Event

When end() is called and no more data is to be written, the stream emits a finish event. It too, provides no additional data. Unlike drain, which can potentially be emitted many times, finish can be used to detect the end of the stream.

The `close` and `error` Events

Like readable streams, writable streams have `close` and `error` events that behave in the same fashion.

An Example of a Writable Stream

Let's look now at a very simple custom writable stream. Custom streams are useful in situations where you want to use the streams API in a situation that is not supported out of the box by Node. In the code in Listing 7-11, adapted from James Halliday's example (`https://github.com/substack/stream-handbook`), the stream counts the number of bytes that it processes. Each time the `write()` method is called, the total byte count increases by the number of bytes in the buffer. When `end()` is called, it checks whether a buffer has been passed in. If it has, the buffer is passed to `write()`. The stream is then shut down by setting the `writable` property to `false` and emitting a `finish` event. Finally, the total number of bytes processed by the stream is displayed.

Listing 7-11. A Custom Writable Stream That Counts the Bytes It Processes

```
var Stream = require("stream");
var stream = new Stream();
var bytes = 0;

stream.writable = true;

stream.write = function(buffer) {
  bytes += buffer.length;
};

stream.end = function(buffer) {
  if (buffer) {
    stream.write(buffer);
  }

  stream.writable = false;
  stream.emit("finish");
  console.log(bytes + " bytes written");
};
```

Pipes

Let's return to the garden hose analogy. What if your hose wasn't long enough to reach from the water supply to your lawn? You might take multiple hoses and connect them. In a similar fashion, data streams can also be chained together in order to accomplish a bigger task. For example, assume we have two programs, Program A and Program B. Program A, whose code is shown in Listing 7-12, generates a random single-digit integer (0–9) once a second and outputs it to `stdout`. Program B, shown in Listing 7-13, reads an arbitrary number of integers from `stdin` and outputs a running sum to `stdout`. All you need now is a hose to connect the two programs.

Listing 7-12. A Random Single-Digit Integer Generator

```
setInterval(function() {
  var random = Math.floor(Math.random() * 10);

  console.log(random);
}, 1000);
```

Listing 7-13. An Application That Sums Numbers Read from `stdin`

```
var sum = 0;

process.stdin.on("data", function(data) {
  var number = parseInt(data.toString(), 10);

  if (isFinite(number)) {
    sum += number;
  }

  console.log(sum);
});

process.stdin.resume();
```

■ **Note** `Math.random()` returns a pseudo-random floating-point number between 0 (inclusive) and 1 (exclusive). Multiplying this value by 10, as shown in Listing 7-12, gives a random floating-point number between 0 (inclusive) and 10 (exclusive). `Math.floor()` returns the largest integer that is less than the argument passed in. Therefore, Listing 7-12 generates a random integer between 0 (inclusive) and 9 (inclusive).

These metaphorical hoses are called pipes. If you've done any shell programming, you have undoubtedly come across pipes. They allow an output stream from one process to feed directly into the input stream of another. In shell programming, the pipe operator, |, implements pipes. Listing 7-14 shows how to use a pipe to connect the two example programs from the command line. In the example, the output from Program A is piped to the input of Program B. When you run this command, you will see a stream of numbers, representing the value of the sum variable in Program B, print to the console at a rate of one per second.

Listing 7-14. Piping Output from One Program to Another

```
$ node Program-A.js | node Program-B.js
```

The `pipe()` Method

Within Node applications, streams can be piped together using the `pipe()` method, which takes two arguments: a required writable stream that acts as the destination for the data and an optional object used to pass in options. In the simple example in Listing 7-15, a pipe is created from `stdin` to `stdout`. When this program is run, it listens for input from the user. When the `Enter` key is pressed, any data typed by the user echoes back to `stdout`.

Listing 7-15. Piping `stdin` to `stdout` Using the `pipe()` Method

```
process.stdin.pipe(process.stdout);
```

The optional second argument to `pipe()` is an object that can hold a single Boolean property, end. If end is `true` (the default behavior), the destination stream is closed when the source stream emits its end event. If end is set to `false`, however, the destination stream stays open, and so additional data can be written to the destination stream without the need to reopen it.

■ **Note**   The standard streams behave synchronously when associated with a file or terminal window. For example, a write to stdout will block the rest of the program. However, when they are piped, they behave asynchronously, just like any other stream. Additionally, the writable standard streams, stdout and stderr, cannot be closed until the process terminates, regardless of the value of the end option.

Back to the Writable Stream Example

When Listing 7-11 introduced a custom writable stream, you weren't able to see it do anything. Now that you have learned about pipes, that example stream can be fed some data. Listing 7-16 shows how this is done. The final three lines are particularly noteworthy. First, a pipe with the same source and destination is created. Next, the stream emits a data event followed by an end event.

Listing 7-16. Piping Data to the Custom Writable Stream from Listing 7-11

```
var Stream = require("stream");
var stream = new Stream();
var bytes = 0;

stream.writable = true;

stream.write = function(buffer) {
  bytes += buffer.length;
};

stream.end = function(buffer) {
  if (buffer) {
    stream.write(buffer);
  }

  stream.writable = false;
  stream.emit("finish");
  console.log(bytes + " bytes written");
};

stream.pipe(stream);
stream.emit("data", new Buffer("foo"));
stream.emit("end");
```

These events trigger the write() and end() methods of the writable stream. The resulting output is shown in Listing 7-17.

Listing 7-17. The Resulting Output from Running the Code in Listing 7-16

```
$ node custom-stream.js
3 bytes written
```

File Streams

In Chapter 6 you saw how to read from and write to files using the fs module's readFile() and writeFile() methods, as well as their synchronous counterparts. These methods are extremely convenient but have the potential to cause memory issues in your applications. As a refresher, take the example of readFile() shown in Listing 7-18, where a file named foo.txt is read asynchronously. Once the read is complete, the callback function is invoked, and the contents of the file are printed to the console.

Listing 7-18. Reading a File Using fs.readFile()

```
var fs = require("fs");

fs.readFile(__dirname + "/foo.txt", function(error, data) {
  console.log(data);
});
```

To understand the problem, assume that your application is a web server that receives hundreds or thousands of connections every second. Assume too that all the files being served are, for whatever reason, significantly large and that readFile() is used to read the files from disk into memory on every request before returning the data to the clients. When readFile() is invoked, it buffers the entire contents of the file before invoking its callback function. Since your busy server is buffering many large files simultaneously, memory consumption can spike.

So how can all this nastiness be avoided? As it turns out, the file system module provides methods for reading and writing files as streams. These methods, createReadStream() and createWriteStream(), however, unlike most other fs methods, have no synchronous equivalent. Thus, Chapter 6 intentionally skipped over them until the reader had a more thorough introduction to streams.

createReadStream()

As the name implies, createReadStream() is used to open a file as a readable stream. In its simplest form, createReadStream() takes a file name as an argument and returns a readable stream of the type ReadStream. Since the ReadStream type, defined in the fs module, inherits from the standard readable stream, it can be used in the same fashion.

The example in Listing 7-19 shows createReadStream() reading the contents of a file. The data event handler is used to print out chunks of data as they come through the stream. Since a file can consist of multiple chunks, process.stdout.write() is used to display the chunks. If console.log() was used and the file was more than one chunk large, the output would contain extra line breaks not present in the original file. When the end event is received, console.log() is used to simply print one trailing new line to the output.

Listing 7-19. Reading a File Using fs.createReadStream()

```
var fs = require("fs");
var stream;

stream = fs.createReadStream(__dirname + "/foo.txt");

stream.on("data", function(data) {
  var chunk = data.toString();

  process.stdout.write(chunk);
});
```

```
stream.on("end", function() {
  console.log();
});()
```

The ReadStream's open Event

As previously mentioned, the ReadStream type inherits from the base readable stream. This means that the ReadStream can augment the base stream's behavior. The open event is a perfect example of this. When the file name passed to createReadStream() is successfully opened, the stream emits an open event. The open event's handler function is invoked with a single parameter, the file descriptor used by the stream. By getting a handle on the file descriptor, createReadStream() can be used in conjunction with other file system methods that work with such file descriptors as fstat(), read(), write(), and close(). In the example in Listing 7-20, when an open event handler is invoked, the file descriptor is passed to fstat() to display the file's statistics.

Listing 7-20. Calling fstat() Using a File Descriptor from the open Event Handler

```
var fs = require("fs");
var stream;

stream = fs.createReadStream(__dirname + "/foo.txt");

stream.on("open", function(fd) {
  fs.fstat(fd, function(error, stats) {
    if (error) {
      console.error("fstat error:  " + error.message);
    } else {
      console.log(stats);
    }
  });
});
```

The options Argument

The optional second argument that createReadStream() takes is named options. If present, this argument is an object whose properties allow you to modify the behavior of createReadStream(). The various properties supported by the options argument are described in Table 7-1.

Table 7-1. *Description of the Properties Supported by the* options *Argument*

Property Name	Description
fd	An existing file descriptor. This defaults to null. If a value is provided, it is not necessary to specify a file name as the first argument to createReadStream().
encoding	Specifies the character encoding of the stream. Defaults to null. The supported encoding types are described in Table 5-1.
autoClose	If true, the file is automatically closed when an error or end event is emitted. If false, the file is not closed. Defaults to true.
flags	flags argument passed to open(). See Table 6-3 for a list of available values. Defaults to "r".

(continued)

Table 7-1. (*continued*)

Property Name	Description
mode	The mode argument passed to open(). Defaults to "0666".
start	The byte index within the file (inclusive) to begin reading. Defaults to zero (the beginning of the file).
end	The byte index within the file (inclusive) to stop reading. This can only be used if start is also specified. Defaults to Infinity (the end of the file).

In the example in Listing 7-21, which utilizes the options argument of createReadStream(), a file descriptor returned by open() is passed to createReadStream(). Since an existing file descriptor is being used, null, instead of a file name, is passed as the first argument to createReadStream(). The example also uses the start and end options to skip the file's first and last bytes. The fstat() method is used to determine the file size in order to set end appropriately. The example also includes a number of checks for errors. For example, the code will not work properly if a directory is used instead of a normal file.

Listing 7-21. Utilizing the options Argument of createReadStream()

```
var fs = require("fs");

fs.open(__dirname + "/foo.txt", "r", function(error, fd) {
  if (error) {
    return console.error("open error:  " + error.message);
  }

  fs.fstat(fd, function(error, stats) {
    var stream;
    var size;

    if (error) {
      return console.error("fstat error:  " + error.message);
    } else if (!stats.isFile()) {
      return console.error("files only please");
    } else if ((size = stats.size) < 3) {
      return console.error("file must be at least three bytes long");
    }

    stream = fs.createReadStream(null, {
      fd: fd,
      start: 1,
      end: size - 2
    });

    stream.on("data", function(data) {
      var chunk = data.toString();

      process.stdout.write(chunk);
    });
```

```
    stream.on("end", function() {
      console.log();
    });
  });
});
```

createWriteStream()

To create a writable stream associated with a file, use createWriteStream(). Much like createReadStream(), createWriteStream() takes a file path as its first argument and an optional options object as its second, and returns an instance of WriteStream, a data type defined in the fs module that inherits from the base writable stream type.

The example in Listing 7-22, shows how data can be piped to a writable file stream created with createWriteStream(). In this example, a readable file stream is created which pulls data from foo.txt. The data is then piped through a writable stream to a file named bar.txt.

Listing 7-22. Piping a Readable File Stream to a Writable File Stream

```
var fs = require("fs");
var readStream = fs.createReadStream(__dirname + "/foo.txt");
var writeStream = fs.createWriteStream(__dirname + "/bar.txt");

readStream.pipe(writeStream);
```

The options argument to createWriteStream() is slightly different from the one used by createReadStream(). Table 7-2 describes the various properties that the options object passed to createWriteStream() can include.

Table 7-2. The Properties Supported by the options Argument to createWriteStream()

Property Name	Description
fd	An existing file descriptor. This defaults to null. If a value is provided, it is not necessary to specify a file name as the first argument to createWriteStream().
flags	flags argument passed to open(). See Table 6-3 for a list of available values. Defaults to "w".
encoding	Specifies the character encoding of the stream. Defaults to null.
mode	The mode argument passed to open(). Defaults to "0666".
start	The byte index within the file (inclusive) to begin writing. Defaults to zero (the beginning of the file).

The WriteStream's open Event

The WriteStream type also implements its own open event, which is emitted when the destination file is successfully opened. The open event's handler accepts the file descriptor as its sole argument. An example open event handler for a writable file stream is shown in Listing 7-23. This example simply prints out the integer representing the file descriptor of the open file.

Listing 7-23. An open Event Handler for a Writable File Stream

```
var fs = require("fs");
var stream = fs.createWriteStream(__dirname + "/foo.txt");

stream.on("open", function(fd) {
  console.log("File descriptor:  " + fd);
});
```

The `bytesWritten` Property

The `WriteStream` type keeps track of the number of bytes written to the underlying stream. This count is available via the stream's bytesWritten property. Listing 7-24 shows how bytesWritten is used. Returning to the example in Listing 7-22, the contents of a file are read using a readable stream and then piped to another file using a writable stream. However, Listing 7-24 includes a handler for the writable stream's finish event. When the finish event is emitted, this handler is invoked, and the number of bytes that have been written to the file are displayed.

Listing 7-24. Using the WriteStream's bytesWritten Property

```
var fs = require("fs");
var readStream = fs.createReadStream(__dirname + "/foo.txt");
var writeStream = fs.createWriteStream(__dirname + "/bar.txt");

readStream.pipe(writeStream);

writeStream.on("finish", function() {
  console.log(writeStream.bytesWritten);
});
```

Compression Using the `zlib` Module

Compression is the process of encoding information using fewer bits than its original representation does. Compression is useful because it allows data to be stored or transmitted using fewer bytes. When the data needs to be retrieved, it is simply uncompressed to its original state. Compression is used extensively in web servers to improve response time by reducing the number of bytes sent over the network. However, it should be noted that compression is not free, and can increase response times. Compression is also commonly used to reduce file sizes when archiving data.

Node's core `zlib` module provides compression and decompression APIs that are implemented using streams. Because the `zlib` module is based on streams, it allows easy compression and decompression of data using pipes. Specifically, `zlib` provides bindings for compression using Gzip, Deflate, and DeflateRaw as well as decompression using Gunzip, Inflate, and InflateRaw. As all three of these schemes provide the same interface, switching between them is just a matter of changing method names.

The example in Listing 7-25, which uses Gzip to compress a file, begins by importing the `fs` and `zlib` modules. Next, the `zlib.createGzip()` method is used to create a Gzip compression stream. The data source, `input.txt`, is used to create a readable file stream. Similarly, a writable file stream is created to output the compressed data to `input.txt.gz`. The listing's final line performs the actual compression by reading the uncompressed data and piping it through the Gzip compressor. The compressed data is then piped to the output file.

Listing 7-25. Compressing a File Using Gzip Compression

```
var fs = require("fs");
var zlib = require("zlib");
var gzip = zlib.createGzip();
var input = fs.createReadStream("input.txt");
var output = fs.createWriteStream("input.txt.gz");

input.pipe(gzip).pipe(output);
```

To test the compression application, simply create `input.txt`, and store 100 A characters in it (the file's size should be 100 bytes). Next, run the Gzip compressor. The file `input.txt.gz` should be created with a file size of 24 bytes. Of course, the size of the compressed file depends on a few things. The first factor is the size of the uncompressed data.

However, the compression's effectiveness also depends on the number of repeating patterns in the original data. Our example achieved excellent compression because all the characters in the file were the same. By replacing a single A with a B, the compressed file size jumps from 24 to 28 bytes, even though the source data is the same size.

The compressed data may be smaller, but it isn't particularly useful. To work with the compressed data, we need to decompress it. A sample Gzip decompression application is shown in Listing 7-26. The zlib.createGunzip() method creates a stream that performs the decompression. The input.txt.gz file from Listing 7-25 is used as the readable stream, which is piped through the Gunzip stream. The decompressed data is then piped to a new output file, output.txt.

Listing 7-26. Decompressing a Gzip Compressed File Using Gunzip

```
var fs = require("fs");
var zlib = require("zlib");
var gunzip = zlib.createGunzip();
var input = fs.createReadStream("input.txt.gz");
var output = fs.createWriteStream("output.txt");

input.pipe(gunzip).pipe(output);
```

Deflate/Inflate and DeflateRaw/InflateRaw

The Deflate compression scheme can be used as an alternative to Gzip. The DeflateRaw scheme is similar to Deflate, but omits the zlib header that is present in Deflate. As previously mentioned, the usage for these schemes are the same as for Gzip. The methods used to create Deflate and DeflateRaw streams are zlib.createDeflate() and zlib.createDeflateRaw(). Similarly, zlib.createInflate() and zlib.createInflateRaw() are used to create the corresponding decompression streams. An additional method, zlib.createUnzip(), is used in the same way, and it can decompress both Gzip and Deflate compressed data by automatically detecting the compression scheme.

Convenience Methods

All of the previously mentioned stream types have a corresponding convenience method for one-step compression/decompression of a string or Buffer. These methods are gzip(), gunzip(), deflate(), inflate(), deflateRaw(), inflateRaw(), and unzip(). Each of them takes a Buffer or string as its first argument and a callback function as its second. The callback function takes an error condition as its first argument and the result of the compression/decompression (as a Buffer) as its second. Listing 7-27 shows how deflate() and unzip() are used to compress and decompress a string. After compression and decompression, the data is printed to the console. If everything works properly, the same string stored in the data variable is displayed.

Listing 7-27. Compression and Decompression Using the Convenience Methods

```
var zlib = require("zlib");
var data = "This is some data to compress!";

zlib.deflate(data, function(error, compressed) {
  if (error) {
    return console.error("Could not compress data!");
  }
```

```
  zlib.unzip(compressed, function(error, decompressed) {
    if (error) {
      return console.error("Could not decompress data!");
    }

    console.log(decompressed.toString());
  });
});
```

Summary

This chapter has introduced the concept of data streams. You have seen how to create your own streams and how to use existing stream APIs, such as file streams. The coming chapters show streams in the context of network programming. You will also learn how to spawn and control child processes, which expose their own standard streams.

CHAPTER 8

Binary Data

Up to this point, we have only studied applications that process textual data. Often, however, applications must work with binary data rather than text in order to save space and time. Additionally, some application data, such as images and audio, are inherently binary. As web applications increase in sophistication, the use of binary data is becoming more popular, even in the browser. Thus, this chapter's focus shifts to applications that handle pure binary data. It examines what binary data is and how it is handled in the JavaScript standard, as well as features unique to Node.

An Overview of Binary Data

So what exactly is binary data? If you were thinking, "on a computer, all data is binary data," you would be correct. At the most basic level, just about every piece of data on a computer is stored in binary form—as a series of ones and zeros representing binary numbers and Boolean logic values. However, when the term "binary data" is used in the context of programming languages, it refers to data containing no additional abstractions or structure. For example, consider the simple JSON object shown in Listing 8-1. This object is considered JSON because it adheres to a certain syntax. The braces, quotation marks, and colon are all necessary in order for it to be a valid JSON object.

Listing 8-1. A Simple JSON Object

```
{"foo": "bar"}
```

You could also view the example as simply a series of characters. In this case, the braces suddenly lose semantic importance. Instead of marking the beginning and end of a JSON object, the braces are simply two more characters in a string. Replacing them with any other characters would make no difference. Ultimately, you have a string containing 14 characters that just so happen to conform to JSON syntax. However, the data is still being interpreted as text, not as true binary data.

In dealing with text, pieces of data are defined in terms of characters. For example, the string in Listing 8-1 is 14 characters long. In dealing with binary data, one speaks of bytes, or *octets*. For bytes to be interpreted as text, some type of character encoding must be used. Depending on the type of encoding, there may or may not be one-to-one mapping of characters to bytes.

■ **Note** An octet is an 8-bit piece of data. The term *byte* is also commonly used to describe 8-bit data. However, historically the byte has not always been 8 bits. This book assumes the common 8-bit definition of *byte* and uses the term interchangeably with *octet*.

Node supports a number of character encodings but normally defaults to UTF-8. UTF-8 is a variable-width encoding that is backward-compatible with ASCII, but it can also represent all Unicode characters. Since UTF-8 encoding is variable-width, some characters are represented using a single byte, but many are not. More specifically, a single UTF-8 character can require between 1 and 4 bytes.

Listing 8-2 shows the string from Listing 8-1 represented as binary data. Since they consist of long strings of ones (1) and zeros (0), binary data is often displayed using hexadecimal notation, in which each digit represents 4 bits. Therefore, each pair of hex digits represents an octet. In this example, each textual character is UTF-8 encoded as a single byte. Therefore, Listing 8-2 contains 14 bytes. By examining the value of each byte, you can begin to see a pattern in the mapping to characters. For example, the byte value 22 occurs four times—where the quotation marks are located in Listing 8-1. The value 6f, corresponding to the "oo" in "foo", also occurs two times in a row.

Listing 8-2. The String in Listing 8-1 Represented As Binary Data Written in Hexadecimal

```
7b 22 66 6f 6f 22 3a 20 22 62 61 72 22 7d
```

In the last example, each text character conveniently mapped to a single byte. However, this may not always happen. For example, consider the snowman Unicode character (see Listing 8-3), which although rarely used, is perfectly valid string data in JavaScript. Listing 8-4 shows the binary representation of the snowman. Notice that 3 bytes are required to represent this single character in UTF-8 encoding.

Listing 8-3. The Snowman Unicode Character

☃

Listing 8-4. The Snowman Character Represented As Binary Data

```
e2 98 83
```

Endianness

Another subject that sometimes arises when dealing with binary data is endianness. Endianness refers to the way a given machine stores data in memory, and comes into play when storing multibyte data such as integers and floating-point numbers. The two most common types of endianness are *big-endian* and *little-endian*. A big-endian machine stores a data item's most significant byte first. In this case, "first" refers to the lowest memory address. A little-endian machine, on the other hand, stores the *least* significant byte in the lowest memory address. To illustrate the difference between big-endian and little-endian storage, let's examine how the number 1 is stored in each scheme. Figure 8-1 shows the number 1 encoded as a 32-bit unsigned integer. The most significant and least significant bytes are labeled for your convenience. Since the data's length is 32 bits, 4 bytes are required to store the data in memory.

This is the most significant byte

This is the least significant byte

00 00 00 01

Figure 8-1. *The number 1, encoded as a 32-bit unsigned integer, shown in hexadecimal*

Figure 8-2 shows how the data is stored on a big-endian machine, while Figure 8-3 shows the same data represented in little-endian format. Notice that the byte containing 01 swaps sides from one representation to the other. The labels 0x00000000 and 0xFFFFFFFF denote the ascending addresses of the memory space.

0x00000000   0xFFFFFFFF

00 00 00 01

Figure 8-2. *The number 1, as it is stored in memory on a big-endian machine*

After examining Figures 8-2 and 8-3, you can see why understanding endianness matters. If a number stored in one endianness is interpreted in the other, the results will be completely wrong. To illustrate this point, let's return to the example of the number 1. Assume that the data has been written to a file on a machine that uses little-endian storage. What if that file were moved to another machine and read as big-endian data? As it turns out, the number 00 00 00 01 would be interpreted as 01 00 00 00. If you do the math, this turns out to be 2^{24}, or 16,777,216—a difference of nearly 17 million!

0x00000000   0xFFFFFFFF

01 00 00 00

Figure 8-3. *The number 1, as it is stored in memory on a little-endian machine*

Determining Endianness

The os core module provides a method, endianness(), that, as the name implies, is used to determine the endianness of the current machine. The endianness() method takes no arguments and returns a string indicating the machine's endianness. If the machine employs big-endian storage, endianness() returns the string "BE". Conversely, if little-endian is used, "LE" is returned. The example in Listing 8-5 calls endianness() and prints the result to the console.

Listing 8-5. Determining a Machine's Endianness Using the os.endianness() Method

```
var os = require("os");

console.log(os.endianness());
```

The Typed Array Specification

Before looking at the Node-specific way of handling binary data, let's look at JavaScript's standard binary data handlers, known as the *typed array specification*. This name comes from the fact that, unlike normal JavaScript variables, a binary data array has a specific data type that does not change. Because the typed array specification is part of the JavaScript language, the material in this section is applicable in the browser (if supported), as well as in Node. Most modern browsers at least partially support binary data, but which browsers support which features are details beyond the scope of this book.

ArrayBuffers

JavaScript's binary data API consists of two parts, a buffer and a view. The buffer, implemented using the ArrayBuffer data type, is a generic container holding an array of bytes. As ArrayBuffers are fixed-length structures, once created, they cannot be resized. It is also advisable not to work directly with the contents of an ArrayBuffer. Instead, create a view to manipulate the ArrayBuffer's contents (the topic of views is revisited shortly).

An ArrayBuffer is created by calling the ArrayBuffer() constructor. The constructor function takes a single argument, an integer representing the number of bytes in the ArrayBuffer. The example in Listing 8-6 creates a new ArrayBuffer that can hold a total of 1,024 bytes.

Listing 8-6. Creating a 1,024-Byte ArrayBuffer

```
var buffer = new ArrayBuffer(1024);
```

Working with an existing ArrayBuffer is very similar to working with a normal array. Individual bytes are read and written using array subscript notation. However, since an ArrayBuffer cannot be resized, writing to a nonexistent index does not change the underlying data structure. Instead, the write does not occur and fails silently. In the example in Listing 8-7, showing an attempt to write past the end of an ArrayBuffer, an empty 4-byte ArrayBuffer is initialized. Next, a value is written to each byte, including a write past the end of the ArrayBuffer. Finally, the ArrayBuffer is printed to the console.

Listing 8-7. Writing Values to an ArrayBuffer and Printing the Result

```
var foo = new ArrayBuffer(4);

foo[0] = 0;
foo[1] = 1;
foo[2] = 2;
foo[3] = 3;
// this assignment will fail silently
foo[4] = 4;
console.log(foo);
```

Listing 8-8 shows the output resulting from Listing 8-7. Notice that although the code wrote past the end of the buffer, the written value is not present in the output. The failed write also did not generate any exceptions.

Listing 8-8. The Results of Running the Code in Listing 8-7

```
$ node array-buffer-write.js
{ '0': 0,
  '1': 1,
  '2': 2,
  '3': 3,
  slice: [Function: slice],
  byteLength: 4 }
```

In the previous output, you may have noticed the byteLength property, which denotes the size of the ArrayBuffer in bytes. This value is assigned when the ArrayBuffer is created and cannot be changed. Like a normal array's length property, byteLength is useful for looping over the contents of an ArrayBuffer. Listing 8-9 shows how the byteLength property is used in a for loop to display the contents of an ArrayBuffer.

Listing 8-9. Looping over an ArrayBuffer Using the byteLength Property

```
var foo = new ArrayBuffer(4);

foo[0] = 0;
foo[1] = 1;
foo[2] = 2;
foo[3] = 3;

for (var i = 0, len = foo.byteLength; i < len; i++) {
  console.log(foo[i]);
}
```

slice()

You can extract a new ArrayBuffer from an existing one using the slice() method. The slice() method takes two arguments, which specify the starting position (inclusive) and ending position (exclusive) of the range to copy. The ending index can be omitted. If it is not specified, the slice span goes from the start index to the end of the ArrayBuffer. Both indexes can be negative as well. A negative index is used to calculate a position from the end of the ArrayBuffer as opposed to the beginning. Listing 8-10 shows several examples that slice the same two bytes from an ArrayBuffer. The first two examples use explicit start and end indexes, while the third omits the end index. Finally, the fourth example creates a slice using a negative starting index.

Listing 8-10. Creating a New ArrayBuffer Using the slice() Method

```
var foo = new ArrayBuffer(4);

foo[0] = 0;
foo[1] = 1;
foo[2] = 2;
foo[3] = 3;

console.log(foo.slice(2, 4));
console.log(foo.slice(2, foo.byteLength));
console.log(foo.slice(2));
console.log(foo.slice(-2));
// returns [2, 3]
```

It is important to note that the new ArrayBuffer returned by slice() is just a copy of the original data. Therefore, if the buffer returned by slice() is modified, the original data is not changed (see the example in Listing 8-11).

Listing 8-11. Creating a New ArrayBuffer Using the slice() Method

```
var foo = new ArrayBuffer(4);
var bar;

foo[0] = 0;
foo[1] = 1;
foo[2] = 2;
foo[3] = 3;

// Create a copy of foo and modify it
bar = foo.slice(0);
bar[0] = 0xc;

console.log(foo);
console.log(bar);
```

In Listing 8-11, an ArrayBuffer named foo is created and populated with data. Next, the entire contents of foo are copied into bar using slice(). Then the hex value 0xc (binary 12) is written to the first position in bar. Finally, both foo and bar are printed to the console. Listing 8-12 shows the resulting output. Notice that the two ArrayBuffers are identical, except for the first byte. The value 0xc, which was written to bar, did not propagate to foo.

Listing 8-12. The Output from Running the Code in Listing 8-11

```
$ node array-buffer-slice.js
{ '0': 0,
  '1': 1,
  '2': 2,
  '3': 3,
  slice: [Function: slice],
  byteLength: 4 }
{ '0': 12,
  '1': 1,
  '2': 2,
  '3': 3,
  slice: [Function: slice],
  byteLength: 4 }
```

ArrayBuffer Views

Working directly with arrays of bytes is both tedious and error prone. By adding a layer of abstraction to an ArrayBuffer, views give the illusion of more traditional data types. For example, instead of working with an 8-byte ArrayBuffer, you can use a view to make the data appear as an array of two 4-byte integers, each 32 bits long, for a total of 64 bits, or 8 bytes. Table 8-1 lists the various types of views as well as the size in bytes of each array element. So in our example scenario, we would want either an Int32Array or an Uint32Array view, depending on whether our application required signed or unsigned numbers.

Table 8-1. *Description of JavaScript's Various ArrayBuffer Views*

View Type	Element Size (Bytes)	Description
Int8Array	1	Array of 8-bit signed integers.
Uint8Array	1	Array of 8-bit unsigned integers.
Uint8ClampedArray	1	Array of 8-bit unsigned integers. Values are clamped to be in the 0–255 range.
Int16Array	2	Array of 16-bit signed integers.
Uint16Array	2	Array of 16-bit unsigned integers.
Int32Array	4	Array of 32-bit signed integers.
Uint32Array	4	Array of 32-bit unsigned integers.
Float32Array	4	Array of 32-bit IEEE floating point numbers.
Float64Array	8	Array of 64-bit IEEE floating-point numbers.

■ **Note**   Though the Uint8Array and Uint8ClampedArray are very similar, there is a key difference in the way values outside the 0–255 range are treated. The Uint8Array simply looks at the least significant 8 bits in determining a value. Thus, 255, 256, and 257 are interpreted as 255, 0, and 1, respectively. On the other hand, the Uint8ClampedArray interprets any value greater than 255 as 255 and any value less than 0 as 0. That is to say, 255, 256, and 257 are all interpreted as 255.

The example in Listing 8-13 shows how views are used in practice. In this case, a view consisting of two 32-bit unsigned integers is created based on an 8-byte ArrayBuffer. Next, two integers are written to the view, and the view is displayed.

Listing 8-13. An Example Using the Uint32Array View

```
var buf = new ArrayBuffer(8);
var view = new Uint32Array(buf);

view[0] = 100;
view[1] = 256;

console.log(view);
```

Listing 8-14 shows the resulting output. Its first two lines show the two values, 100 and 256, written to the view. Following the array values is the BYTES_PER_ELEMENT property. This read-only property, included in each type of view, represents the number of raw bytes in each array element. Following the BYTES_PER_ELEMENT property is a collection of methods to be revisited shortly.

Listing 8-14. Output from Running the Code in Listing 8-13

```
$ node array-buffer-view.js
{ '0': 100,
  '1': 256,
  BYTES_PER_ELEMENT: 4,
```

```
  get: [Function: get],
  set: [Function: set],
  slice: [Function: slice],
  subarray: [Function: subarray],
  buffer:
   { '0': 100,
     '1': 0,
     '2': 0,
     '3': 0,
     '4': 0,
     '5': 1,
     '6': 0,
     '7': 0,
     slice: [Function: slice],
     byteLength: 8 },
  length: 2,
  byteOffset: 0,
  byteLength: 8 }
```

Notice that the underlying ArrayBuffer is also displayed as the buffer property. Examine the value of each byte in the ArrayBuffer, and you will see its correspondence with the value stored in the view. In this example, bytes 0 through 3 correspond with the value 100, and bytes 4 through 7 represent the value 256.

■ **Note** As a reminder, 256 is equivalent to 2^8, meaning that it cannot be represented in a single byte. A single unsigned byte can hold a maximum of 255. Therefore, the hex representation of 256 is 01 00.

This brings up another important aspect of views. Unlike the ArrayBuffer slice() method, which returns a new copy of data, views manipulate the original data directly. So modifying the values of a view changes the contents of the ArrayBuffer, and vice versa. Also, two views having the same ArrayBuffer can accidentally (or intentionally) change each other's values. The example shown in Listing 8-15, where a 4-byte ArrayBuffer is shared by a Uint32Array view and a Uint8Array view, begins by writing 100 to the Uint32Array, then printing the value. Then the Uint8Array writes the value 1 to its second byte (effectively writing the value 256). The data from the Uint32Array is then printed again.

Listing 8-15. Views Interacting with Each Other

```
var buf = new ArrayBuffer(4);
var view1 = new Uint32Array(buf);
var view2 = new Uint8Array(buf);

// write to view1 and print the value
view1[0] = 100;
console.log("Uint32 = " + view1[0]);

// write to view2 and print view1's value
view2[1] = 1;
console.log("Uint32 = " + view1[0]);
```

Listing 8-16 shows the output from Listing 8-15. As expected, the first print statement displays the value 100. However, by the time the second print statement occurs, the value has increased to 356. In the example this behavior is expected. However, in more complex applications you must be cautious when creating multiple views of the same data.

Listing 8-16. The Output from Running the Code in Listing 8-15

```
$ node view-overwrite.js
Uint32 = 100
Uint32 = 356
```

A Note on View Sizing

Views must be sized such that each element can be fully composed from data in the ArrayBuffer. That is, a view can only be constructed from data whose length in bytes is a multiple of the view's BYTES_PER_ELEMENT property. For example, a 4-byte ArrayBuffer can be used to construct an Int32Array view holding a single integer. However, the same 4-byte buffer cannot be used to construct a Float64Array view whose elements are 8 bytes long.

Constructor Information

Each type of view has four constructors. One form, which you've already seen, takes an ArrayBuffer as its first argument. This constructor function can also optionally specify both a starting byte offset in the ArrayBuffer and the view's length. The byte offset defaults to 0 and ***must*** be a multiple of BYTES_PER_ELEMENT, or else a RangeError exception is thrown. If omitted, the length will try to consume the entire ArrayBuffer, starting at the byte offset. These arguments, if specified, allow the view to be based on a piece of the ArrayBuffer instead of the entire thing. This is especially useful if the ArrayBuffer length is not an exact multiple of the view's BYTES_PER_ELEMENT.

In the example in Listing 8-17, which shows how a view can be constructed from a buffer whose size is not an exact multiple of BYTES_PER_ELEMENT, an Int32Array view is built on a 5-byte ArrayBuffer. The byte offset of 0 indicates that the view should begin at the first byte of the ArrayBuffer. Meanwhile, the length argument specifies that the view should contain a single integer. Without these arguments, it would not be possible to construct the view from this ArrayBuffer. Also, notice that the example contains a write to the byte at buf[4]. Since the view uses only the first four bytes, this write to the fifth byte does not alter the data in the view.

Listing 8-17. Building a View Based on Part of an ArrayBuffer

```
var buf = new ArrayBuffer(5);
var view = new Int32Array(buf, 0, 1);

view[0] = 256;
buf[4] = 5;
console.log(view[0]);
```

Creating an Empty View

The second constructor is used to create an empty view of a predefined length, n. This form of the constructor also creates a new ArrayBuffer big enough to accommodate n view elements. For example, the code in Listing 8-18 creates an empty Float32Array view that holds two floating-point numbers. Behind the scenes the constructor also creates an 8-byte ArrayBuffer to hold the floats. During construction, all the bytes in the ArrayBuffer are initialized to 0.

Listing 8-18. Creating an Empty Float32Array View

```
var view = new Float32Array(2);
```

Creating a View from Data Values

The third form of constructor accepts an array of values that are used to populate the view data. The values in the array are converted to the appropriate data type and then stored in the view. The constructor also creates a new ArrayBuffer to hold the values. Listing 8-19 shows an example that creates a Uint16Array view populated with the values 1, 2, and 3.

Listing 8-19. Creating a Uint16Array View from an Array Containing Three Values

```
var view = new Uint16Array([1, 2, 3]);
```

Creating a View from Another View

The fourth version of the constructor is very similar to the third. The only difference is that instead of passing in a standard array, this version accepts another view as its only argument. The newly created view also instantiates its own backing ArrayBuffer—that is, the underlying data is not shared. Listing 8-20 shows how this version of the constructor is used in practice. In this example, a 4-byte ArrayBuffer is used to create an Int8Array view containing four numbers. The Int8Array view is then used to create a new Uint32Array view. The Uint32Array also contains four numbers, corresponding to the data in the Int8Array view. However, its underlying ArrayBuffer is 16 bytes long instead of 4. Of course, because the two views have different ArrayBuffers, updating one view does not affect the other.

Listing 8-20. Creating a Uint32Array View from an Int8Array View

```
var buf = new ArrayBuffer(4);
var view1 = new Int8Array(buf);
var view2 = new Uint32Array(view1);

console.log(buf.byteLength);    // 4
console.log(view1.byteLength);  // 4
console.log(view2.byteLength);  // 16
```

View Properties

You've already seen that a view's ArrayBuffer can be accessed via the buffer property and that the BYTES_PER_ELEMENT property represents the number of bytes per view element. Views also have two properties, byteLength and length, related to the data size, and a byteOffset property indicating the first byte of a buffer used by the view.

byteLength

The byteLength property represents the view's data size in bytes. This value is not necessarily equal to the byteLength property of the underlying ArrayBuffer. In the example of this case, shown in Listing 8-21, an Int16Array view is built from a 10-byte ArrayBuffer. However, because the Int16Array constructor specifies that it is to contain only two integers, its byteLength property is 4, while the ArrayBuffer's byteLength is 10.

Listing 8-21. Differing byteLengths of a View and Its `ArrayBuffer`

```
var buf = new ArrayBuffer(10);
var view = new Int16Array(buf, 0, 2);

console.log(buf.byteLength);
console.log(view.byteLength);
```

length

The `length` property, which works like that of a standard array, indicates the number of data elements in the view. This property is useful for looping over the view's data, as shown in Listing 8-22.

Listing 8-22. Looping over View Data Using the `length` Property

```
var view = new Int32Array([5, 10]);

for (var i = 0, len = view.length; i < len; i++) {
  console.log(view[i]);
}
```

byteOffset

The `byteOffset` property specifies the offset into the `ArrayBuffer` corresponding to the first byte used by the view. This value is always 0, unless an offset was passed in as the second argument to the constructor (see Listing 8-17). The `byteOffset` can be used in conjunction with the `byteLength` property to loop over the bytes of the underlying `ArrayBuffer`. In the example in Listing 8-23, which shows how only the bytes used by a view can be looped over using `byteOffset` and `byteLength`, the source `ArrayBuffer` is 10 bytes long, but the view only uses bytes 4 through 7.

Listing 8-23. Looping over the Utilized Subset of Bytes in an `ArrayBuffer`

```
var buf = new ArrayBuffer(10);
var view = new Int16Array(buf, 4, 2);
var len = view.byteOffset + view.byteLength;

view[0] = 100;
view[1] = 256;

for (var i = view.byteOffset; i < len; i++) {
  console.log(buf[i]);
}
```

get()

The `get()` method is used to retrieve the data value at a given index in the view. However, as you've already seen, the same task can be accomplished using array index notation, which requires fewer characters. If you elect to use `get()` for whatever reason, an example of its usage is shown in Listing 8-24.

Listing 8-24. Using the View get() Method

```
var view = new Uint8ClampedArray([5]);

console.log(view.get(0));
// could also use view[0]
```

set()

set() is used to assign one or more values in the view. To assign a single value, pass the index to write, followed by the value to write as an argument to set() (you can also accomplish this using array index notation). An example assigning the value 3.14 to the fourth view element is shown in Listing 8-25.

Listing 8-25. Assigning a Single Value Using set()

```
var view = new Float64Array(4);

view.set(3, 3.14);
// could also use view[3] = 3.14
```

In order to assign multiple values, set() also accepts arrays and views as its first argument. Optionally use this form of set() to provide a second argument that specifies the offset to begin writing values. If this offset is not included, set() begins writing values at the first index. In Listing 8-26, set() is used to populate all four elements of an Int32Array.

Listing 8-26. Assigning Multiple Values Using set()

```
var view = new Int32Array(4);

view.set([1, 2, 3, 4], 0);
```

There are two important things to know about this version of set(). First, an exception is thrown if you attempt to write past the end of the view. In the example in Listing 8-26, if the second argument had been larger than 0, the four-element boundary would have been exceeded, resulting in an error. Second, note that because set() accepts a view as its first argument, the argument's ArrayBuffer might possibly be shared with the calling object. If the source and destination are the same, Node must intelligently copy the data such that bytes are not overwritten before they've had a chance to be copied. Listing 8-27 is an example of a scenario where two Int8Array views have the same ArrayBuffer. The second view, view2, is also smaller, representing the first half of the larger view, view1. When the call to set() occurs, 0 is assigned to view1[1], and 1 is assigned to view1[2]. Since view1[1] is part of the source (as well as the destination in this operation), you need to ensure that the original value is copied before it is overwritten.

Listing 8-27. Showing Where a Single ArrayBuffer Is Shared in set()

```
var buf = new ArrayBuffer(4);
var view1 = new Int8Array(buf);
var view2 = new Int8Array(buf, 0, 2);

view1[0] = 0;
view1[1] = 1;
view1[2] = 2;
view1[3] = 3;
view1.set(view2, 1);
console.log(view1.buffer);
```

According to the specification, "setting the values takes place as if all the data is first copied into a temporary buffer that does not overlap either of the arrays, and then the data from the temporary buffer is copied into the current array." Essentially, this means that Node takes care of everything for you. To verify this, the resulting output from the previous example is shown in Listing 8-28. Notice that bytes 1 and 2 hold the correct values of 0 and 1.

Listing 8-28. The Output from Running the Code in Listing 8-27

```
$ node view-set-overlap.js
{ '0': 0,
  '1': 0,
  '2': 1,
  '3': 3,
  slice: [Function: slice],
  byteLength: 4 }
```

subarray()

subarray(), which returns a new view of the data type that relies on the same ArrayBuffer, takes two arguments. The first argument specifies the first index to be referenced in the new view. The second, which is optional, represents the last index to be referenced in the new view. If the ending index is omitted, the new view's span goes from the start index to the end of the original view. Either index can be negative, meaning that the offset is computed from the end of the data array. Note that the new view returned by subarray() has the same ArrayBuffer as the original view. Listing 8-29 shows how subarray() is used to create several identical Uint8ClampedArray views making up a subset of another.

Listing 8-29. Using subarray() to Create New Views from an Existing One

```
var view1 = new Uint8ClampedArray([1, 2, 3, 4, 5]);
var view2 = view1.subarray(3, view1.length);
var view3 = view1.subarray(3);
var view4 = view1.subarray(-2);
```

Node Buffers

Node provides its own Buffer data type for working with binary data. This is the preferred method of processing binary data in Node because it is slightly more efficient than typed arrays. Up to this point, you have encountered a number of methods that work with Buffer objects—for example, the fs module's read() and write() methods. This section explores in detail how Buffers work, including their compatibility with the typed array specification.

The Buffer Constructor

Buffer objects are created using one of the three Buffer() constructor functions. The Buffer constructor is global, meaning that it can be called without requiring any modules. Once a Buffer is created, it cannot be resized. The first form of the Buffer() constructor creates an empty Buffer of a given number of bytes. The example in Listing 8-30, which creates an empty 4-byte Buffer, also demonstrates that individual bytes within the Buffer can be accessed using array subscript notation.

Listing 8-30. Creating a 4-Byte Buffer and Accessing Individual Bytes

```
var buf = new Buffer(4);

buf[0] = 0;
buf[1] = 1;

console.log(buf);
```

Listing 8-31 shows the stringified version of the `Buffer`. The first two bytes in the `Buffer` hold the values 00 and 01, which were individually assigned in the code. Notice that the final two bytes also have values, although they were never assigned. These are actually the values already in memory when the program ran (if you run this code, the values you see will likely differ), indicating that the `Buffer()` constructor does not initialize the memory it reserves to 0. This is done intentionally—to save time when requesting a large amount of memory (recall that the `ArrayBuffer` constructor initializes its buffer to 0). As `ArrayBuffer`s are commonly used in web browsers, leaving the memory uninitialized could be a security hazard—you probably wouldn't want arbitrary web sites to read the contents of your computer's memory. Since the `Buffer` type is specific to Node, it isn't subject to the same security risks.

Listing 8-31. The Output Resulting from Running the Code in Listing 8-30

```
$ node buffer-constructor-1.js
<Buffer 00 01 05 02>
```

The second form of the `Buffer()` constructor accepts an array of bytes as its only argument. The resulting `Buffer` is populated with the values stored in the array. An example of this form of the constructor is shown in Listing 8-32.

Listing 8-32. Creating a `Buffer` from an Array of Octets

```
var buf = new Buffer([1, 2, 3, 4]);
```

The final version of the constructor is used to create a `Buffer` from string data. The code in Listing 8-33 shows how a `Buffer` is created from the string `"foo"`.

Listing 8-33. Creating a `Buffer` from a String

```
var buf = new Buffer("foo");
```

Earlier in this chapter, you learned that in order to convert from binary data to text, a character encoding must be specified. When a string is passed as the first argument to `Buffer()`, a second optional argument can be used to specify the encoding type. In Listing 8-33, no encoding is explicitly set, so UTF-8 is used by default. Table 8-2 breaks down the various character encodings supported by Node. (The astute reader might recognize this table from Chapter 5. However, it is worth repeating the information at this point in the book.)

Table 8-2. *The Various String Encoding Types Supported by Node*

Encoding Type	Description
utf8	Multibyte encoded Unicode characters. UTF-8 encoding is used by many web pages and to represent string data in Node.
ascii	7-bit American Standard Code for Information Interchange (ASCII) encoding.
utf16le	Little-endian-encoded Unicode characters. Each character is 2 or 4 bytes.
ucs2	This is simply an alias for utf16le encoding.
base64	Base64 string encoding. Base64 is commonly used in URL encoding, e-mail, and similar applications.
binary	Allows binary data to be encoded as string using only the first 8 bits of each character. As this is deprecated in favor of the Buffer object, it will be removed in future versions of Node.
hex	Encodes each byte as two hexadecimal characters.

Stringification Methods

Buffers can be stringified in two ways. The first uses the toString() method, which attempts to interpret the contents of the Buffer as string data. The toString() method accepts three arguments, all optional. They specify the character encoding and the starting and ending indexes of the Buffer to stringify. If unspecified, the entire Buffer is stringified using UTF-8 encoding. The example in Listing 8-34 stringifies an entire Buffer using toString().

Listing 8-34. Using the Buffer.toString() Method

```
var buf = new Buffer("foo");

console.log(buf.toString());
```

The second stringification method, toJSON(), returns the Buffer data as a JSON array of bytes. You get a similar result by calling JSON.stringify() on the Buffer object. Listing 8-35 shows an example of the toJSON() method.

Listing 8-35. Using the Buffer.toJSON() Method

```
var buf = new Buffer("foo");

console.log(buf.toJSON());
console.log(JSON.stringify(buf));
```

Buffer.isEncoding()

The isEncoding() method is a class method (i.e., a specific instance is not needed to invoke it) that accepts a string as its only argument and returns a Boolean indicating whether the input is a valid encoding type. Listing 8-36 shows two examples of isEncoding(). The first tests the string "utf8" and displays true. The second, however, prints false because "foo" is not a valid character encoding.

Listing 8-36. Two Examples of the Buffer.isEncoding() Class Method

```
console.log(Buffer.isEncoding("utf8"));
console.log(Buffer.isEncoding("foo"));
```

Buffer.isBuffer()

The class method isBuffer() is used to determine whether a piece of data is a Buffer object. It is used in the same fashion as the Array.isArray() method. Listing 8-37 shows an example use of isBuffer(). This example prints true because the buf variable is, in fact, a Buffer.

Listing 8-37. The Buffer.isBuffer() Class Method

```
var buf = new Buffer(1);

console.log(Buffer.isBuffer(buf));
```

Buffer.byteLength() and length

The byteLength() class method is used to calculate the number of bytes in a given string. This method also accepts an optional second argument to specify the string's encoding type. This method is useful for calculating byte lengths without actually instantiating a Buffer instance. However, if you have already constructed a Buffer, its length property serves the same purpose. In the example in Listing 8-38, which shows byteLength() and length, byteLength() is used to calculate the byte length of the string "foo" with UTF-8 encoding. Next, an actual Buffer is constructed from the same string. The Buffer's length property is then used to inspect the byte length.

Listing 8-38. Buffer.byteLength() and the length Property

```
var byteLength = Buffer.byteLength("foo");
var length = (new Buffer("foo")).length;

console.log(byteLength);
console.log(length);
```

fill()

There are a number of ways to write data to a Buffer. The appropriate method can depend on several factors, including the type of data and its endianness. The simplest method, fill(), which writes the same value to all or part of a Buffer, takes three arguments—the value to write, an optional offset to start filling, and an optional offset to stop filling. As with the other writing methods, the starting offset defaults to 0, and the ending offset defaults to the end of the Buffer. Since a Buffer is not set to zero by default, fill() is useful for initializing a Buffer to a value. The example in Listing 8-39 shows how all the memory in a Buffer can be zeroed out.

Listing 8-39. Zeroing Out the Memory in a Buffer Using fill()

```
var buf = new Buffer(1024);

buf.fill(0);
```

write()

To write a string to a Buffer, use the write() method. It accepts the following four arguments.

- The string to write.
- The offset to begin writing. This is optional and defaults to index 0.

- The number of bytes to write. If not specified, the entire string is written. However, if the Buffer lacks space for the entire string, it is truncated.

- The character encoding of the string. If omitted, this defaults to UTF-8.

The example in Listing 8-40 fills a 9-byte Buffer with three copies of the string "foo". As the first write starts at the beginning of the Buffer, an offset is not required. However, the second and third writes require an offset value. In the third, the string length is included though it is not necessary.

Listing 8-40. Several Writes to the Same Buffer Using write()

```
var buf = new Buffer(9);
var data = "foo";

buf.write(data);
buf.write(data, 3);
buf.write(data, 6, data.length);
```

Writing Numeric Data

There is a collection of methods used to write numeric data to a Buffer, each method being used to write a specific type of number. This is analogous to the various typed array views, each of which stores a different type of data. Table 8-3 lists the methods used to write numbers.

Table 8-3. *The Collection of Methods Used for Writing Numeric Data to a Buffer*

Method Name	Description
writeUInt8()	Writes an unsigned 8-bit integer.
writeInt8()	Writes a signed 8-bit integer.
writeUInt16LE()	Writes an unsigned 16-bit integer using little-endian format.
writeUInt16BE()	Writes an unsigned 16-bit integer using big-endian format.
writeInt16LE()	Writes a signed 16-bit integer using little-endian format.
writeInt16BE()	Writes a signed 16-bit integer using big-endian format.
writeUInt32LE()	Writes an unsigned 32-bit integer using little-endian format.
writeUInt32BE()	Writes an unsigned 32-bit integer using big-endian format.
writeInt32LE()	Writes a signed 32-bit integer using little-endian format.
writeInt32BE()	Writes a signed 32-bit integer using big-endian format.
writeFloatLE()	Writes a 32-bit floating-point number using little-endian format.
writeFloatBE()	Writes a 32-bit floating-point number using big-endian format.
writeDoubleLE()	Writes a 64-bit floating-point number using little-endian format.
writeDoubleBE()	Writes a 64-bit floating-point number using big-endian format.

All the methods in Table 8-3 take three arguments—the data to write, the offset in the Buffer to write the data, and an optional flag to turn off validation checking. If the validation flag is set to false (the default), an exception is thrown if the value is too large or the data overflows the Buffer. If this flag is set to true, large values are truncated, and overflow writes fail silently. In the example using writeDoubleLE() in Listing 8-41, the value 3.14 is written to the first 8 bytes of a Buffer, with no validation checking.

Listing 8-41. Using writeDoubleLE()

```
var buf = new Buffer(16);

buf.writeDoubleLE(3.14, 0, true);
```

Reading Numeric Data

Reading numeric data from a Buffer, like writing, also requires a collection of methods. Table 8-4 lists various methods used for reading data. Notice the one-to-one correspondence with the write methods in Table 8-3.

Table 8-4. *The Collection of Methods Used for Reading Numeric Data from a Buffer*

Method Name	Description
readUInt8()	Reads an unsigned 8-bit integer.
readInt8()	Reads a signed 8-bit integer.
readUInt16LE()	Reads an unsigned 16-bit integer using little-endian format.
readUInt16BE()	Reads an unsigned 16-bit integer using big-endian format.
readInt16LE()	Reads a signed 16-bit integer using little-endian format.
readInt16BE()	Reads a signed 16-bit integer using big-endian format.
readUInt32LE()	Reads an unsigned 32-bit integer using little-endian format.
readUInt32BE()	Reads an unsigned 32-bit integer using big-endian format.
readInt32LE()	Reads a signed 32-bit integer using little-endian format.
readInt32BE()	Reads a signed 32-bit integer using big-endian format.
readFloatLE()	Reads a 32-bit floating-point number using little-endian format.
readFloatBE()	Reads a 32-bit floating-point number using big-endian format.
readDoubleLE()	Reads a 64-bit floating-point number using little-endian format.
readDoubleBE()	Reads a 64-bit floating-point number using big-endian format.

All the numeric read methods take two arguments. The first is the offset in the Buffer to read the data from. The optional second argument is used to disable validation checking. If it is false (the default), an exception is thrown if the offset exceeds the Buffer size. If the flag is true, no validation occurs, and the returned data might be invalid. Listing 8-42 shows how a 64-bit floating-point number is written to a buffer and then read back using readDoubleLE().

Listing 8-42. Writing and Reading Numeric Data

```
var buf = new Buffer(8);
var value;

buf.writeDoubleLE(3.14, 0);
value = buf.readDoubleLE(0);
```

slice()

The slice() method returns a new Buffer that shares memory with the original Buffer. In other words, updates to the new Buffer affect the original, and vice versa. The slice() method takes two optional arguments, representing the starting and ending indexes to slice. The indexes can also be negative, meaning that they are relative to the end of the Buffer. Listing 8-43 shows how slice() is used to extract the first half of a 4-byte Buffer.

Listing 8-43. Using slice() to Create a New Buffer

```
var buf1 = new Buffer(4);
var buf2 = buf1.slice(0, 2);
```

copy()

The copy() method is used to copy data from one Buffer to another. The first argument to copy() is the destination Buffer. The second, if present, represents the starting index in the target to copy. The third and fourth arguments, if present, are the starting and ending indexes in the source Buffer to copy. An example that copies the full contents of one Buffer to another is shown in Listing 8-44.

Listing 8-44. Copying the Contents of One Buffer to Another Using copy()

```
var buf1 = new Buffer([1, 2, 3, 4]);
var buf2 = new Buffer(4);

buf1.copy(buf2, 0, 0, buf1.length);
```

Buffer.concat()

The concat() class method allows concatenation of multiple Buffers into a single larger Buffer. The first argument to concat() is an array of Buffer objects to be concatenated. If no Buffers are provided, concat() returns a zero-length Buffer. If a single Buffer is provided, a reference to that Buffer is returned. If multiple Buffers are provided, a new Buffer is created. Listing 8-45 provides an example that concatenates two Buffer objects.

Listing 8-45. Concatenating Two Buffer Objects

```
var buf1 = new Buffer([1, 2]);
var buf2 = new Buffer([3, 4]);
var buf = Buffer.concat([buf1, buf2]);

console.log(buf);
```

Typed Array Compatibility

Buffers are compatible with typed array views. When a view is constructed from a `Buffer`, the contents of the `Buffer` are cloned into a new `ArrayBuffer`. The cloned `ArrayBuffer` does not share memory with the original `Buffer`. In the example in Listing 8-46, which creates a view from a `Buffer`, a 4-byte `Buffer` is cloned into a 16-byte `ArrayBuffer`, which backs a `Uint32Array` view. Notice that the `Buffer` is initialized to all 0s prior to creating the view. Without doing so, the view would contain arbitrary data.

Listing 8-46. Creating a View from a `Buffer`

```
var buf = new Buffer(4);
var view;

buf.fill(0);
view = new Uint32Array(buf);
console.log(buf);
console.log(view);
```

It is also worth pointing out that while a view can be constructed from a `Buffer`, `ArrayBuffers` cannot be. A `Buffer` also cannot be constructed from an `ArrayBuffer`. A `Buffer` *can* be constructed from a view, but be cautious when doing so, as the views are likely to contain data that will not transfer well. In the simple example in Listing 8-47 illustrating this point, the integer 257, when moved from a `Uint32Array` view to a `Buffer`, becomes the byte value 1.

Listing 8-47. Data Loss when Constructing a `Buffer` from a View

```
var view = new Uint32Array([257]);
var buf = new Buffer(view);

console.log(buf);
```

Summary

A lot of material has been covered in this chapter. Starting with an overview of binary data, you were exposed to topics including character encoding and endianness at a high level. From there, the chapter progressed into the typed array specification. Hopefully, you found this material useful. After all, it is part of the JavaScript language and can be used in the browser as well as in Node. After presenting `ArrayBuffers` and views, the chapter moved on to Node's `Buffer` data type and, finally, looked at how the `Buffer` type works with typed arrays.

CHAPTER 9

■ ■ ■

Executing Code

This chapter's concern is the execution of *untrusted code*. In this case, "untrusted" refers to code that is not part of your application or imported modules but can still be executed. This chapter's specific focus is on two main use cases for running untrusted code. The first involves executing applications and scripts by spawning child processes. This use case allows Node applications to behave like a shell script, orchestrating multiple utility programs to achieve a larger goal. The second use case concerns the execution of JavaScript source code. While this scenario is not as common as process spawning, it is supported in the Node core and should be understood as an alternative to eval().

The child_process Module

The child_process core module, used to spawn and interact with child processes, provides several methods for running those processes, with each method providing different levels of control and implementation complexity. This section explains how each method works and indicates the trade-offs associated with each.

exec()

The exec() method is perhaps the simplest way to launch a child process. The exec() method takes a command (e.g., one issued from the command line) as its first argument. When exec() is invoked, a new shell—cmd.exe in Windows, /bin/sh otherwise—is launched and used to execute the command string. Additional configuration options can be passed to exec() via an optional second argument. This argument, if present, should be an object containing one or more of the properties shown in Table 9-1.

Table 9-1. *The Configuration Options Supported by exec()*

Property	Description
cwd	The value used to set the child process's working directory.
env	env should be an object whose key-value pairs specify the child process's environment. This object is equivalent to process.env in the child. If not specified, the child process inherits its environment from the parent process.
encoding	The character encoding used by the child process's stdout and stderr streams. It defaults to utf8 (UTF-8)
timeout	The property used to terminate the child process after a certain amount of time. If this value is greater than 0, the process is killed after timeout milliseconds. Otherwise the process runs indefinitely. The property defaults to 0.
maxBuffer	The maximum amount of data that can be buffered in the child process's stdout or stderr stream. It defaults to 200 KB. If this value is exceeded by either stream, the child process is killed.
killSignal	The signal used to terminate the child process. It is sent to the child process if, for example, a time-out occurs or if the maximum buffer size is exceeded. It defaults to SIGTERM.

The final argument to exec() is a callback function called after the child process terminates. This function is invoked with three arguments. Following Node convention, the first argument is any error condition. On success, this argument is null. If an error is present, the argument is an instance of Error. The second and third arguments are the buffered stdout and stderr data from the child process. Since the callback is invoked after the child process terminates, the stdout and stderr arguments are not streams, but rather strings containing the data that passed through the streams while the child was executing. stdout and stderr can each hold a total of maxBuffer bytes. Listing 9-1 shows an example use of exec() that executes the ls command (Windows users would substitute dir) to display the contents of the root directory (note that the example does not utilize the configuration options argument). An equivalent example, one that does pass in configuration options, is shown in Listing 9-2. In the second example, the directory to list is no longer specified in the actual command string. However, the cwd option is used to set the working directory to the root directory. Though the output from Listings 9-1 and 9-2 should be the same, they will depend on the contents of your local machine.

Listing 9-1. Displaying the Output of a Process Using exec()

```
var cp = require("child_process");

cp.exec("ls -l /", function(error, stdout, stderr) {
  if (error) {
    console.error(error.toString());
  } else if (stderr !== "") {
    console.error(stderr);
  } else {
    console.log(stdout);
  }
});
```

Listing 9-2. A Display Equivalent to Listing 9-1 (with Configuration Options)

```
var cp = require("child_process");

cp.exec("ls -l", {
  cwd: "/"
}, function(error, stdout, stderr) {
  if (error) {
    console.error(error.toString());
  } else if (stderr !== "") {
    console.error(stderr);
  } else {
    console.log(stdout);
  }
});
```

execFile()

The execFile() method is similar to exec(), with two slight differences. The primary one is that execFile() does not spawn a new shell. Instead, execFile() directly executes the file passed to it, making execFile() slightly less resource intensive than exec(). The second difference is that the first argument to execFile() is the name of the file to execute, with no additional arguments. Listing 9-3 shows how the ls command would be invoked to display the contents of the current working directory.

Listing 9-3. Executing a File with No Additional Arguments Using execFile()

```
var cp = require("child_process");

cp.execFile("ls", function(error, stdout, stderr) {
  if (error) {
    console.error(error.toString());
  } else if (stderr !== "") {
    console.error(stderr);
  } else {
    console.log(stdout);
  }
});
```

■ **Warning**   Because execFile() does not spawn a new shell, Windows users cannot make it issue a command such as dir. In Windows, dir is a built-in feature of the shell. Additionally, execFile() cannot be used to run .cmd and .bat files, which rely on the shell. You can, however, use execFile() to run .exe files.

If you need to pass additional arguments to the command, specify an array of arguments as the second argument to execFile(). Listing 9-4 shows how this is accomplished. In this example, the ls command is executed again. However, this time the -l flag and / are also passed in to display the contents of the root directory.

Listing 9-4. Passing Arguments to the File Executed by execFile()

```
var cp = require("child_process");

cp.execFile("ls", ["-l", "/"], function(error, stdout, stderr) {
  if (error) {
    console.error(error.toString());
  } else if (stderr !== "") {
    console.error(stderr);
  } else {
    console.log(stdout);
  }
});
```

The third argument—or second, if no command arguments are passed in—to execFile() is an optional configuration object. As execFile() supports the same options as exec(), an explanation of the supported properties can be obtained from Table 9-1. The example in Listing 9-5, which uses the cwd option of the configuration object, is semantically equivalent to the code in Listing 9-4.

Listing 9-5. An Equivalent to Listing 9-4 That Utilizes the cwd Option

```
var cp = require("child_process");

cp.execFile("ls", ["-l"], {
  cwd: "/"
}, function(error, stdout, stderr) {
  if (error) {
    console.error(error.toString());
  } else if (stderr !== "") {
    console.error(stderr);
  } else {
    console.log(stdout);
  }
});
```

■ **Note** Behind the scenes, exec() invokes execFile(), with your operating system's shell as the file argument. The command to execute is then passed to execFile() in the array argument.

---

spawn()

The exec() and execFile() methods are simple, and they work well when you just need to issue a command and capture its output. However, some applications require more complex interactions. That is where spawn(), the most powerful and flexible abstraction that Node provides for working with child processes, comes into play (from the developer's perspective it also requires the most work). spawn() is also called by execFile()—and by extension, exec()—as well as fork() (which is covered later in this chapter).

spawn() takes a maximum of three arguments. The first, the command to execute, should be the path to the executable only. It should not contain any arguments to the command. To pass arguments to the command, use the optional second argument. If present, it should be an array of values to pass to the command. The third and final argument, also optional, is used to pass options to spawn() itself. Table 9-2 lists the options supported by spawn().

Table 9-2. *A Listing of the Options Supported by* spawn( )

Property	Description
cwd	The value used to set the child process's working directory.
env	env should be an object whose key-value pairs specify the child process's environment. This object is equivalent to process.env in the child. If not specified, the child process inherits its environment from the parent process.
stdio	Either an array or a string used to configure the child process's standard streams. This argument is covered below.
detached	A Boolean specifying if the child process will be a process group leader. If true, the child can continue executing even if the parent terminates. This defaults to false.
uid	This number, representing the user identity to run the process as, allows programs to be run as another user and to temporarily elevate privileges. It defaults to null, causing the child to be run as the current user.
gid	A number used to set the process's group identity. It defaults to null, with the value to be set based on the current user.

The stdio Option

The stdio option is used to configure the stdin, stdout, and stderr streams of the child process. This option can be a three-item array or one of the following strings: "ignore", "pipe", and "inherit". Before the string arguments can be explained, you must first understand the array form. If stdio is an array, the first element sets the file descriptor for the child process's stdin stream. Similarly, the second and third elements set the file descriptors for the child's stdout and stderr streams, respectively. Table 9-3 enumerates the possible values for each array element.

Table 9-3. *The Possible Values for* stdio *Array Entries*

Value	Description
"pipe"	Creates a pipe between the child process and the parent process. spawn( ) returns a ChildProcess object (explained in more detail later). The parent can access the child's standard streams via the ChildProcess object's stdin, stdout, and stderr streams.
"ipc"	Creates an interprocess communication (IPC) channel between child and parent that can be used to pass messages and file descriptors. A child process can have, at most, one IPC file descriptor. (IPC channels are covered in more detail in a later section.)
"ignore"	Causes the child's corresponding stream to simply be ignored.
A stream object	A readable or writable stream that can be shared with the child process. The stream's underlying file descriptor is duplicated in the child process. For example, the parent could set up a child process to read commands from a file stream.
A positive integer	Corresponds to a file descriptor currently open in the parent process that is shared with the child process.
null or undefined	Use the default values of 0, 1, and 2 for stdin, stdout, and stderr, respectively.

If stdio is a string, it can be "ignore", "pipe", or "inherit". These values are shorthand for certain array configurations. The meaning of each value is shown in Table 9-4.

Table 9-4. *A Translation of Each* stdio *String Value*

String	Value
"ignore"	["ignore", "ignore", "ignore"]
"pipe"	["pipe", "pipe", "pipe"]
"inherit"	[process.stdin, process.stdout, process.stderr] or [0, 1, 2]

The ChildProcess Class

spawn() does not accept callback functions like exec() and execFile(). Instead, it returns a ChildProcess object. The ChildProcess class inherits from EventEmitter and is used to interact with the spawned child process. ChildProcess objects provide three stream objects, stdin, stdout, and stderr, representing the standard streams of the underlying child process. The example in Listing 9-6 uses spawn() to run the ls command in the root directory. The child process is then set up to inherit its standard streams from the parent process. Because the child's standard streams are hooked up to the parent's streams, the child output is printed to the console. Since our only real interest is in the output of the ls command, the stdio option could also have been set up using the array ["ignore", process.stdout, "ignore"].

Listing 9-6. Executing a Command Using spawn()

```
var cp = require("child_process");
var child = cp.spawn("ls", ["-l"], {
  cwd: "/",
  stdio: "inherit"
});
```

■ **Note** For a refresher on working with the standard streams, revisit Chapters 5 and 7. This chapter focuses on material not covered earlier.

In the last example, the child process's stdout stream was essentially managed by using the stdio property's "inherit" value. However, the stream could also have been explicitly controlled. The example in Listing 9-7 taps directly into the child's stdout stream and its data event handler.

Listing 9-7. An Alternative Implementation of Listing 9-6

```
var cp = require("child_process");
var child = cp.spawn("ls", ["-l", "/"]);

child.stdout.on("data", function(data) {
  process.stdout.write(data.toString());
});
```

The error Event

A ChildProcess object emits an error event when the child cannot be spawned or killed, or when sending it an IPC message has failed. The generic format of a ChildProcess error event handler is shown in Listing 9-8.

Listing 9-8. A ChildProcess error Event Handler

```
var cp = require("child_process");
var child = cp.spawn("ls");

child.on("error", function(error) {
  // process error here
  console.error(error.toString());
});
```

The exit Event

When the child process terminates, the ChildProcess object emits an exit event. The exit event handler is passed two arguments. The first is the exit code of the process if it is terminated by the parent (if the process is not terminated by the parent, the code argument is null). The second is the signal used to kill the process. If the child isn't terminated by a signal from the parent process, this is also null. Listing 9-9 shows a generic exit event handler.

Listing 9-9. A ChildProcess exit Event Handler

```
var cp = require("child_process");
var child = cp.spawn("ls");

child.on("exit", function(code, signal) {
  console.log("exit code:  " + code);
  console.log("exit signal:  " + signal);
});
```

The close Event

The close event is emitted when the standard streams of a child process are closed. This is distinct from the exit event because it is possible for multiple processes to share the same streams. Like the exit event, close also provides the exit code and signal as arguments to the event handler. A generic close event handler is shown in Listing 9-10.

Listing 9-10. A ChildProcess close Event Handler

```
var cp = require("child_process");
var child = cp.spawn("ls");

child.on("close", function(code, signal) {
  console.log("exit code:  " + code);
  console.log("exit signal:  " + signal);
});
```

The pid Property

A ChildProcess's pid property is used to obtain the child's process identifier. Listing 9-11 shows how the pid property is accessed.

Listing 9-11. Accessing a Child Process's pid Property

```
var cp = require("child_process");
var child = cp.spawn("ls");

console.log(child.pid);
```

kill()

kill() is used to send a signal to a child process. This signal to the child is the only argument to kill(). If no argument is provided, kill() sends the SIGTERM signal in an attempt to kill the child process. In the example in Listing 9-12, which calls kill(), an exit event handler is also included to display the terminating signal.

Listing 9-12. Sending a Signal to a Child Process Using kill()

```
var cp = require("child_process");
var child = cp.spawn("cat");

child.on("exit", function(code, signal) {
  console.log("Killed using " + signal);
});

child.kill("SIGTERM");
```

fork()

fork(), a special case of spawn(), is used to create Node processes (see Listing 9-13). The modulePath argument is the path to the Node module that is run in the child process. The optional second argument is an array used to pass arguments to the child process. The final argument is an optional object used to pass options to fork(). The options that fork() supports are shown in Table 9-5.

Listing 9-13. Using the child_process.fork() Method

```
child_process.fork(modulePath, [args], [options])
```

Table 9-5. *The Options Supported by fork()*

Option	Description
cwd	Value used to set the child process's working directory.
env	env should be an object whose key-value pairs specify the child process's environment. The object is equivalent to process.env in the child. If not specified, the child process inherits its environment from the parent process.
encoding	The character encoding used by the child process. It defaults to "utf8" (UTF-8).

▪ **Note** The process returned by `fork()` is a new instance of Node, containing a complete instance of V8. Take care not to create too many of these processes, as they consume considerable resources.

The `ChildProcess` object returned by `fork()` comes equipped with a built-in IPC channel that allows the different Node processes to communicate via JSON messages. The child process's standard streams are also associated with the parent process's by default.

To demonstrate how `fork()` works, two test applications are needed. The first application (see Listing 9-14) represents the child module to be executed. The module simply prints the arguments passed to it, its environment, and its working directory. Save this code in a file named `child.js`.

Listing 9-14. A Child Module

```
console.log("argv:  " + process.argv);
console.log("env:   " + JSON.stringify(process.env, null, 2));
console.log("cwd:   " + process.cwd());
```

Listing 9-15 shows the corresponding parent process. This code forks a new instance of Node, which runs the child module from Listing 9-14. The call to `fork()` passes a `-foo` argument to the child. It also sets the child's working directory to / and provides a custom environment. When the application is run, the print statements from the child process are displayed on the parent process's console.

Listing 9-15. The Parent for the Child Module Shown in Listing 9-14

```
var cp = require("child_process");
var child;

child = cp.fork(__dirname + "/child", ["-foo"], {
  cwd: "/",
  env: {
    bar: "baz"
  }
});
```

send()

The `send()` method uses the built-in IPC channel to pass JSON messages between Node processes. The parent process can send data by invoking the `ChildProcess` object's `send()` method. The data can then be handled in the child process by setting up a `message` event handler on the `process` object. Similarly, the child can send data to its parent by calling the `process.send()` method. In the parent process, the data is received via the `ChildProcess`'s `message` event handler.

The following example contains two Node applications that pass messages back and forth indefinitely. The child module (see Listing 9-16) should be stored in a file named `message-counter.js`. The entire module is simply the `process` object's `message` handler. Each time a message is received, the handler displays the message counter. Next, we verify that the parent process is still alive and the IPC channel is intact by inspecting the value of `process.connected`. If the channel is connected, the counter is incremented, and the message is sent back to the parent process.

Listing 9-16. A Child Module That Passes Messages Back to Its Parent

```
process.on("message", function(message) {
  console.log("child received:   " + message.count);

  if (process.connected) {
    message.count++;
    process.send(message);
  }
});
```

Listing 9-17 shows the corresponding parent process. The parent begins by forking a child process and then sets up two event handlers. The first handles `message` events from the child. The handler displays the message count and checks whether the IPC channel is connected via the `child.connected` value. If it is, the handler increments the counter and then passes the message back to the child process.

The second handler listens for the `SIGINT` signal. If `SIGINT` is received, the child is killed, and the parent process exits. This handler has been added to permit the user to terminate both programs, which are running in an infinite message passing loop. At the end of Listing 9-17, the message passing is started by sending a message with a count of 0 to the child. To test this program, simply run the parent process. To terminate, simply press `Ctrl+C`.

Listing 9-17. A Parent Module That Works in Conjunction with the Child in Listing 9-16

```
var cp = require("child_process");
var child = cp.fork(__dirname + "/message-counter");

child.on("message", function(message) {
  console.log("parent received:   " + message.count);

  if (child.connected) {
    message.count++;
    child.send(message);
  }
});

child.on("SIGINT", function() {
  child.kill();
  process.exit();
});

child.send({
  count: 0
});
```

■ **Note**   If the object transmitted via `send()` has a property named `cmd` whose value is a string beginning with `"NODE_"`, then the message is not emitted as a `message` event. An example is the object `{cmd: "NODE_foo"}`. These are special messages used by the Node core, and cause `internalMessage` events to be emitted. The official documentation strongly discourages the use of this feature, as it is subject to change without notice.

---

disconnect()

To close the IPC channel between the parent and child process, use the disconnect() method. From the parent process, invoke the ChildProcess's disconnect() method. From the child process, disconnect() is a method of the process object.

disconnect(), which does not accept any arguments, causes several things to occur. First, ChildProcess.connected and process.connected are set to false in the parent and child processes. Second, a disconnect event is emitted in both processes. Once disconnect() is called, an attempt to send more messages will cause an error.

Listing 9-18 shows a child module consisting of only a disconnect event handler. When the parent disconnects, the child process prints a message to the console. Store this code in a file named disconnect.js. Listing 9-19 shows the corresponding parent process. The parent forks a child process, sets up a disconnect event handler, and then immediately disconnects from the child. When the disconnect event is emitted by the child process, the parent also prints a goodbye message to the console.

Listing 9-18. A Child Module Implementing a disconnect Event Handler

```
process.on("disconnect", function() {
  console.log("Goodbye from the child process");
});
```

Listing 9-19. The Parent Corresponding to the Child Shown in Listing 9-18

```
var cp = require("child_process");
var child = cp.fork(__dirname + "/disconnect");

child.on("disconnect", function() {
  console.log("Goodbye from the parent process");
});

child.disconnect();
```

The vm Module

The vm (virtual machine) core module is used to execute raw strings of JavaScript code. At first glance it appears to be just another implementation of JavaScript's built-in eval() function, but vm is much more powerful. For starters, vm allows you to parse a piece of code and run it at a later time—something that cannot be done with eval(). vm also allows you to define the *context* in which the code executes, making it a safer alternative to eval(). With regard to vm, a context is a V8 data structure consisting of a global object and a set of built-in objects and functions. The context that code is executed in can be thought of as the JavaScript environment. The remainder of this section describes the various methods vm provides for working with contexts and executing code.

■ **Note**   eval(), a global function that is not associated with any object, takes a string as its only argument. This string can contain arbitrary JavaScript code, which eval() will attempt to execute. The code executed by eval() has all of the same privileges as the caller, as well as access to any variables currently in scope. eval() is considered a security risk because it gives arbitrary code read/write access to your data, and should generally be avoided.

---

runInThisContext()

The runInThisContext() method allows code to execute using the same context as the rest of your application. This method takes two arguments. The first is the code string to be executed. The optional second argument represents the "file name" of the executed code. If present, this can be any string, as it is only a virtual file name used to improve the readability of stack traces. Listing 9-20 is a simple example that prints to the console using runInThisContext(). The resulting output is shown in Listing 9-21.

Listing 9-20. Using vm.runInThisContext()

```
var vm = require("vm");
var code = "console.log(foo);";

foo = "Hello vm";
vm.runInThisContext(code);
```

Listing 9-21. The Output Generated by the Code in Listing 9-20

```
$ node runInThisContext-hello.js
Hello vm
```

The code executed by runInThisContext() has access to the same context as your application, meaning that it can access all globally defined data. However, the executing code does not have access to nonglobal variables. This is probably the biggest difference between runInThisContext() and eval(). To illustrate this concept, look first at the example in Listing 9-22, which accesses the global variable foo from within runInThisContext(). Recall that JavaScript variables that are not declared using the var keyword automatically become global variables.

Listing 9-22. Updating a Global Variable Within vm.runInThisContext()

```
var vm = require("vm");
var code = "console.log(foo); foo = 'Goodbye';";

foo = "Hello vm";
vm.runInThisContext(code);
console.log(foo);
```

Listing 9-23 shows the output from running the code in Listing 9-22. In this example, the variable foo initially holds the value "Hello vm". When runInThisContext() is executed, foo is printed to the console and then assigned the value "Goodbye". Finally, the value of foo is printed again. The assignment occurring within runInThisContext() has persisted, and Goodbye is printed.

Listing 9-23. The Output Resulting from the Code in Listing 9-22

```
$ node runInThisContext-update.js
Hello vm
Goodbye
```

As previously mentioned, runInThisContext() cannot access nonglobal variables. Listing 9-22 has been rewritten in Listing 9-24 such that foo is now a local variable (declared using the var keyword). Also, note that an additional parameter, specifying an optional file name, has now been passed into runInThisContext().

Listing 9-24. Attempting to Access a Nonglobal Variable in vm.runInThisContext()

```
var vm = require("vm");
var code = "console.log(foo);";
var foo = "Hello vm";

vm.runInThisContext(code, "example.vm");
```

When the code in Listing 9-24 is executed, a ReferenceError occurs in the attempt to access foo. The exception and stack trace are shown in Listing 9-25. Notice that the stack trace refers to example.vm, the file name associated with runInThisContext().

Listing 9-25. The Stack Trace Output from the Code in Listing 9-24

```
$ node runInThisContext-var.js

/home/colin/runInThisContext-var.js:5
vm.runInThisContext(code, "example.vm");
   ^
ReferenceError: foo is not defined
    at example.vm:1:13
    at Object.<anonymous> (/home/colin/runInThisContext-var.js:5:4)
    at Module._compile (module.js:456:26)
    at Object.Module._extensions..js (module.js:474:10)
    at Module.load (module.js:356:32)
    at Function.Module._load (module.js:312:12)
    at Function.Module.runMain (module.js:497:10)
    at startup (node.js:119:16)
    at node.js:901:3
```

Listing 9-26 replaces the call to runInThisContext() with a call to eval(). The resulting output is also shown in Listing 9-27. Based on the observed output, eval() is clearly able to access foo in the local scope.

Listing 9-26. Successfully Accessing a Local Variable Using eval()

```
var vm = require("vm");
var code = "console.log(foo);";
var foo = "Hello eval";

eval(code);
```

Listing 9-27. The Output Resulting from Listing 9-26

```
$ node runInThisContext-eval.js
Hello eval
```

runInNewContext()

In the previous section you saw how local variables can be protected by using runInThisContext() instead of eval(). However, because runInThisContext()works with the current context, it still gives untrusted code access to your global data. If you need to restrict access even further, use vm's runInNewContext() method. As its name implies, `runInNewContext()` creates a brand new context in which the code can execute. Listing 9-28 shows the usage of `runInNewContext()`. The first argument is the JavaScript string to execute. The second, optional, argument is used as the global object in the new context. The third argument, which is also optional, is the file name shown in stack traces.

Listing 9-28. Using `vm.runInNewContext()`

```
vm.runInNewContext(code, [sandbox], [filename])
```

The `sandbox` argument is used for setting global variables in the context, as well as retrieving values after `runInNewContext()` has completed. Remember, with `runInThisContext()` we were able to modify global variables directly, and the changes would persist. However, because `runInNewContext()` uses a different set of globals, the same tricks do not apply. For example, one might expect the code in Listing 9-29 to display "Hello vm" when run, but this is not the case.

Listing 9-29. Attempting to Execute Code Using `vm.runInNewContext()`

```
var vm = require("vm");
var code = "console.log(foo);";

foo = "Hello vm";
vm.runInNewContext(code);
```

Instead of running successfully, this code crashes, with the error shown in Listing 9-30. The error occurs because the new context does not have access to the application's `console` object. It is worth pointing out that only one error is thrown before the program crashes. However, even if `console` was available, a second exception would be thrown because the global variable `foo` is not available in the new context.

Listing 9-30. The `ReferenceError` Thrown by the Code in Listing 9-29

```
ReferenceError: console is not defined
```

Luckily, we can explicitly pass `foo` and the `console` object to the new context using the `sandbox` argument. Listing 9-31 shows how to accomplish this. When run, this code displays "Hello vm", as expected.

Listing 9-31. A Successful Use of `vm.runInNewContext()`

```
var vm = require("vm");
var code = "console.log(foo);";
var sandbox;

foo = "Hello vm";
sandbox = {
  console: console,
  foo: foo
};
vm.runInNewContext(code, sandbox);
```

Sandboxing Data

A nice thing about `runInNewContext()` is that changes made to the sandboxed data do not actually change your application's data. In the example shown in Listing 9-32, the global variables `foo` and `console` are passed to `runInNewContext()` via a sandbox. Inside of `runInNewContext()`, a new variable named `bar` is defined, `foo` is printed to the console, and then foo is modified. After runInNewContext() completes, foo is printed again, along with several of the sandboxed values.

Listing 9-32. Creating and Modifying Sandboxed Data

```
var vm = require("vm");
var code = "var bar = 1; console.log(foo); foo = 'Goodbye'";
var sandbox;

foo = "Hello vm";
sandbox = {
  console: console,
  foo: foo
};
vm.runInNewContext(code, sandbox);
console.log(foo);
console.log(sandbox.foo);
console.log(sandbox.bar);
```

Listing 9-33 shows the resulting output. The first instance of "Hello vm" comes from the print statement inside runInNewContext(). As expected, this is the value of foo passed in through the sandbox. Next, foo is set to "Goodbye". However, the next print statement shows the original value of foo. This is because the assignment statement inside runInNewContext() updates the sandboxed copy of foo. The final two print statements reflect the sandboxed values of foo ("Goodbye") and bar (1) at the end of runInNewContext().

Listing 9-33. The Output Resulting from Listing 9-32

```
$ node runInNewContext-sandbox.js
Hello vm
Hello vm
Goodbye
1
```

runInContext()

Node allows you to create individual V8 context objects and execute code in them using the runInContext() method. Individual contexts are created using vm's createContext() method. runInContext() can be called with no arguments, causing it to return a bare context. Alternatively, a sandbox object can be passed to createContext(), which is shallow-copied to the context's global object. The usage of createContext() is shown in Listing 9-34.

Listing 9-34. Using vm.createContext()

```
vm.createContext([initSandbox])
```

Context objects returned by createContext() can then be passed as the second argument to vm's runInContext() method, which is nearly identical to runInNewContext(). The only difference is that the second argument to runInContext() is a context object instead of a sandbox. Listing 9-35 shows how Listing 9-32 can be rewritten using runInContext(). The differences are that runInContext() has replaced runInNewContext() and context, created with createContext(), has replaced the sandbox variable. The output from running this code is the same as what is shown in Listing 9-33.

Listing 9-35. Rewriting Listing 9-34 Using vm.createContext()

```
var vm = require("vm");
var code = "var bar = 1; console.log(foo); foo = 'Goodbye'";
var context;

foo = "Hello vm";
context = vm.createContext({
  console: console,
  foo: foo
});
vm.runInContext(code, context);
console.log(foo);
console.log(context.foo);
console.log(context.bar);
```

createScript()

The createScript() method, used to compile a JavaScript string for future execution, is useful when you want to execute code multiple times. The createScript() method, which returns a vm.Script object that can be executed repeatedly without the need to reinterpret the code, accepts two arguments. The first is the code to be compiled. The optional second argument represents the file name that will be displayed in stack traces.

The vm.Script object returned by createScript() has three methods for executing the code. These methods are modified versions of runInThisContext(), runInNewContext(), and runInContext(). The usage of these three methods is shown in Listing 9-36. They behave the same as the vm methods of the same names. The difference is that these methods do not accept the JavaScript code string or file name arguments, as they are already part of the script object.

Listing 9-36. The Script Execution Methods of the vm.Script Type

```
script.runInThisContext()
script.runInNewContext([sandbox])
script.runInContext(context)
```

Listing 9-37 shows an example that runs a script multiple times within a loop. In the example, a simple script is compiled using createScript(). Next, a sandbox is created with a single value, i, that is set to 0. The script is then executed ten times within a for loop using runInNewContext(). Each iteration increments the sandboxed value of i. When the loop completes, the sandbox is printed. When the sandbox is displayed, the cumulative effect of the increment operations is apparent, as the value of i is 10.

Listing 9-37. Executing a Compiled Script Multiple Times

```
var vm = require("vm");
var script = vm.createScript("i++;", "example.vm");
var sandbox = {
    i: 0
  }

for (var i = 0; i < 10; i++) {
  script.runInNewContext(sandbox);
}

console.log(sandbox);
// displays {i: 10}
```

Summary

This chapter has shown you how to execute code in a variety of manners. Covered first was the common case where your program needs to execute another application. In these situations, the methods in the child_process module are used. The methods exec(), execFile(), spawn(), and fork() were examined in detail, as well as the different levels of abstraction offered by each. Covered next was the execution of strings of JavaScript code. The vm module was explored, and its various methods were compared with JavaScript's native eval() function. The concept of contexts and the various types of contexts offered by vm were also covered. Finally, you learned how to compile scripts and execute them at a later time using the vm.Script type.

CHAPTER 10

■ ■ ■

Network Programming

Until this point, the example code provided in this book has focused on your local machine. Whether accessing the file system, parsing command line arguments, or executing untrusted code, all examples were isolated to a single computer. This chapter starts to explore the world outside of localhost. It covers network programming and introduces many important topics, including sockets, client-server programming, Transmission Control Protocol (TCP), User Datagram Protocol (UDP), and Domain Name Service (DNS). A full explanation of all these concepts is beyond this book's scope, but a basic understanding of them is crucial, as they are the foundation for the material on web applications covered in the next few chapters.

Sockets

When two applications communicate over a network, they do so using sockets. A socket is a combination of an Internet Protocol (IP) address and a port number. An IP address is used to uniquely identify a device on a network, which can be a small home network or the entire Internet itself. The device can be a PC, tablet, smartphone, printer, or any other Internet-enabled device. IP addresses are 32-bit numbers formatted as four 8-bit numbers separated by dots. Examples of IP addresses are 184.168.230.128 and 74.125.226.193. These correspond to web servers at www.cjihrig.com and www.google.com.

■ **Note** The IP addresses described here are referred to as IPv4 addresses, the most common variety. These addresses are based on Internet Protocol version 4. Due to the growth of the Internet, it is anticipated that the number of IPv4 addresses will run out. To mitigate this problem, Internet Protocol version 6 (IPv6) was developed. IPv6 addresses are 128 bits long, meaning that more addresses can be represented. IPv6 address strings are also longer and include hexadecimal values, with colons as separators instead of dots.

The port component of a socket is a 16-bit number used to uniquely identify a communication endpoint on a computer. Ports allow a single computer to maintain many socket connections simultaneously. To better understand the concept of ports, envision yourself calling someone working in a large corporate office building. When you make the call, you need to know the office's phone number. In this analogy, the office is a remote computer, and its phone number is its IP address. Corporate offices provide extensions for reaching individuals. The phone extension is analogous to the port number, and the party you are trying to reach represents a process or thread on the remote machine. Once you enter your party's extension and are connected, you can carry on a conversation. Similarly, once two sockets have established a communication channel, they can begin sending data back and forth.

It was previously mentioned that the IP address 74.125.226.193 corresponds to a web server at www.google.com. To verify this, type http://74.125.226.193 into your browser's address bar. Clearly this request includes the server's IP address, but where is the port number? As it turns out, Google's web server accepts connections on port 80. URL syntax allows you to explicitly identify the port to connect to by including a colon and the port number after the host. To verify this, try connecting to http://74.125.226.193:80 (or www.google.com:80) in your browser. You should see the Google home page once again. Now try connecting to http://74.125.226.193:81 (www.google.com:81). Suddenly the page can no longer be found. How does a browser know to connect to port 80 when www.google.com is typed into its address bar? To answer that question, let's return to our telephone analogy. In the United States, how do you know to call 911 and not 912 in an emergency? The answer: because every child in the country has been taught to call 911 in case of an emergency. It is an agreed-upon convention in society.

On the Internet, common services follow a similar convention. The port numbers from 0 to 1023 are referred to as the *well-known ports*, or *reserved ports*. For example, port 80 is reserved for serving HTTP traffic. Therefore, when you navigate to a URL beginning with http://, your browser assumes that the port number is 80, unless you explicitly state otherwise. That is why Google's web server responded to our request on port 80, but not 81. A similar experiment can be conducted with the HTTPS (secure HTTP) protocol. Port 443 is reserved for HTTPS traffic. If you enter the URL http://74.125.226.193:443 in your browser's address bar, you will encounter an error. However, if you change the URL to https://74.125.226.193:443, you will land on the Google home page over a secure connection. Note that you may encounter a browser warning during the navigation process. This warning can safely be ignored in this case.

If you plan to implement a common service, such as a web server, using its well-known port number is advisable. However, there is nothing stopping you from running a web server on a nonstandard port. For example, you can run a web server on port 8080, as long as everyone trying to connect to the server explicitly specifies port 8080 in the URLs. Similarly, if you are creating a custom application, avoid using ports customarily used for other purposes. Before selecting a port for your application, you may want to conduct a quick Internet search for other common services that may conflict with it. Also, avoid using one of the reserved port numbers.

Client-Server Programming

The client-server model is a paradigm in which computational tasks are split between servers (machines that provide resources) and clients (machines that request and consume those resources). The Web is a perfect example of the client-server model in action. When you open a browser window and navigate to a web site, your computer acts as a client. The resource that your computer requests and consumes is a web page. That web page is provided by a server, which your computer connects to over the Internet using sockets. A high-level abstraction of this model is shown in Figure 10-1.

Clients

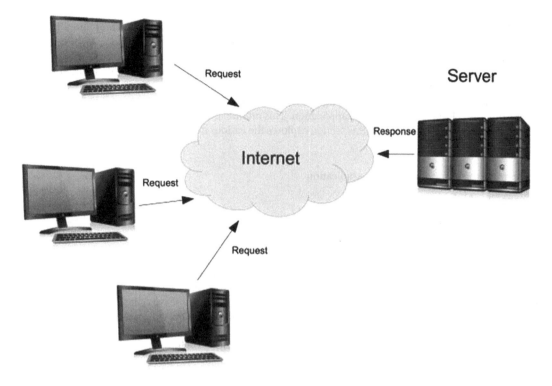

Figure 10-1. *The client-server model working over the Internet*

■ **Tip**   The IP address 127.0.0.1 is used to identify the local machine, known as localhost. Many client-server applications can be tested using a single machine by having clients connect to the server running on localhost.

■ **Note**   The last section discussed well-known ports. In the client-server model, this concept generally applies only to server applications. Since a client initiates connections to a server, the client must know which port to connect to. A server, on the other hand, doesn't need to worry about the port being used on the client's side of the connection.

Transmission Control Protocol

Transmission Control Protocol, or TCP, is a communication protocol used for transmitting data over the Internet. Internet data transfer is unreliable. When your computer sends a message onto the network, the message is first broken up into smaller pieces known as packets, which are then sent out onto the network and begin making their way to their destination. Because your computer does not have a direct connection to every other computer in the world, each packet must traverse a number of intermediate machines until it finds a route to its destination. Each packet can potentially take a unique route to the destination, meaning that the order of the packets' arrival can be different from the order they were sent in. Furthermore, the Internet is unreliable, and individual packets can be lost or damaged along the way.

TCP helps bring reliability to the chaos that is the Internet. TCP is what is known as a *connection-oriented protocol*, a term referring to the virtual connection established between machines. Two machines enter into a TCP connection by sending small pieces of data back and forth in a defined pattern known as a handshake. At the end of the multistep handshake, the two machines have established a connection. Using this connection, TCP enforces ordering among packets and confirms that packets are successfully received at the destination. Additionally, among the features TCP provides are error checking and retransmission of lost packets.

In the Node ecosystem, network programming using TCP is implemented using the net core module. Listing 10-1 shows how the net module is imported into a Node application. This module includes methods for creating both client and server applications. The remainder of this section explores the various methods provided by net for working with TCP.

Listing 10-1. Importing the Net Module into an Application

```
var net = require("net");
```

Creating a TCP Server

TCP servers can be created easily using the createServer() method (see Listing 10-2). This method takes two optional arguments. The first is an object containing configuration options. createServer() supports a single option, allowHalfOpen, that defaults to false. If this option is explicitly set to true, the server leaves client connections open, even if the client terminates them. In this situation the socket becomes nonreadable but still writable by the server. Additionally, if allowHalfOpen is true, the connection must be explicitly closed on the server side, regardless of what the client does. This matter is explained in more detail later, when the end() method is covered.

Listing 10-2. Creating a TCP Server Using net.createServer()

```
var net = require("net");
var server = net.createServer({
  allowHalfOpen: false
}, function(socket) {
  // handle connection
});
```

The second argument to createServer() in Listing 10-2 is an event handler used to handle connections from clients. The event handler accepts a single argument, a net.Socket object representing the socket connection to the client. The net.Socket class is also examined in greater detail later in this chapter. Finally, createServer() returns the newly created TCP server as a net.Server instance. The net.Server class inherits from EventEmitter and emits socket-related events.

Listening for Connections

The server returned by createServer() cannot be accessed by clients, because it is not associated with a specific port. To make the server accessible, it must listen for incoming client connections on a port. The listen() method, whose use is shown in Listing 10-3, is used to bind the server to a specified port. The only required argument to listen() is the port number to bind to. To listen on a randomly selected port, pass 0 as the port argument. (Note that doing this should generally be avoided, as clients will not know what port to connect to.)

Listing 10-3. Using the net.Server.listen() Method

```
server.listen(port, [host], [backlog], [callback])
```

If the host argument is omitted, the server accepts connections directed to any valid IPv4 address. To restrict the connections that the server accepts, specify the host that the server will respond as. This feature is useful on servers that have multiple network interfaces, as it allows an application to be scoped to an individual network. You can experiment with this feature if your machine has only one IP address. As an example, the code in Listing 10-4 only accepts connections directed at localhost (127.0.0.1). This allows you to create a web interface for your application while not exposing it to remote, potentially malicious, connections.

Listing 10-4. Code That Accepts Only localhost Connections on Port 8000

```
var net = require("net");
var server = net.createServer(function(socket) {
  // handle connection
});

server.listen(8000, "127.0.0.1");
```

A server's backlog is a queue of client connections that have been made to the server but that have not yet been handled. Once the backlog is full, any new incoming connections to that port are dropped. The backlog argument is used to specify the maximum length of this queue. This value defaults to 511.

The final argument to listen() is an event handler that responds to listening events. When the server successfully binds to a port and is listening for connections, it emits a listening event. The listening event does not provide arguments to its handler function, but it is very useful for things like debugging and logging. For example, the code in Listing 10-5 attempts to listen on a random port. A listening event handler is included which displays the randomly selected port.

Listing 10-5. A Server with a listening Event Handler

```
var net = require("net");
var server = net.createServer(function(socket) {
  // handle connection
});

server.listen(0, function() {
  var address = server.address();

  console.log("Listening on port " + address.port);
});
```

■ **Note**   The event handler for listen() is provided strictly for convenience. It is also possible to add listening event handlers using the on() method.

---

address()

In Listing 10-5, the server's address() method was used to display the randomly selected port. The address() method returns an object containing the server's bound address, address family, and port. As already shown, the port property represents the bound port. The bound address gets its value from the host argument to listen() or "0.0.0.0" if the host is not specified. The address family represents the type of address (IPv4, IPv6, etc.). Note that since the values returned by address() depend on the arguments passed to listen(), this method should not be invoked until the listening event has been emitted. In the example in Listing 10-6, which shows another use of address(), a random port is used, along with the address ::1 (localhost in IPv6). The resulting output is shown in Listing 10-7. Of course, because it is random, your port number is likely to be different.

Listing 10-6. Using net.Server.address()

```
var net = require("net");
var server = net.createServer(function(socket) {
  // handle connection
});

server.listen(0, "::1", function() {
  var address = server.address();

  console.log(address);
});
```

Listing 10-7. The Output Resulting from the Code in Listing 10-6

```
$ node server-address.js
{ address: '::1', family: 'IPv6', port: 64269 }
```

Variations of listen()

The listen() method has two less commonly used signatures. The first variation allows a server to listen on an existing server/socket that has already been bound. The new server begins accepting connections that would otherwise have been directed at the existing server/socket. An example which creates two servers, server1 and server2, is shown in Listing 10-8 (with sample output shown in Listing 10-9). Next, a listening event handler is set up on server2, which calls address() and displays the results. Next, server1's listen() method is invoked with its own listening event handler. This handler also displays the results of address() but then tells server2 to listen on server1's configuration.

Listing 10-8. Passing a Server Instance to listen()

```
var net = require("net");
var server1 = net.createServer();
var server2 = net.createServer(function(socket) {
  // handle connection
});

server2.on("listening", function() {
  console.log("server2:");
  console.log(server2.address());
});
```

```
server1.listen(0, "127.0.0.1", function() {
  console.log("server1:");
  console.log(server1.address());
  server2.listen(server1);
});
```

Listing 10-9. The Output Resulting from Running the Code in Listing 10-8

```
$ node server-listen-handle.js
server1:
{ address: '127.0.0.1', family: 'IPv4', port: 53091 }
server2:
{ address: '127.0.0.1', family: 'IPv4', port: 53091 }
```

Notice that the results of address() (see Listing 10-9) are the same for both servers. You haven't seen how to actually process connections yet, but it is worth pointing out that connections to server1 are directed to server2 in this example. It is also worth noting that this incarnation of listen() accepts a listening event handler as an optional second argument.

The final variation of listen() accepts a Unix socket file name or Windows named pipe as its first argument and a listening event handler as its optional second argument. An example using a Unix socket is shown in Listing 10-10.

Listing 10-10. Passing a Unix Socket File to listen()

```
var net = require("net");
var server = net.createServer(function(socket) {
  // handle connection
});

server.listen("/tmp/foo.sock");
```

Handling Connections

Once the server is bound and listening, it can begin accepting connections. Each time the server receives a new connection, a connection event is emitted. In order to process incoming connections, a connection event handler must be passed to createServer() or attached using a method such as on(). The connection handler takes a net.Socket object as its only argument. This socket is then used to send data to and receive data from the client. The same socket class is used to implement TCP clients, and so the full API is covered in that section. For now, Listing 10-11 shows a server that listens on port 8000 and responds to client requests.

Listing 10-11. A Server That Responds to Clients with a Simple Message

```
var net = require("net");
var server = net.createServer(function(socket) {
  socket.end("Hello and Goodbye!\n");
});

server.listen(8000);
```

To test the server, run the code in Listing 10-11 as you would any other Node application. Next, connect to the server using telnet or a web browser (telnet is a command line utility used for establishing network connections and sending/receiving data). To test the server with telnet, issue the command telnet localhost 8000 from a terminal window. If using a web browser, simply navigate to http://localhost:8000. If everything is working properly, the terminal or browser should display the message "Hello and Goodbye!" Listing 10-12 shows the output using telnet. Note that the telnet application prints several additional lines that are not actually related to the server.

Listing 10-12. The telnet Output from Connecting to the Server in Listing 10-11

```
$ telnet localhost 8000
Trying 127.0.0.1...
Connected to localhost.
Escape character is '^]'.
Hello and Goodbye!
Connection closed by foreign host.
```

Shutting Down the Server

To terminate the server, use the close() method. Calling close() prevents the server from accepting new connections. However, any existing connections are allowed to finish their work. Once no connections remain, the server emits a close event. The close() method optionally accepts an event handler that handles the close event. The example in Listing 10-13 starts up a new server and then, once it is listening, immediately shuts down. A close event handler has also been defined using on() rather than as an argument to close().

Listing 10-13. A Server That Listens and Then Immediately Shuts Down

```
var net = require("net");
var server = net.createServer();

server.on("close", function() {
  console.log("And now it's closed.");
});

server.listen(function() {
  console.log("The server is listening.");
  server.close();
});
```

ref() and unref()

Chapter 4 introduced two methods, ref() and unref(), in the context of timers and intervals. These methods are used to prevent or allow termination of a Node application if the timer/interval is the only remaining item in the event loop. TCP servers have equivalent methods of the same names. If a *bound* server is the only item left in the event loop's queue, calling unref() allows the program to terminate. This scenario is demonstrated in Listing 10-14. Conversely, calling ref() restores the default behavior preventing the application from exiting if the server is the only item remaining in the event loop.

Listing 10-14. A Server That Immediately Shuts Down After Calling unref()

```
var net = require("net");
var server = net.createServer();

server.listen();
server.unref();
```

error Events

When things go wrong, net.Server instances emit error events. A commonly encountered exception is the EADDRINUSE error, which occurs when an application attempts to use a port that is already in use by another application. Listing 10-15 shows how this type of error can be detected and handled. Once the error has been detected, your application can try connecting to another port, wait before trying to connect to the same port again, or simply exit.

Listing 10-15. A Handler That Detects Port-Already-In-Use Errors

```
server.on("error", function(error) {
  if (error.code === "EADDRINUSE") {
    console.error("Port is already in use");
  }
});
```

Another commonly encountered error is EACCES, an exception thrown when you have insufficient permissions to bind to a port. On Unix-flavored operating systems, these errors occur when you attempt to bind to a reserved port. For example, web servers typically require admin privileges to bind to port 80.

Creating a TCP Client

The net module provides two methods, connect() and createConnection(), that can be used interchangeably to create TCP client sockets. These client sockets are used to connect to the server applications created in this chapter. Throughout this book, connect() is used because its name is shorter. Just be aware that createConnection() can be substituted for connect() in any scenario. connect() has three incarnations, the first of which is shown in Listing 10-16.

Listing 10-16. One Use of the net.connect() Method

```
net.connect(port, [host], [connectListener])
```

In Listing 10-16, a TCP connection is created to the machine specified by host on the port specified by port. If host is unspecified, the connection is made to localhost. If the connection is successfully established, the client emits a connect event with no arguments. The optional third argument, connectListener, is an event handler that will process the connect event. Listing 10-17 shows a client that connects to port 8000 on localhost. This client can be tested with the server created in Listing 10-11. Begin by opening a terminal window and running the server application. Next, open a separate terminal window and run the client application. The client displays a message upon successfully connecting to the server. The actual data returned by the server is not displayed (more on that later).

Listing 10-17. A Client That Connects to localhost on Port 8000

```
var net = require("net");
var client = net.connect(8000, "localhost", function() {
  console.log("Connection established");
});
```

The second version of connect() takes a Unix socket file name or Windows named pipe as its first argument and an optional connect event handler as its second. Listing 10-17 has been rewritten to use a Unix socket file in Listing 10-18. To test this client, use the modified server shown in Listing 10-19, which binds to the same socket file.

Listing 10-18. A Client That Connects to the Socket File /tmp/foo.sock

```
var net = require("net");
var client = net.connect("/tmp/foo.sock", function() {
  console.log("Connection established");
});
```

Listing 10-19. A Server Used to Test the Client from Listing 10-18

```
var net = require("net");
var server = net.createServer(function(socket) {
  socket.end("Hello and Goodbye!\n");
});

server.listen("/tmp/foo.sock");
```

The final version of connect() takes a configuration object and an optional connect event handler as arguments. Table 10-1 shows the properties supported by the configuration object. Listing 10-20 rewrites Listing 10-17 to use this form of connect(). Similarly, Listing 10-21 rewrites Listing 10-18.

Table 10-1. List of Configuration Options Supported by connect()

Property	Description
port	If connecting over a TCP socket (as opposed to a Unix socket file or Windows named pipe), this specifies the port number that the client should connect to. This is required.
host	If connecting over a TCP socket, this specifies the host to connect to. If omitted, this defaults to localhost.
localAddress	The local interface to use when creating the connection. This option is useful when a single machine has multiple network interfaces.
path	If connecting to a Unix socket file or Windows named pipe, this is used to specify the path.
allowHalfOpen	If true, the client does not close the connection when the server does. Instead, the connection must be manually closed. This defaults to false.

Listing 10-20. A Client That Connects to localhost on Port 8000

```
var net = require("net");
var client = net.connect({
  port: 8000,
  host: "localhost"
}, function() {
  console.log("Connection established");
});
```

Listing 10-21. A Client That Connects to the Socket File /tmp/foo.sock

```
var net = require("net");
var client = net.connect({
  path: "/tmp/foo.sock"
}, function() {
  console.log("Connection established");
});
```

The net.Socket Class

Understanding the net.Socket class is imperative for both client and server development. On the server side, a socket is passed to the connection event handler. On the client side, connect() returns a socket. Since the socket class uses streams to move data, you already know some of the basics (if you need a review, revisit Chapter 7). For example, reading data from a socket uses all of the readable stream fundamentals you've come to know and love, including data events and the pause() and resume() methods. Listing 10-22 shows how simple it is to read data from a socket using streams. This client, which works with the server from Listing 10-11, uses a data event handler to read data from the socket and print the data to the console.

Listing 10-22. A Client Displaying Data Read from the Server in Listing 10-11

```
var net = require("net");
var clientSocket = net.connect({
  port: 8000,
  host: "localhost"
});

clientSocket.setEncoding("utf8");

clientSocket.on("data", function(data) {
  process.stdout.write(data);
});
```

Writing data to a socket can also be accomplished using the stream write() method. Sockets have an additional method, end(), that closes the connection. end() can optionally be passed data and encoding arguments similar to write(). Thus, a socket can be written and closed using a single function call (end() is used in this fashion in the server in Listing 10-11). Note that end() must be called at least once for the connection to close. Additionally, attempting to write to the socket after calling end() will cause an error.

The socket class has several other events and methods that you should already recognize. For example, sockets have ref() and unref() methods, which affect an application's ability to terminate if the socket is the only item remaining in the event loop. Sockets also have an address() method, which returns the bound address, port number, and address family of a connected socket. With regard to events, a drain event is emitted when the write buffer becomes empty, and an error event is emitted when an exception occurs.

Local and Remote Addresses

As previously mentioned, the address() method returns an object containing the local bound address, its family type, and the port in use. There are also four properties—remoteAddress, remotePort, localAddress, and localPort—that provide information on the remote and local end points of the socket. An example of these properties is shown in Listing 10-23.

Listing 10-23. An example which displays local and remote addresses and ports

```
var net = require("net");
var client = net.connect(8000, function() {
  console.log("Local endpoint " + client.localAddress + ":" +
              client.localPort);
  console.log("is connected to");
  console.log("Remote endpoint " + client.remoteAddress + ":" +
              client.remotePort);
});
```

Closing a Socket

As previously mentioned, a socket is closed using the end() method. Technically, end() only half-closes the socket. It is still possible for the other end of the connection to continue sending data. If you need to completely shut down the socket—for example, in the case of an error—you can use the destroy() method, which ensures that no more I/O occurs on the socket.

When the remote host calls end() or destroy(), the local side emits an end event. If the socket was created with the allowHalfOpen option set to false (the default), the local side writes out any pending data and closes its side of the connection as well. However, if allowHalfOpen is true, the local side must explicitly call end() or destroy(). Once both sides of the connection are closed, a close event is emitted. If a close event handler is present, it accepts a single Boolean argument, which is true if the socket had any transmission errors, or false otherwise.

Listing 10-24 includes a client that sets its allowHalfOpen option to true. The example also includes end and close event handlers. Notice that the end() method is explicitly called in the end handler. If this line were not present, the connection would not be completely closed, and the close event would never be emitted.

Listing 10-24. A Client with end and close Event Handlers

```
var net = require("net");
var client = net.connect({
  port: 8000,
  host: "localhost",
  allowHalfOpen: true
});

client.on("end", function() {
  console.log("end handler");
  client.end();
});

client.on("close", function(error) {
  console.log("close handler");
  console.log("had error:   " + error);
});
```

Timeouts

By default, sockets do not have a timeout. This can be bad, because if the network or remote host fails, the connection sits idle indefinitely. However, you can define a timeout on the socket using its setTimeout() method (not to be confused with the core JavaScript method used to create timers). This version of setTimeout() takes a timeout in milliseconds as its first argument. If the socket is idle for this amount of time, a timeout event is emitted. A one-time timeout event handler can optionally be passed as the second argument to setTimeout(). A timeout event does not close the socket; you are responsible for closing it using end() or destroy(). Additionally, you can remove an existing timeout by passing 0 to setTimeout(). Listing 10-25 shows how a ten-second timeout is created on a socket. In this example, an error message is printed and the socket is closed when a timeout occurs.

Listing 10-25. A Client with a Ten-Second Timeout

```
var net = require("net");
var client = net.connect(8000, "localhost");

client.setTimeout(10000, function() {
  console.error("Ten second timeout elapsed");
  client.end();
});
```

Sockets, Servers, and Child Processes

Chapter 9 showed how to create Node child processes using the fork() method. Data can be transferred between these processes on an interprocess communication channel using the send() method. The data to be transmitted is passed as the first argument to send(). Not mentioned in Chapter 9 is that the send() method takes an optional second argument, a TCP socket or server, that allows a single network connection to be shared among multiple processes. As you know by now, Node processes are single-threaded. Spawning multiple processes that share a single socket allows better utilization of modern multicore hardware. This use case is revisited in more detail in Chapter 16, when the cluster module is covered.

Listing 10-26 contains code that creates a new TCP server, forks a child process, and passes the server to the child as a server message. The code for the child process (see Listing 10-27) should be saved in a file named child.js. The child process detects server messages and sets up a connection handler. To verify that the socket is shared by two processes, make a number of connections to port 8000. You will see that some of the connections respond with "Handled by parent process" and others respond with "Handled by child process".

Listing 10-26. Passing a TCP Server to a Forked Child Process

```
var cp = require("child_process");
var net = require("net");
var server = net.createServer();
var child = cp.fork("child");

server.on("connection", function(socket) {
  socket.end("Handled by parent process");
});

server.listen(8000, function() {
  child.send("server", server);
});
```

Listing 10-27. The Code for child.js That Works with Listing 10-26

```
process.on("message", function(message, server) {
  if (message === "server") {
    server.on("connection", function(socket) {
      socket.end("Handled by child process");
    });
  }
});
```

User Datagram Protocol

The User Datagram Protocol, or UDP, is an alternative to TCP. UDP, like TCP, operates on top of IP. However, UDP does not include many of the features that make TCP so dependable. For example, UDP does not establish a connection during communication. It also lacks message ordering, guaranteed delivery, and retransmission of lost data. Because there is less protocol overhead, UDP communication is typically faster and simpler than TCP. The flip side of the coin is that UDP is only as reliable as the underlying network, and so data can easily be lost. UDP is typically useful in applications, such as streaming audio and video, where performance is key and some data can afford to be lost. In these applications, a few lost packets might minimally affect playback quality, but the media will still be usable. On the other hand, UDP would not be suitable for viewing a web page, as even one dropped packet could ruin a page's ability to render.

To include UDP functionality in Node applications, use the dgram core module. Listing 10-28 shows how this module is imported. The remainder of this section explores the various methods provided by the dgram module.

Listing 10-28. Importing the dgram Core Module

```
var dgram = require("dgram");
```

Creating UDP Sockets

Both client and server sockets are created using the createSocket() method. The first argument to createSocket(), which specifies the socket type, should be either "udp4" or "udp6" (corresponding to IPv4 and IPv6). The second argument (optional) is a callback function used to handle message events that are emitted when data is received over the socket. An example that creates a new UDP socket is shown in Listing 10-29. This example includes a message event handler, which will be revisited when receiving data is covered.

Listing 10-29. Creating a UDP Socket and message Event Handler

```
var dgram = require("dgram");
var socket = dgram.createSocket("udp4", function(msg, rinfo) {
  console.log("Received data");
});
```

Binding to a Port

When a socket is created, it uses a randomly assigned port number. However, server applications normally need to listen on a predefined port. UDP sockets can listen on a specified port using the bind() method, whose usage is shown in Listing 10-30. The port argument is the port number to bind to. The optional address argument specifies the IP address to listen on (useful if the server has multiple network interfaces). If this is omitted, the socket listens on all addresses. The optional callback function is a one-time listening event handler.

Listing 10-30. Using the bind() Method

```
socket.bind(port, [address], [callback])
```

An example of bind() is shown in Listing 10-31. This example creates a UDP socket and binds it to port 8000. To verify that everything worked properly, the bound address is printed to the console. Listing 10-32 shows the resulting output.

Listing 10-31. Binding a UDP Socket to Port 8000

```
var dgram = require("dgram");
var server = dgram.createSocket("udp4");

server.bind(8000, function() {
  console.log("bound to ");
  console.log(server.address());
});
```

Listing 10-32. The Output from Running the Code in Listing 10-31

```
$ node udp-bind.js
bound to
{ address: '0.0.0.0', family: 'IPv4', port: 8000 }
```

Receiving Data

When data is received on a UDP socket, a message event is emitted that triggers any existing message event handlers. A message event handler takes two arguments, a Buffer representing the data and an object containing information on the sender. In Listing 10-33, a UDP server is created that binds to port 8000. When messages are received, the server displays the message size, the IP address and port of the remote host, and the message payload.

Listing 10-33. A Server That Receives and Displays Messages

```
var dgram = require("dgram");
var server = dgram.createSocket("udp4", function(msg, rinfo) {
  console.log("received " + rinfo.size + " bytes");
  console.log("from " + rinfo.address + ":" + rinfo.port);
  console.log("message is:  " + msg.toString());
});

server.bind(8000);
```

Next, let's see how to send data to test the server.

Sending Data

Data is sent over a UDP socket using the send() method. Listing 10-34 shows how this method is used. The data transmitted by send() comes from a Buffer, represented by the buffer argument. The offset argument specifies the starting position of the relevant data in the buffer, and length specifies the number of bytes to send, starting from the offset. Since UDP is a connectionless protocol, it is not necessary to connect to a remote machine before sending. Therefore, the remote port and address are arguments to send(). The final argument to send() is an optional callback function invoked after the data has been sent. The callback function takes two arguments, representing potential errors and the number of bytes sent. Including this callback is the only way to verify that the data was actually sent. However, UDP has no built-in mechanism for verifying that the data was received.

Listing 10-34. Using the send() Method

```
socket.send(buffer, offset, length, port, address, [callback])
```

The client code in Listing 10-35 can be used in conjunction with the server from Listing 10-33. The client sends a message to the server, which the server then displays. Notice that the client's callback function checks for errors and reports the number of bytes sent, then closes the connection. Once the socket is closed, a close event is emitted, and no new message events are emitted.

Listing 10-35. A Client That Sends Data to the Server from Listing 10-33

```
var dgram = require("dgram");
var client = dgram.createSocket("udp4");
var message = new Buffer("Hello UDP");
```

```
client.send(message, 0, message.length, 8000, "127.0.0.1", function(error, bytes) {
  if (error) {
    console.error("An error occurred while sending");
  } else {
    console.log("Successfully sent " + bytes + " bytes");
  }

  client.close();
});
```

Domain Name System

The Domain Name System (DNS) is a distributed network that, among other things, maps domain names to IP addresses. DNS is needed because people remember names better than long strings of numbers. DNS can be thought of as a phone book for the Internet. When you want to reach a web site, you type its domain name into the navigation bar. Your browser then makes a DNS lookup request for that domain name. The DNS lookup then returns the corresponding IP address for that domain, assuming it exists.

In the Node ecosystem, DNS is normally handled under the hood, meaning that the developer provides either an IP address or a domain name, and everything just works. However, should the need arise, DNS can be accessed directly using the dns core module. This section explores the most important methods used for DNS lookups and reverse lookups, which map IP addresses to domain names.

Performing Lookups

The most important DNS method is likely lookup(), which takes a domain name as input and returns the first IPv4 or IPv6 DNS record found. The lookup() method accepts an optional second argument specifying the address family to search for. This argument defaults to null, but it can also be 4 or 6, corresponding to the IPv4 or IPv6 address family. If the family argument is null, both IPv4 and IPv6 addresses are searched.

The final argument to lookup() is a callback function that is invoked once the DNS lookup finishes. The callback function takes three arguments, error, address, and family. The error argument represents any exceptions that occur. If the lookup fails for any reason, error.code is set to the string "ENOENT". The address argument is the resulting IP address as a string, and the family argument is either 4 or 6.

In Listing 10-36, a DNS lookup of google.com is performed. Its output is shown in Listing 10-37. In this example, the DNS lookup is limited to IPv4 addresses. Please note that because Google uses multiple IP addresses, the IP address you observe may be different.

Listing 10-36. Performing a DNS Lookup

```
var dns = require("dns");
var domain = "google.com";

dns.lookup(domain, 4, function(error, address, family) {
  if (error) {
    console.error("DNS lookup failed with code " + error.code);
  } else {
    console.log(domain + " -> " + address);
  }
});
```

Listing 10-37. The Resulting Output of the Code in Listing 10-36

```
$ node dns-lookup.js
google.com -> 74.125.226.229
```

resolve()

The lookup() method returns the first IPv4 or IPv6 DNS record found. There are other types of records, however, and there can be multiple records of each type. To retrieve multiple DNS records of a specific type in array format, use resolve() instead. The usage of resolve() is shown in Listing 10-38.

Listing 10-38. Using the resolve() Method

```
dns.resolve(domain, [recordType], callback)
```

The domain argument is the domain name to be resolved. The optional recordType argument specifies the type of DNS record to look up. Table 10-2 lists the various DNS record types supported by resolve(). If no recordType is provided, resolve() looks up A records (IPv4 address records). The third argument is a callback function invoked following the DNS lookup. A possible Error object and an array of DNS responses are passed to the callback function.

■ **Note** There are also a number of methods (shown in the third column of Table 10-2) used to resolve specific types of records. Each method behaves like resolve() but works only with a single type of record and therefore does not require a recordType argument. For example, if you are interested in retrieving CNAME records, simply call dns.resolveCname().

Table 10-2. The Various DNS Record Types Supported by resolve()

Record Type	Description	Method
A	IPv4 address records. This is the default behavior of resolve().	dns.resolve4()
AAAA	IPv6 address records.	dns.resolve6()
MX	Mail exchange records. These records map a domain to message transfer agents.	dns.resolveMx()
TXT	Text records. These records should include human-readable text.	dns.resolveTxt()
SRV	Service locator records. These records map a service to a location. These are used for mapping new protocols instead of creating new DNS record types for each protocol.	dns.resolveSrv()
PTR	Pointer records. These records are used in reverse DNS lookups.	None
NS	Name server records. These delegate a DNS zone to use the given server names.	dns.resolveNs()
CNAME	Canonical name records. These are used to alias one domain to another.	dns.resolveCname()

Listing 10-39 shows an example use of resolve() by looking up IPv6 addresses (AAAA DNS records) associated with the domain google.com. If no errors occur, the domain and array of addresses are printed to the console.

Listing 10-39. Using resolve() to Look Up IPv6 Addresses for google.com

```
var dns = require("dns");
var domain = "google.com";

dns.resolve(domain, "AAAA", function(error, addresses) {
  if (error) {
    console.error("DNS lookup failed with code " + error.code);
  } else {
    console.log(domain + " -> " + addresses);
  }
});
```

Reverse Lookups

A reverse DNS lookup resolves an IP address to a domain. In Node, this type of lookup is achieved using the dns module's reverse() method. This method takes two arguments, an IP address and a callback function. The callback function's arguments are error, representing potential errors, and domains, an array of domain names. In the example using reverse(), shown in Listing 10-40, a DNS lookup is performed for www.google.com. The resulting IP address is then used to perform a reverse DNS lookup.

Listing 10-40. Performing a DNS Lookup, Followed by a Reverse Lookup

```
var dns = require("dns");
var domain = "www.google.com";

dns.lookup(domain, 4, function(error, address, family) {
  dns.reverse(address, function(error, domains) {
    console.log(domain + " -> " + address + " -> " + domains);
  });
});
```

■ **Note**   Depending on the site's DNS configuration, the results of a reverse lookup may surprise you. If a site hasn't set up any PTR records, a reverse lookup may not be possible. For example, when the code in Listing 10-40 is run for www.nodejs.org, the reverse lookup returns undefined.

Detecting Valid IP Addresses

To finish off this chapter, let's return to the net module and examine some useful utility methods. The net module provides three methods for identifying valid IP addresses: isIP(), isIPv4(), and isIPv6(). Each method takes a single argument to test as input. isIP() checks whether its input is a valid IPv4 or IPv6 address. isIP() returns 4, 6, or 0 if the input is IPv4, IPv6, or invalid. isIPv4() and isIPv6() are more specific, and return true or false to indicate whether the input is in the given address family. Listing 10-41 shows all three methods called on various input strings. Listing 10-42 shows the results.

Listing 10-41. Classifying IP addresses

```
var net = require("net");
var input1 = "127.0.0.1";
var input2 = "fe80::1610:9fff:fee4:d63d";
var input3 = "foo";

function classify(input) {
  console.log("isIP('" + input + "') = " + net.isIP(input));
  console.log("isIPv4('" + input + "') = " + net.isIPv4(input));
  console.log("isIPv6('" + input + "') = " + net.isIPv6(input));
  console.log();
}

classify(input1);
classify(input2);
classify(input3);
```

Listing 10-42. The Output of the Code in Listing 10-41

```
$ node ip-address-classification.js
isIP('127.0.0.1') = 4
isIPv4('127.0.0.1') = true
isIPv6('127.0.0.1') = false

isIP('fe80::1610:9fff:fee4:d63d') = 6
isIPv4('fe80::1610:9fff:fee4:d63d') = false
isIPv6('fe80::1610:9fff:fee4:d63d') = true

isIP('foo') = 0
isIPv4('foo') = false
isIPv6('foo') = false
```

Summary

This chapter has presented a large amount of information on network programming. A lot of its content is applicable outside the world of Node. A general knowledge of popular networking topics such as IP, TCP, UDP, and DNS will come in handy no matter the language you develop in. Of course, this chapter's primary focus has been network programming as it relates to Node. By now, you should have a solid understanding of the net, dgram, and dns core modules. However, as all the material in these modules cannot be covered in a single chapter, you are encouraged to browse the Node documentation to see what else is possible.

The book's next few chapters focus on creating web applications. Most people associate Node with web servers/apps (although you should realize by now that Node can do much more). Since Web apps work primarily with higher-level protocols (such as HTTP) that are built on top of the protocols discussed in this chapter, you need to understand the material covered here.

CHAPTER 11

HTTP

The Hypertext Transfer Protocol, or HTTP, drives the Web. HTTP is a stateless, text-based protocol that works on top of TCP. An encrypted version of HTTP, named HTTP Secure, or HTTPS, is also commonly used when dealing with sensitive data. HTTP is a request-response protocol that is implemented using the client-server programming model discussed in Chapter 10. Traditionally, a browser is used as the client in an HTTP transaction, but you'll see that this is not always the case. When a browser navigates to a given URL, an HTTP request is made to the server that hosts the URL. As you learned in Chapter 10, this request is normally made on TCP port 80 (or 443 if HTTPS is in use). The server processes the request and then responds to the client. This is how HTTP works at a *very* high level. This chapter takes a deeper dive into HTTP in the Node.js world.

A Basic Server

Before we look under the hood of HTTP, let's create a simple server application using the code in Listing 11-1. Node's HTTP API is implemented in the http core module, which is imported on the first line of Listing 11-1. On the following line, the http module's createServer() method is used to create a new instance of an HTTP server. Much like the equivalent TCP method of the same name, the server returned by createServer() is an event emitter, and is not bound to any specific port. On the last line of Listing 11-1, the server is bound to port 8000 using the listen() method. The http version of listen() is also used in the same fashion as the TCP listen() method.

Listing 11-1. A Bare Bones HTTP Server

```
var http = require("http");
var server = http.createServer(function(request, response) {
  response.write("Hello <strong>HTTP</strong>!");
  response.end();
});

server.listen(8000);
```

The function passed to createServer() is an optional request event handler that is invoked each time a new HTTP request is received. The event handler takes two arguments, request and response. The request argument is an instance of http.IncomingMessage, and contains information about the client's request. The response argument, on the other hand, is an instance of http.ServerResponse, and is used to respond to the client. The handler in Listing 11-1 responds to all connections with a simple string of HTML using the write() and end() methods. As you might have guessed, these methods behave like the TCP methods of the same names.

Anatomy of an HTTP Request

Now that we have a simple HTTP server, we can begin sending requests to it. An example HTTP request is shown in Listing 11-2. The first line of the request, referred to as the *request line*, specifies the request method, the requested URL, and the protocol in use. In this example, the request method is GET, the URL is /, and the protocol is HTTP version 1.1. The meaning of each of these will be explained shortly, but first let's examine the rest of the example HTTP request. Following the request line is a collection of *request headers*, which are used to parameterize the request. In Listing 11-2, only the Host header has been included. This header is mandatory in HTTP 1.1, and is used to specify the domain name and port of the server that is being requested. Although not included in this example, a request can also include a *body*, which is used to pass additional information to the server.

Listing 11-2. A Hand Crafted HTTP Request

```
GET / HTTP/1.1
Host: localhost:8000
```

Since HTTP is a text-based protocol, we can easily hand craft a request using telnet. Listing 11-3 shows how the request from Listing 11-2 is made to the example server using telnet. It is important to note that HTTP requests must be terminated with a blank line. In Listing 11-3, this blank line is shown following the Host header.

Listing 11-3. A telnet Session Connecting to the Server in Listing 11-1

```
$ telnet localhost 8000
Trying 127.0.0.1...
Connected to localhost.
Escape character is '^]'.
GET / HTTP/1.1
Host: localhost:8000

HTTP/1.1 200 OK
Date: Sun, 21 Jul 2013 22:14:26 GMT
Connection: keep-alive
Transfer-Encoding: chunked

1c
Hello <strong>HTTP</strong>!
0
```

Everything following the request's terminating blank line is part of the response sent from the server. The response begins with a *status line,* which specifies the protocol, *status code*, and *reason phrase*. Again, the protocol is HTTP 1.1. The 200 status code indicates that the request was successful, and the reason phrase is used to provide a short description of the status code. A collection of *response headers* follow the status line. The server uses response headers in the same way the client uses request headers. Following the response headers is another blank line, then the *response body*. The value 1c is a hex value indicating the length of the body. In this case, the body is the HTML string returned by the server.

Request Methods

The request line of an HTTP request begins with a request method, followed by the requested resource's URL. The request method, also referred to as an HTTP verb, is used to specify the action to be performed on the specified URL. For example, in Listing 11-2, a GET request was made for the resource located at /. The purpose of the GET request is to view the specified resource (for example, to GET a web page to be displayed in a browser). Another common HTTP verb is POST, which allows the client to submit data to the server. POST requests are commonly used to submit HTML forms. Table 11-1 lists the various HTTP verbs supported by HTTP 1.1. Previously, HTTP 1.0 (which is still in use) only supported GET, POST, and HEAD requests.

Table 11-1. *Various HTTP Request Methods*

Method	Description
GET	Retrieves a representation of the specified resource. A GET request should not alter the state of the server, and is essentially a read operation.
HEAD	Retrieves the same data as an equivalent GET request, except the response body should be omitted. This is useful for quickly retrieving a resource's response headers without incurring the overhead of transferring the entire body. An example use case for a HEAD request is simply checking if a resource exists without downloading its entire contents.
POST	Used to create new resources on the server. Typical uses of POST requests are the submission of HTML forms and the addition of data to a database.
PUT	PUT requests are similar to POST requests; however, PUTs are used to update existing resources on the server. If the resource does not exist, the server can create it.
DELETE	Used to delete a resource from a server.
TRACE	Echoed back to the client. This is useful for detecting any changes made by intermediary servers.
OPTIONS	Returns a list of the verbs supported for the given URL.
CONNECT	Used to create a tunnel through a proxy server. The proxy will make the connection on the client's behalf. After the connection is established, the proxy simply forwards the TCP traffic between the client and remote server. This technique allows encrypted HTTPS traffic to be proxied through an unencrypted HTTP channel.
PATCH	The PATCH method is similar to PUT. However, PATCH is used to make partial updates to an existing resource. This is different from PUT, which should resubmit the entire resource during an update.

The example in Listing 11-4 displays the request line for each connection. All of the information in the request line is accessible via the http.IncomingMessage class. Specifically, this example uses the method, url, and httpVersion properties to re-create the request line.

Listing 11-4. A Server that Displays the Request Line of Each Incoming Connection

```
var http = require("http");
var server = http.createServer(function(request, response) {
  var requestLine = request.method + " " + request.url +
                    " HTTP/" + request.httpVersion;

  console.log(requestLine);
  response.end();
});

server.listen(8000);
```

Request Headers

The collection of request headers sent from the client tells the server how to properly handle the request. You've already seen an example including the Host header; however, there are many other commonly used request headers. For example, the Accept header is used to request data in a certain format. This header is useful when a resource is available in multiple formats (JSON, XML, HTML, and so on). In this scenario, a client could simply request a certain data format by setting the Accept header to the proper Content-Type (application/json, application/xml, text/html, and so on). Content-Types are discussed in more detail when response headers are covered. A non-exhaustive list of common request headers is shown in Table 11-2.

Table 11-2. *Several Common HTTP Request Headers*

Header	Description
Accept	Specifies the Content-Types that the client is willing to accept for this request.
Accept-Encoding	Provides a list of acceptable encodings. Many servers can compress data to speed up network transmission times. This header tells the server which compression types (gzip, deflate, and so on) the client can handle.
Cookie	Small pieces of data that the server stores on the client. The Cookie header contains all of the cookies that the client is currently storing for the server.
Content-Length	The length of the request body in octets.
Host	The domain and port of the server. This header is mandatory in HTTP 1.1. This header is useful when multiple servers are hosted on the same machine.
User-Agent	A string identifying the type of client. This normally contains information such as the browser name and version and operating system.

The request headers are accessible via the headers property of the http.IncomingMessage class. Listing 11-5 provides an example that prints out the headers on each request.

Listing 11-5. A Server that Displays the Request Headers of Each Incoming Connection

```
var http = require("http");

http.createServer(function(request, response) {
  console.log(request.headers);
  response.end();
}).listen(8000);
```

Response Codes

The status line of every HTTP response includes a numeric status code, as well as a reason phrase that describes the code. The reason phrase is simply cosmetic, while the status code is actually used by the client and, in conjunction with the response headers, it dictates how the response is handled. Table 11-3 contains a listing of several common (and one uncommon) HTTP response status codes and reason phrases.

Table 11-3. *Several Common (and One Comical) HTTP Response Codes and Reason Phrases*

Status Code and Reason Phrase	Description
200 OK	Indicates that the HTTP request was handled successfully.
201 Created	Indicates that the request has been fulfilled, and a new resource has been created on the server.
301 Moved Permanently	The requested resource has permanently moved to a new URL. The Location response header should contain the new URL to redirect to.
303 See Other	The requested resource can be found via a GET request to the URL specified in the Location response header.
304 Not Modified	Indicates that a cached resource has not been modified. To improve performance, a 304 response should not contain a body.
400 Bad Request	Indicates that the request was malformed and could not be understood. An example of this is a request that is missing a required parameter.
401 Unauthorized	If a resource requires authentication, and the provided credentials are refused, then the server will respond with this status code.
404 Not Found	The server could not locate the requested URL.
418 I'm a Teapot	This status code was introduced as an April Fools' Day joke. Actual servers should not return this status code.
500 Internal Server Error	The server encountered an error while attempting to fulfill the request.

A more extensive listing of the HTTP status codes is available in the http module, via its STATUS_CODES property. STATUS_CODES is an object that maps numeric status codes to reason phrase strings. The example in Listing 11-6 displays the reason phrase corresponding to the 404 status code.

Listing 11-6. An Example of Using http.STATUS_CODES

```
var http = require("http");

console.log(http.STATUS_CODES[404]);
// displays "Not Found"
```

You can set the status code of a response object using its statusCode property. If you do not explicitly provide a status code, this value defaults to 200. An example server that sets the statusCode property is shown in Listing 11-7. If a request is made for the URL /foo, the server will respond with a 200 status code and an HTML response body. However, if any other URL is requested, the server responds with a 404 error.

Listing 11-7. This Example Provides Different Responses Depending on the Requested URL

```
var http = require("http");

http.createServer(function(request, response) {
  if (request.url === "/foo") {
    response.end("Hello <strong>HTTP</strong>");
  } else {
    response.statusCode = 404;
    response.end();
  }
}).listen(8000);
```

Response Headers

The response headers, combined with the response status code, are used to interpret the data sent back from the server. Some of the more commonly encountered response headers are shown in Table 11-4.

Table 11-4. *Several Common HTTP Response Headers*

Header	Description
Cache-Control	Specifies whether a resource can be cached. If it can, this header designates the length of time, in seconds, that it can be stored in any cache.
Content-Encoding	Specifies the encoding used on the data. This allows the server to compress responses for faster transmission over the network.
Content-Length	The length of the response body in bytes.
Content-Type	Specifies the MIME type of the response body. Essentially, this header tells the client how to interpret the data.
Location	When the client is redirected, the target URL is stored in this header.
Set-Cookie	Creates a new cookie on the client. This cookie will be included in the Cookie header of future requests.
Vary	Used to dictate which request headers affect caching. For example, if a given resource has more than one representation, and the Accept request header is used to differentiate between them, then Accept should be included in the Vary header.
WWW-Authenticate	If an authentication scheme is implemented for a given resource, this header is used to identify the scheme. An example value is Basic, corresponding to HTTP Basic authentication.

One particularly important header in Table 11-4 is Content-Type. This is because the Content-Type header tells the client what kind of data it is dealing with. To demonstrate this point, connect to the example server from Listing 11-1 using a browser. Figure 11-1 shows the result using Google's Chrome browser. Additionally, Chrome's developer tools have been used to record the HTTP request. Notice that the HTML tags in the response are showing up onscreen, instead of marking up the text. By examining the response, you can see that no Content-Type header has been sent back from the server.

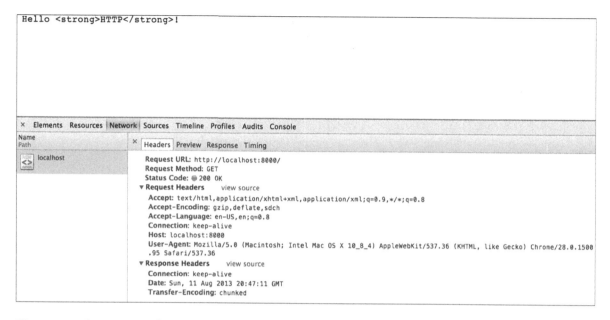

Figure 11-1. *Connecting to the server in Listing 11-1 using Google's Chrome browser*

Luckily, the http module provides several ways to create response headers. The simplest way is with the response argument's setHeader() method. This method takes two arguments, the header name and value(s). The header name is always a string. The value should either be a string or an array of strings, if you need to create multiple headers with the same name. In Listing 11-8, the server has been modified to return a Content-Type header. Since the server is sending back a string of HTML, the Content-Type header should tell the client to interpret the response as HTML. This is accomplished by setting the header's value to the text/html MIME type.

Listing 11-8. Setting a Content-Type Response Header Using the setHeader() Method

```
var http = require("http");
var server = http.createServer(function(request, response) {
  response.setHeader("Content-Type", "text/html");
  response.write("Hello <strong>HTTP</strong>!");
  response.end();
});

server.listen(8000);
```

■ **Note**   Response headers created with setHeader() can be removed using the response.removeHeader() method. This method takes a single argument, the name of the header to remove. You may be asking why this is important. Assume that you have a resource that is set to be cached using a cache header. However, before the response can be sent, an error is encountered. Since you don't want to cache an error response, the removeHeader() method can be used to remove the cache header.

Now, try connecting to the server in Listing 11-8 using a browser. This time, the word HTTP should display as boldface text. Figure 11-2 shows the resulting page using Chrome, as well as the recorded HTTP request. Notice that the response headers now include the Content-Type header.

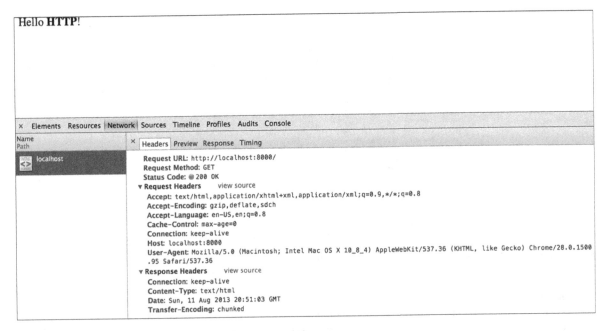

Figure 11-2. *Connecting to the server in Listing 11-8 using Chrome*

The second way to write response headers is with the writeHead() method. This method takes three arguments. The first is the status code to return. The second argument is an optional reason phrase. The final argument is an optional object containing the response headers. Listing 11-9 shows how the server from Listing 11-8 is implemented using writeHead() instead of setHeader().

Listing 11-9. An Example Using the writeHead() Method

```
var http = require("http");
var server = http.createServer(function(request, response) {
  response.writeHead(200, {
    "Content-Type": "text/html"
  });
  response.write("Hello <strong>HTTP</strong>!");
  response.end();
});

server.listen(8000);
```

Please note that header information must be set before calling write() or end(). Once write() or end() is called, Node will implicitly call writeHead() if you have not already explicitly done so. If you attempt to write the headers again after this point, you will get a "Can't set headers after they are sent" error. Additionally, writeHead() must be called only once per request. If you are unsure whether the headers have already been written, you can use the response.headersSent property to find out. headersSent holds a Boolean value that is true if the headers have already been sent, and false otherwise.

Working with Cookies

Because HTTP is a stateless protocol, it cannot directly remember details about a client's previous interactions with a server. For example, if you were to visit the same page 1,000 times, HTTP would treat each request as if it were the first. Obviously, web pages can remember details about you, such as whether you are logged in. So, how is state maintained over a stateless protocol? There are a few options. The state could be maintained on the server using a database or a session. The alternative is to store the data on the client in a cookie. Each approach has advantages and disadvantages. The advantage to storing data on the server is that it is less prone to tampering. The drawback is that all of the state information consumes memory on the server. For a heavily loaded server, memory consumption can quickly become a problem. On the flip side of the coin, maintaining state on the client using cookies is far more scalable, yet less secure.

▪ **Tip** Although cookies are more scalable than server-stored state, you should still use them sparingly. A site's cookies are sent back to the server in the `Cookie` header of *every* HTTP request, including requests for images, scripts, stylesheets, and so on. All of this data can increase network latencies. One way to mitigate this problem is to store static assets like images on a separate domain or subdomain that doesn't use any cookies.

In its simplest form, a cookie is just a name/value pair, separated with an equals sign. Multiple cookies are concatenated together using a semicolon as the delimiter. An example of two `Set-Cookie` response headers is shown in Listing 11-10. These cookies names are `name` and `foo`, while the values are `Colin` and `bar`, respectively. Once these cookies are set, they will be included in future `Cookie` request headers, as shown in Listing 11-11.

Listing 11-10. An Example of Two `Set-Cookie` Headers

```
Set-Cookie: name=Colin
Set-Cookie: foo=bar
```

Listing 11-11. The Cookie Header Resulting from the `Set-Cookie` Headers in Listing 11-10

```
Cookie: name=Colin; foo=bar
```

Cookies can also be parameterized using attributes. The various cookie attributes are shown in Table 11-5. Some of these attributes—such as `Domain` and `Path`—are given values, while others—such as `Secure` and `HttpOnly`—are Boolean attributes whose value is either set or not set.

Table 11-5. *Description of Various Cookie Attributes*

Attribute	Description
Domain	Limits the scope of the cookie, such that it is sent to the server only on requests of the given domain. If omitted, this defaults to the domain of the resource that set the cookie.
Path	Limits the scope of the cookie to all resources contained in the provided path. If omitted, Path defaults to /, applying to all resources.
Expires	Includes the date when the cookie should be deleted and is no longer valid.
Max-Age	Also specifies when the cookie should expire. However, Max-Age is specified as the number of seconds that the cookie should persist from the time it is set.
Secure	Cookies marked with the Secure flag are used only over secure connections. Browsers should send these cookies only over a secure (HTTPS) connection, while servers should set them only when the client makes a secure connection.
HttpOnly	Cookies marked with HttpOnly can be accessed only by HTTP and HTTPS. These cookies cannot be accessed via JavaScript in the browser, helping to mitigate cross-site scripting attacks.

An example use of setHeader() that creates two cookies with attributes is shown in Listing 11-12. In this example, the name cookie is set to expire on January 10, 2015. This cookie is also secure, and is an HTTP-only cookie. The foo cookie, on the other hand, uses the Max-Age attribute, and expires in one hour.

Listing 11-12. Setting Two Cookies that Include Attributes

```
response.setHeader("Set-Cookie",
  ["name=Colin; Expires=Sat, 10 Jan 2015 20:00:00 GMT;\
  Domain=foo.com; HttpOnly; Secure",
  "foo=bar; Max-Age=3600"]);
```

Middleware

Even with the help of Node's core modules, implementing all of the features of a stock web server is a daunting task. Examples might include implementing HTTP Basic authentication and gzip compression. You could write all of this code yourself, but the more popular alternative is to use *middleware*. Middleware are functions that process requests in an assembly line fashion. This means that one piece of middleware initially processes an incoming request. This middleware can either process the request completely, or perform an operation on the request and then pass it to another piece of middleware for additional processing.

An example of middleware that performs no processing is shown in Listing 11-13. Notice that the middleware takes three arguments, request, response, and next. request and response are the exact same objects used to process requests that you've become acquainted with. next is a function that is called to invoke the next piece of middleware. Note that next() has been included in a return statement in this example. This is not required, but it is good practice to return when calling next() to ensure that execution does not continue when the next middleware completes.

Listing 11-13. An Example Middleware Function

```
function middleware(request, response, next) {
  return next();
}
```

Connect

Now that we've seen what middleware looks like, let's build something with it. The first step is to install the Connect module (npm install connect). Connect touts itself as "high-quality middleware for node.js." Connect not only allows you to build applications using your own middleware, but it also comes bundled with some very useful middleware. There is also an abundance of freely available, third-party middleware built using Connect.

After installing Connect, create a new server containing the code shown in Listing 11-14. The first two lines of this example import the http and connect modules. On the third line, a Connect app is initialized using the connect module. Next, a piece of middleware is added to the app via its use() method. The body of the middleware should look familiar, as we've been using it in previous examples. That is one of the beautiful things about Connect middleware—it is built on top of the http module, and is therefore compatible with everything you've already learned. Finally, an HTTP server is constructed based on the Connect app. You may recall that createServer() takes a request event handler (function) as an argument. As it turns out, the app object returned by connect() is just a function that can be used to handle request events.

Listing 11-14. An Example Server Built Using Middleware

```
var http = require("http");
var connect = require("connect");
var app = connect();

app.use(function(request, response, next) {
  response.setHeader("Content-Type", "text/html");
  response.end("Hello <strong>HTTP</strong>!");
});

http.createServer(app).listen(8000);
```

We've just shown how our simple HTTP server can be re-created using middleware. However, to truly appreciate middleware, let's look at another example that uses multiple pieces of middleware. The server in Listing 11-15 uses three middleware functions. The first is Connect's built-in query() middleware. query() automatically parses the requested URL, and augments the request object with a query object containing all of the query string parameters and their values. The second piece of middleware is custom, and iterates over all of the parsed query string parameters, printing each one along the way. After calling next(), control is passed to the third and final middleware, which responds to the client. Note that the middleware are executed in the same order that they are attached (by calling use()). In this example, query() must be called before the custom middleware. If the order is reversed, an error will not occur, but no console output will be observed in the custom middleware.

Listing 11-15. Chaining Together Multiple Pieces of Connect Middleware

```
var http = require("http");
var connect = require("connect");
var app = connect();

app.use(connect.query());

app.use(function(request, response, next) {
  var query = request.query;

  for (q in query) {
    console.log(q + ' = ' + query[q]);
  }
```

```
  next();
});

app.use(function(request, response, next) {
  response.setHeader("Content-Type", "text/html");
  response.end("Hello <strong>HTTP</strong>!");
});

http.createServer(app).listen(8000);
```

■ **Note** The query string is an optional part of a URL used to pass request-specific parameters. A question mark (?) is used to separate the requested resource from the query string. Within the query string, individual parameters are formatted as `parameter=value`. An ampersand (&) is used to separate parameter-value pairs.

Example console output from Listing 11-15 is shown in Listing 11-16. To re-create this output, simply point a browser to `http://localhost:8000?foo=bar&fizz=buzz`. Notice that `query()` successfully extracts the two query string parameters, `foo` and `fizz`, and their values, `bar` and `buzz`.

Listing 11-16. Example Output After Connecting to the Server in Listing 11-15

```
$ node connect-query.js
foo = bar
fizz = buzz
```

`query()` is just one of the over 20 middleware methods that comes bundled with Connect. The `bodyParser()` and `cookieParser()` middleware provide similar functionality for working with request bodies and cookies, respectively. For a listing of all the middleware provided with Connect, the reader is encouraged to check out the project's GitHub page at `https://github.com/senchalabs/connect`. The Connect home page, located at `http://www.senchalabs. org/connect/`, also provides links to popular third-party middleware.

Issuing HTTP Requests

In addition to creating servers, the `http` module also allows you to make requests using the aptly named `request()` method. `request()` takes two arguments, `options` and `callback`. `options` is an object used to parameterize the HTTP request. A description of various properties supported by `options` is shown in Table 11-6. The `callback` argument is a function that is invoked when a response to the request is received. An instance of `http. IncomingMessage` is the only argument passed to the callback function. `request()` also returns an instance of `http. ClientRequest`, which is a writable stream.

Table 11-6. *Various Properties Supported by the* options *Argument to* request()

Option	Description
hostname	The domain or IP address to connect to. If omitted, this defaults to localhost. You can also specify this using the host property, but hostname is preferred.
port	The server port to connect to. This defaults to 80.
method	The HTTP method of the request. This defaults to GET.
path	The path of the resource being requested. If the request includes a query string, it should be specified as part of the path. If omitted, this defaults to /.
headers	An object containing the request headers.
auth	If Basic authentication is in use, the auth property is used to generate an Authorization header. The username and password used to authenticate should be formatted as username:password. Setting the Authorization header in the headers field will override this option.
socketPath	The UNIX socket to use. If this option is used, hostname and port should be omitted, and vice versa.

A client that works with our example server is shown in Listing 11-17. The client makes a GET request to http://localhost:8000/. Several of the options passed to request() could be omitted because they are the default values (namely, hostname, path, and method), but have been included for the sake of the example. When a response is received, the callback function re-creates the HTTP response by printing out the status line, headers, and body. The body is displayed as UTF-8 data using a stream data event handler. An important thing to note is the call to end() on the final line of the example. Had this been a POST or PUT request, there would have likely been a request body created by calling request.write(). To mark the end of the request body, even if there is none, end() is called. Had end() not been called, the request would have never been made.

Listing 11-17. Making an HTTP Request Using the request() Method

```
var http = require("http");
var request = http.request({
  hostname: "localhost",
  port: 8000,
  path: "/",
  method: "GET",
  headers: {
    "Host": "localhost:8000"
  }
}, function(response) {
  var statusCode = response.statusCode;
  var headers = response.headers;
  var statusLine = "HTTP/" + response.httpVersion + " " +
                   statusCode + " " + http.STATUS_CODES[statusCode];

  console.log(statusLine);

  for (header in headers) {
    console.log(header + ": " + headers[header]);
  }
```

```
  console.log();
  response.setEncoding("utf8");
  response.on("data", function(data) {
    process.stdout.write(data);
  });

  response.on("end", function() {
    console.log();
  });
});

request.end();
```

request() has a simpler, yet less powerful signature that takes a URL string as its first argument. Listing 11-17 has been rewritten in Listing 11-18 to use this version of request(). The drawback to this version is that the request method and headers cannot be specified. Therefore, this example makes a GET request with no headers. Also notice that we must still call end().

Listing 11-18. An Alternative Use of http.request()

```
var http = require("http");
var request = http.request("http://localhost:8000/", function(response) {
  response.setEncoding("utf8");

  response.on("data", function(data) {
    process.stdout.write(data);
  });

  response.on("end", function() {
    console.log();
  });
});

request.end();
```

As a convenience, the http module also provides a get() method for making GET requests, without calling end(). An example of get() is shown in Listing 11-19. It is worth pointing out that get() supports both of the argument signatures supported by request().

Listing 11-19. An Example of http.get()

```
var http = require("http");

http.get("http://localhost:8000/", function(response) {
  response.setEncoding("utf8");

  response.on("data", function(data) {
    process.stdout.write(data);
  });

  response.on("end", function() {
    console.log();
  });
});
```

Form Data

Thus far, we've only dealt with GET requests, which do not include request bodies. Now we'll look at requests that post data to the server. The example in Listing 11-20 makes a POST request to our example server (which will need to be updated to handle the additional data). The first thing to note is that the querystring core module is imported on the second line of the example. The querystring module's stringify() method creates a query string from an object. In this example, stringify() creates the query string foo=bar&baz=1&baz=2. It is worth pointing out that arrays, such as baz, can be stringified, but nested objects cannot.

Listing 11-20. An Example POST Request

```
var http = require("http");
var qs = require("querystring");
var body = qs.stringify({
     foo: "bar",
     baz: [1, 2]
   });
var request = http.request({
     hostname: "localhost",
     port: 8000,
     path: "/",
     method: "POST",
     headers: {
       "Host": "localhost:8000",
       "Content-Type": "application/x-www-form-urlencoded",
       "Content-Length": Buffer.byteLength(body)
     }
   }, function(response) {
     response.setEncoding("utf8");

     response.on("data", function(data) {
       process.stdout.write(data);
     });

     response.on("end", function() {
       console.log();
     });
   });

request.end(body);
```

The options passed to request() are the next thing to note. Obviously, the request method is set to POST, but also notice the Content-Type and Content-Length headers. The Content-Type header signifies to the server that the request body contains URL-encoded form data (which is generated by querystring.stringify()). The Content-Length header tells the server how many bytes (not characters) are included in the request body. Finally, the request body is sent to the server using end() (write() followed by end() could also be used alternatively).

Our current server will work fine with the updated client, but it has no way of processing the form data. Listing 11-21 shows how the request body can be parsed using the familiar stream API and the querystring module. The request stream's data handler is used to collect the entire request body in the bodyString variable. When the end event is emitted, the request body is parsed into an object using the querystring.parse() method. Next, each field in the body is iterated over, and written back to the client.

Listing 11-21. An Example Server that Handles POST Requests

```
var http = require("http");
var qs = require("querystring");
var server = http.createServer(function(request, response) {
  var bodyString = "";

  request.setEncoding("utf8");

  request.on("data", function(data) {
    bodyString += data;
  });

  request.on("end", function() {
    var body = qs.parse(bodyString);

    for (var b in body) {
      response.write(b + ' = ' + body[b] + "\n");
    }

    response.end();
  });
});

server.listen(8000);
```

Now that the server has been configured to handle POST requests, we can test our client. If everything works properly, the client should generate the output shown in Listing 11-22.

Listing 11-22. Example Output from the POST Request Client and Server

```
$ node post-client.js
foo = bar
baz = 1,2
```

Processing the incoming request body isn't terribly difficult, but it is a bit more tedious than it needs to be. To mitigate this problem, we can turn to Connect's bodyParser() middleware. Listing 11-23 shows how the server can be rewritten using Connect. The bodyParser() middleware parses the incoming request body and stores the result in request.body for future processing.

Listing 11-23. Using Connect's bodyParser() Middleware to Handle POST Requests

```
var http = require("http");
var connect = require("connect");
var app = connect();

app.use(connect.bodyParser());

app.use(function(request, response, next) {
  var body = request.body;
```

```
  for (b in body) {
    response.write(b + ' = ' + body[b] + "\n");
  }

  response.end();
});

http.createServer(app).listen(8000);
```

Nested Objects

It was previously mentioned that querystring.stringify() does not handle nested objects. The workaround is to define query parameters using square bracket notation, as shown in Listing 11-24. In this example, an object called name is created with two properties, first and last.

Listing 11-24. Passing Nested Objects to querystring.stringify()

```
var body = qs.stringify({
  "name[first]": "Colin",
  "name[last]": "Ihrig"
});
```

Connect's bodyParser() middleware will interpret this request as the object shown in Listing 11-25. Unfortunately, if you are parsing the request by hand using querystring.parse(), this trick will not work, and the data will be stored as shown in Listing 11-26.

Listing 11-25. Connect's Interpretation of the Data in Listing 11-24

```
{
  name: {
    first: "Colin",
    last: "Ihrig"
  }
}
```

Listing 11-26. The Data from Listing 11-24 as Parsed Using querystring.parse()

```
{
  "name[first]": "Colin",
  "name[last]": "Ihrig"
}
```

The request Module

request is a third-party module, written by Mikeal Rogers, that simplifies the process of making HTTP requests. At the time of writing, request is the third most depended upon module in the npm registry. request's popularity is due to the simplistic abstraction that it provides on top of Node's core functionality. To demonstrate request's simplicity, Listing 11-20 has been rewritten in Listing 11-27. Immediately you will notice that there are no streams and no querystring module—all of that occurs under the hood in request. All of the parameters of the request are passed in the first argument to request(). Most of these parameters will be self-explanatory at this point, but a rundown of many common options supported by request is provided in Table 11-7.

Listing 11-27. An Example Use of the request Module

```
var request = require("request");

request({
  uri: "http://localhost:8000/",
  method: "POST",
  headers: {
    Host: "localhost:8000"
  },
  form: {
    foo: "bar",
    baz: [1, 2]
  }
}, function(error, response, body) {
  console.log(body);
});
```

Table 11-7. *Common Options Used with the request Module*

Option	Description
uri (or url)	The URL being requested. This is the only required option.
method	The HTTP request method. This defaults to GET.
headers	The request headers to send. This defaults to an empty object.
body	The request body as a string or Buffer.
form	An object representation of the request body. Internally, this will set the body option to the URL encoded string equivalent. Additionally, the Content-Type header will be set to application/x-www-form-urlencoded; charset=utf-8.
qs	An object representation of any query string parameters. Internally, this will converted to a URL encoded query string, and appended to the requested URL.
jar	A cookie jar object used to define the cookies for the request. This will be covered in more detail later.
followRedirect	If true (the default), request will automatically follow HTTP 3xx response redirects.
followAllRedirects	If true, request will automatically follow HTTP 3xx response redirects, even on non-GET requests. This defaults to false.
maxRedirects	The maximum number of redirects to follow. This defaults to ten.
timeout	The number of milliseconds to wait for a response before aborting the request.

The second argument to request() is a callback function that is invoked once a response is received. The first argument to the callback is used to pass in any error information. The second argument is the complete response, and is an instance of http.IncomingMessage. The third argument, body, is the response body.

Cookies in `request`

Many sites require cookies in order to function properly. For example, most e-commerce sites use cookies to map requests to shopping carts. If you were able to guess (or steal) another user's cookies, you could manipulate their shopping cart. Using only the Node core, you would have to set the `Cookie` header on every request, and examine `Set-Cookie` headers on every response. `request` abstracts this away through the concept of a cookie jar. A cookie jar is an object containing representations of cookies. This jar is then passed to `request()` instead of a `Cookie` header. Once a response is received, `request` will take care of updating the cookie jar with any `Set-Cookie` headers.

An example `request` client that uses cookies is shown in Listing 11-28. The `request.jar()` method is used to create a new empty cookie jar. Next, a new cookie named `count`, with a value of one, is created using the `request.cookie()` method. The cookie is then added to the jar using the `add()` method. When the request is made, the cookie jar is passed in via the `jar` option. Finally, once the response is received, the contents of the cookie jar are printed.

Listing 11-28. An Example Request Using Cookies

```
var request = require("request");
var jar = request.jar();
var cookie = request.cookie("count=1");

jar.add(cookie);

request({
  url: "http://localhost:8000/",
  jar: jar
}, function(error, response, body) {
  console.log(jar);
});
```

To verify that `request` automagically updates the cookie jar, we're going to create a server that updates the cookie's value. The example server, shown in Listing 11-29, uses Connect's `cookieParser()` middleware to parse the `Cookie` header and create the `request.cookies` object. Next, the value of the `count` cookie is read and converted to an integer. Finally, a `Set-Cookie` response header is created with an incremented count. The client output resulting from connecting to this server is shown in Listing 11-30.

Listing 11-29. An Example Server that Updates a Cookie Value

```
var http = require("http");
var connect = require("connect");
var app = connect();

app.use(connect.cookieParser());

app.use(function(request, response, next) {
  var cookies = request.cookies;
  var count = parseInt(cookies.count, 10);
  var setCookie = "count=" + (count + 1);

  response.setHeader("Set-Cookie", setCookie);
  response.end();
});

http.createServer(app).listen(8000);
```

Listing 11-30. Output from the Cookie Example

```
$ node cookie-update.js
{ cookies:
   [ { str: 'count=2',
       name: 'count',
       value: '2',
       expires: Infinity,
       path: '/' } ] }
```

HTTPS

HTTP transmits data in plaintext, making it inherently insecure. When transmitting sensitive/private data such as social security numbers, credit card information, emails, or even instant messages, a secure protocol should be used. Luckily, HTTP has a secure sister protocol in HTTPS. HTTPS is simply standard HTTP executed over a secure channel. To be more specific, the channel is secured using the SSL/TLS (Secure Socket Layer / Transport Layer Security) protocol.

Under SSL/TLS, each client and server must have a private cryptographic key. Therefore, the first thing we need to do is create a private key. This can be done using the freely available OpenSSL utility. For more information on obtaining OpenSSL, please visit www.openssl.org. Next, create a private key named key.pem using the command shown in Listing 11-31. Make sure to remember where the key is saved, as you'll need it later!

Listing 11-31. Creating a Private Key Using OpenSSL

```
$ openssl genrsa -out key.pem 1024
```

In addition to a private key, each server must have a *certificate*, which is a public cryptographic key that has been signed by a Certificate Authority (CA). Essentially, a certificate is a voucher that the owner of a public key is who they say they are. Anyone can sign a certificate, so its legitimacy really depends on the reputation of the signer. Therefore, CAs are typically trusted third parties. To obtain a certificate, you must first generate a certificate signing request. Using OpenSSL, this can be accomplished via the command shown in Listing 11-32.

Listing 11-32. Creating a Certificate Signing Request Using OpenSSL

```
$ openssl req -new -key key.pem -out request.csr
```

At this point, you would send your request.csr to a CA to be signed. However, this often comes with a fee, and is not needed for the examples shown here. For our purposes, we can just create a self-signed certificate using the OpenSSL command shown in Listing 11-33.

Listing 11-33. Creating a Self-Signed Certificate Using OpenSSL

```
$ openssl x509 -req -in request.csr -signkey key.pem -out cert.pem
```

Using the key.pem and cert.pem files that we've just created, we can build a simple HTTPS server (shown in Listing 11-34). Node provides a core https module that provides secure alternatives to many of the features included in the http module. Notice that the https version of createServer() takes an additional argument prior to the request event listener. This argument is used to pass in the server's private key and certificate. If necessary, adjust the paths to point to the location of your key and certificate. The rest of the server is identical to our old HTTP server.

Listing 11-34. An Example HTTPS Server

```
var fs = require("fs");
var https = require("https");
var server = https.createServer({
  key: fs.readFileSync(__dirname + "/key.pem"),
  cert: fs.readFileSync(__dirname + "/cert.pem")
}, function(request, response) {
  response.writeHead(200, {
    "Content-Type": "text/html"
  });
  response.end("Hello <strong>HTTP</strong>!");
});

server.listen(8000);
```

To test our shiny new HTTPS server, we need a new client. You can just navigate to https://localhost:8000 in a browser. Ignore any warnings about an invalid/untrusted certificate, as they are due to the use of a self-signed certificate. The https module also provides its own request() method, which is demonstrated in Listing 11-35. Nothing special needs to be done in order to use the https request(). In fact, Listing 11-35 is identical to our HTTP example with the exception of the first line, and the use of the https module instead of http. The first line is used to suppress an error that is thrown because of the server's untrusted certificate. In production code, you would want to remove this line, and instead handle the error as needed within your application.

Listing 11-35. An Example HTTPS Client

```
process.env.NODE_TLS_REJECT_UNAUTHORIZED = "0";

var https = require("https");
var request = https.request({
  hostname: "localhost",
  port: 8000
}, function(response) {
  response.setEncoding("utf8");

  response.on("data", function(data) {
    process.stdout.write(data);
  });

  response.on("end", function() {
    console.log();
  });
});

request.end();
```

■ **Note**   While we're on the topic of HTTPS clients, it is worth pointing out that the request module is fully compatible with HTTPS.

Summary

This chapter has introduced a lot of material related to HTTP. While HTTP is not a terribly complicated protocol, there are many associated concepts which must be understood in order to properly use HTTP. This chapter has also touched on subjects like cookies and security via the HTTPS protocol. In addition to the core http, https, and querystring modules, this chapter introduced connect and request, two of the most popular modules in the npm registry. The next chapter is dedicated to Express, a framework for creating web applications that is built on top of http and connect. Therefore, it is important to understand the material covered here before moving on to the next chapter.

CHAPTER 12

■ ■ ■

The Express Framework

In Chapter 10, you learned how to create low-level TCP applications using the net module. Then, in Chapter 11, the low-level details of TCP were abstracted away using the http module. The move to a higher level of abstraction allowed us to do more, while writing less code. Chapter 11 also introduced the concept of middleware via the Connect library. Middleware promotes code reuse and enables you to request processing in an assembly line fashion. However, creating complex applications using the http and connect modules can still be a bit tedious.

The Express framework, created by TJ Holowaychuk, provides another level of abstraction on top of http and connect. Express is based on Ruby's Sinatra framework, and touts itself as "a minimal and flexible Node.js web application framework, providing a robust set of features for building single and multipage, and hybrid web applications." Express provides convenience methods and syntactic sugar for many common tasks that would otherwise be tedious or redundant. This chapter examines the Express framework in detail. And remember, because Express is built on http and connect, everything you learned in Chapter 11 is applicable.

Express Routes

Before looking at what Express has to offer, let's identify some shortcomings of http and connect. Listing 12-1 includes an example that supports three unique GET URLs, and returns a 404 for everything else. Notice that each newly supported verb/URL combination requires an additional branch in the if statement. There is also a fair amount of duplicated code. Some of this duplication could be eliminated by better optimizing the code, but that would require sacrificing code readability and consistency.

Listing 12-1. Supporting Multiple Resources Using the http Module

```
var http = require("http");

http.createServer(function(request, response) {
  if (request.url === "/" && request.method === "GET") {
    response.writeHead(200, {
      "Content-Type": "text/html"
    });
    response.end("Hello <strong>home page</strong>");
  } else if (request.url === "/foo" && request.method === "GET") {
    response.writeHead(200, {
      "Content-Type": "text/html"
    });
    response.end("Hello <strong>foo</strong>");
  } else if (request.url === "/bar" && request.method === "GET") {
```

```
    response.writeHead(200, {
      "Content-Type": "text/html"
    });
    response.end("Hello <strong>bar</strong>");
  } else {
    response.writeHead(404, {
      "Content-Type": "text/html"
    });
    response.end("404 Not Found");
  }
}).listen(8000);
```

HTTP verb and URL combinations are referred to as *routes*, and Express has efficient syntax for handling them. Listing 12-2 shows how the routes from Listing 12-1 are written using Express's syntax. First, the express module must be installed (npm install express) and imported into the application. The http module must also be imported. On line three of Listing 12-2, an Express app is created by calling the express() function. This app behaves like a Connect app, and is passed to the http.createServer() method on the last line of Listing 12-2.

Listing 12-2. Rewriting the Server from Listing 12-1 Using Express

```
var express = require("express");
var http = require("http");
var app = express();

app.get("/", function(req, res, next) {
  res.send("Hello <strong>home page</strong>");
});

app.get("/foo", function(req, res, next) {
  res.send("Hello <strong>foo</strong>");
});

app.get("/bar", function(req, res, next) {
  res.send("Hello <strong>bar</strong>");
});

http.createServer(app).listen(8000);
```

Three calls to the app's get() method are used to define the routes. The get() method defines routes for handling GET requests. Express also defines similar methods for the other HTTP verbs (put(), post(), delete(), and so on). All of these methods take a URL path and a sequence of middleware as arguments. The path is a string or regular expression representing the URL that the route responds to. Note that the query string is not considered part of the route's URL. Also notice that we haven't defined a 404 route, as this is the default behavior of Express when a request does not match any defined routes.

■ **Note**   Express middleware follow the same `request-response-next` signature as Connect. Express also augments the request and response objects with additional methods. An example of this is the `response.send()` method, shown in Listing 12-2 as `res.send()`. `send()` is used to send a response status code and/or body back to the client. If the first argument to `send()` is a number, then it is treated as the status code. If a status code is not provided, Express will send back a 200. The response body can be specified in the first or second argument, and can be a string, `Buffer`, array, or object. `send()` also sets the `Content-Type` header unless you do so explicitly. If the response body is a `Buffer`, the `Content-Type` header is also set to `application/octet-stream`. If the body is a string, Express will set the `Content-Type` header to `text/html`. If the body is an array or object, then Express will send back JSON. Finally, if no body is provided, the status code's reason phrase is used.

Route Parameters

Assume that you are creating an e-commerce site that sells hundreds or thousands of different products, each with its own unique product ID. You certainly would not want to specify hundreds of unique routes by hand. One option is to create a single route, and specify the product ID as a query string argument. Although this is a perfectly valid option, it leads to unattractive URLs. Wouldn't it be better if the sweater's URL looked like /products/sweater instead of /products?productId=sweater?

As it turns out, Express routes, which can be defined as regular expressions, are very good at supporting this scenario. Listing 12-3 shows how a route can be parameterized using a regular expression. In this example, the product ID can be any character except a forward slash. Inside of the route's middleware, any matched parameters are made accessible via the req.params object.

Listing 12-3. Parameterizing an Express Route Using a Regular Expression

```
var express = require("express");
var http = require("http");
var app = express();

app.get(/\/products\/([^\/]+)\/?$/, function(req, res, next) {
  res.send("Requested " + req.params[0]);
});

http.createServer(app).listen(8000);
```

For added convenience, routes can be parameterized even when the URL is described using a string. Listing 12-4 shows how this is accomplished. In this example, a named parameter, productId, is created using the colon (:) character. Inside of the route's middleware, this parameter is accessed by name using the req.params object.

Listing 12-4. A Route with Named Parameters

```
var express = require("express");
var http = require("http");
var app = express();

app.get("/products/:productId", function(req, res, next) {
  res.send("Requested " + req.params.productId);
});

http.createServer(app).listen(8000);
```

You can even define a regular expression for the parameter from within the string. Assuming that the `productId` parameter can now only be made up of digits, Listing 12-5 shows how a regular expression is defined. Please note the additional backslash on the `\d` character class. Because the regular expression is defined within a string constant, an extra backslash is required as an escape character.

Listing 12-5. Defining a Regular Expression Within a Route String

```
var express = require("express");
var http = require("http");
var app = express();

app.get("/products/:productId(\\d+)", function(req, res, next) {
  res.send("Requested " + req.params.productId);
});

http.createServer(app).listen(8000);
```

■ **Note** Optional named parameters are followed by question marks. For example, in the previous examples, if `productId` were optional, it would be written as `:productId?`.

Creating an Express Application

Express includes an executable script named `express(1)`, which is used to generate a skeleton Express application. The preferred way to run `express(1)` is by globally installing the `express` module using the command shown in Listing 12-6. For a refresher on what it means to globally install a module, see Chapter 2.

Listing 12-6. Globally Installing the express Module

```
npm install -g express
```

After globally installing Express, you can create a skeleton application anywhere on your machine by issuing the command shown in Listing 12-7. This listing also includes the command's output, which details the files created as well as instructions for configuring and running the application. Note, the only thing that you actually type in this example is `express testapp`.

Listing 12-7. Creating an Application Skeleton Using express(1)

```
$ express testapp

   create : testapp
   create : testapp/package.json
   create : testapp/app.js
   create : testapp/public
   create : testapp/public/stylesheets
   create : testapp/public/stylesheets/style.css
   create : testapp/routes
   create : testapp/routes/index.js
   create : testapp/routes/user.js
   create : testapp/public/javascripts
```

```
create : testapp/views
create : testapp/views/layout.jade
create : testapp/views/index.jade
create : testapp/public/images

install dependencies:
  $ cd testapp && npm install

run the app:
  $ node app
```

The skeleton Express app will be created in a new folder. In this case, the folder will be named testapp. Next, install the app's dependencies using the command shown in Listing 12-8.

Listing 12-8. Installing the Skeleton App's Dependencies

```
$ cd testapp && npm install
```

After npm has finished installing dependencies, we can run the skeleton program. The entry point to an Express app is located in the file app.js. Therefore, to run testapp, issue the command node app from the project's root directory. You can access the test app by connecting to localhost's port 3000. The skeleton app defines two routes—/ and /users—both of which respond to GET requests. Figure 12-1 shows the result of connecting to the / route using Chrome.

Express

Welcome to Express

Figure 12-1. *The index page returned by the skeleton app*

Examining the Skeleton App

app.js is the heart of an Express app. The contents of the app.js file generated during Listing 12-7 are shown in Listing 12-9. The file begins by importing the express, http, and path modules, as well as two project files, /routes/index.js and /routes/user.js. The two files imported from the routes directory contain the middleware used by the skeleton app's routes. Following the require() statements, an Express app is created using the express() function.

Listing 12-9. The Generated Contents of app.js

```
/**
 * Module dependencies.
 */

var express = require('express');
var routes = require('./routes');
var user = require('./routes/user');
var http = require('http');
var path = require('path');

var app = express();

// all environments
app.set('port', process.env.PORT || 3000);
app.set('views', __dirname + '/views');
app.set('view engine', 'jade');
app.use(express.favicon());
app.use(express.logger('dev'));
app.use(express.bodyParser());
app.use(express.methodOverride());
app.use(app.router);
app.use(express.static(path.join(__dirname, 'public')));

// development only
if ('development' == app.get('env')) {
  app.use(express.errorHandler());
}

app.get('/', routes.index);
app.get('/users', user.list);

http.createServer(app).listen(app.get('port'), function(){
  console.log('Express server listening on port ' + app.get('port'));
});
```

■ **Note** If the module path passed to require() resolves to a directory, Node will look for an index file within the directory. That is why the expression require("./routes") resolves to /routes/index.js.

Next, you'll see three calls to the app's set() method, which is used to define application settings. The first call defines a setting named port, which defines the port number that the server will bind to. The port number defaults to 3000, but this value can be overridden by defining an environment variable named PORT. The next two settings, views and view engine, are used by the Express templating system. The templating system will be revisited later in this chapter. For now, just know that these settings use the Jade templating language to render views stored in the views directory.

Following the setting definitions are several calls to use() that define middleware used to process all requests. Table 12-1 contains a short description of the various middleware included in the skeleton app. Many of these functions just use the Connect middleware of the same name.

Table 12-1. *Middleware Used in* app.js

Middleware	Description
favicon	If you've been testing your web servers using a browser, then you may have noticed requests for the file favicon.ico. This middleware handles such requests by serving your favicon.ico file, or the Connect default if you do not provide one.
logger	This middleware logs information about every request it receives. In dev mode, which is used in the skeleton app, logger displays the request verb and URL, as well as the response code, the time taken to process the request, and the size of the data returned.
bodyParser	This middleware was explained in Chapter 11. It parses the request body string into an object and attaches it to the request object as request.body.
methodOverride	Some browsers only allow HTML forms to make GET and POST requests. To make other types of requests (PUT, DELETE, and so on), the form can include an input named X-HTTP-Method-Override whose value is the desired request type. This middleware detects this situation and sets the request.method property accordingly.
app.router	This is the Express router that's used to map incoming requests to defined routes. If you do not explicitly use this, Express will mount it the first time it encounters a route. However, manually mounting the router will ensure its place in the middleware sequence.
static	This middleware accepts a directory path as input. This directory is treated as the root directory of a static file server. This is useful for serving content like images, stylesheets, and other static resources. In the skeleton app, the static directory is public.
errorHandler	As the name implies, errorHandler is middleware for processing errors. Unlike other middleware, errorHandler accepts four arguments—error, request, response, and next. In the skeleton app, this middleware is used only in development mode (see the development only comment).

Following the set() and use() calls, two GET routes are defined using the get() method. As previously mentioned, the URLs for these routes are / and /users. The /users route uses a single piece of middleware stored in the user.list variable. Looking back to the require() statements, the user variable comes from the file /routes/user, whose contents are shown in Listing 12-10. As you can see, this route simply returns the string "respond with a resource".

Listing 12-10. The Generated Contents of /routes/user.js

```
/*
 * GET users listing.
 */

exports.list = function(req, res){
  res.send("respond with a resource");
};
```

The / route is more interesting. It is defined in /routes/index.js, which is shown in Listing 12-11. The code shown here doesn't look like it could create the page shown in Figure 12-1. The key is the render() method, which ties into the Express templating system. This is probably a good time to explore templating, and how it is handled in Express.

Listing 12-11. The Generated Contents of /routes/index.js

```
/*
 * GET home page.
 */

exports.index = function(req, res){
  res.render('index', { title: 'Express' });
};
```

Templating

Creating dynamic web content often involves building long strings of HTML. Doing this by hand is both tedious and error prone. For example, it's very easy to forget to escape characters properly inside of long string literals. Templating engines are an alternative that greatly simplify the process by providing a skeleton document (the template) inside of which you can embed dynamic data. There are many JavaScript-compatible templating engines in existence, with some of the more popular options being Mustache, Handlebars, Embedded JavaScript (EJS), and Jade. Express supports all of these templating engines, but Jade comes packaged with Express by default. This section explains how to use Jade. Other templating engines can easily be installed and configured to work with Express, but are not covered here.

Configuring Jade is as simple as defining two settings in the app.js file. These settings are views and view engine. The views setting specifies a directory where Express can locate the templates, also referred to as *views*. The view engine specifies the view file extension to use if one is not provided. Listing 12-12 shows how these settings are applied. In this example, the templates are located in a subdirectory named views. This directory should include a number of Jade template files, whose file extension is .jade.

Listing 12-12. Settings Used to Configure Jade in Express

```
app.set("views", __dirname + "/views");
app.set("view engine", "jade");
```

Once Express has been configured to use your favorite templating engine, you can start rendering views. This is accomplished via the response object's render() method. The first argument to render() is the name of the view in your views directory. If your views directory contains subdirectories, this name can include forward slashes. The next argument to render() is an optional argument for passing in data. This is used to embed dynamic data in an otherwise static template. The final argument to render() is an optional callback function that is invoked once the template has finished rendering. If the callback is omitted, Express will automatically respond to the client with the rendered page. If the callback is included, Express will not automatically respond, and the function is invoked with a possible error and the rendered string as arguments.

Let's assume that you are creating a view for a user's account page. Once the user is logged in, you want to greet them by name. Listing 12-13 shows an example use of render() that handles this situation. This example assumes that the template file is named home.jade, and is located in a directory named account within the views folder. The user's name is assumed to be Bob. In a real application, this information would likely come from a data store of some type. The optional callback function has been included here as well. Within the callback, we check for an error. If an error has occurred, a 500 Internal Server Error is returned. Otherwise, the rendered HTML is returned.

Listing 12-13. An Example Use of `render()`

```
res.render("account/home", {
  name: "Bob"
}, function(error, html) {
  if (error) {
    return res.send(500);
  }

  res.send(200, html);
});
```

Of course, in order to render a view, we need to actually create the view. So, within your `views` directory, create a file named `account/home.jade` containing the code shown in Listing 12-14. This is a Jade template, and while an explanation of Jade's syntax is beyond the scope of this book, we're going to introduce the absolute basics. The first line is used to specify the HTML5 DOCTYPE. The second line creates the opening `<html>` tag. Notice that Jade doesn't include any angle brackets or closing tags. Instead, Jade infers these things based on code indentation.

Listing 12-14. An Example Jade Template

```
doctype 5
html
  head
    title Account Home
    link(rel='stylesheet', href='/stylesheets/style.css')
  body
    h1 Welcome back #{name}
```

Next comes the document's `<head>` tag. The head includes the page's title and a link to a stylesheet. The parentheses next to `link` are used to specify tag attributes. The stylesheet links to a static file, which Express is able to locate using the `static` middleware.

The final two lines of Listing 12-14 define the `<body>` of the document. In this case, the body consists of a single `<h1>` tag that welcomes the user. The value of `#{name}` is taken from the JSON object passed to `render()`. Inside of the curly braces, nested objects and arrays can be accessed using JavaScript's standard dot and subscript notations.

The resulting HTML string is shown in Listing 12-15. Please note that the string has been formatted for readability. In reality, Express renders the template with no extraneous indentation and line breaks. For additional information on Jade syntax, see the Jade home page at `http://www.jade-lang.com`.

Listing 12-15. Example HTML Rendered from the Template in Listing 12-14

```
<!DOCTYPE html>
<html>
  <head>
    <title>Account Home</title>
    <link rel="stylesheet" href="/stylesheets/style.css">
  </head>
  <body>
    <h1>Welcome back Bob</h1>
  </body>
</html>
```

express-validator

express-validator is a useful third-party module for ensuring that user input is provided in an expected format. express-validator creates middleware that attaches data-checking methods to the request object. An example that uses express-validator to validate a product ID is shown in Listing 12-16. The express-validator module is imported on the second line of the example, and then later added as middleware with use(). The middleware attaches the assert() and validationErrors() methods to req, which are used within the route.

The assert() method takes a parameter name and error message as arguments. The parameter can be a named URL parameter, a query string parameter, or a request body parameter. The object returned by assert() is used to validate the parameter's data type and/or value. Listing 12-16 demonstrates three validation methods, notEmpty(), isAlpha(), and len(). These methods validate that the productId parameter exists and is between two and ten letters long. As a convenience, these methods can be chained together, as shown by the second assert(). Of course, if you omit the productId parameter completely, the route will not be matched, and the validator will never be run. notEmpty() is more useful in validating query string parameters and form body data.

Listing 12-16. An Example of express-validator

```
var express = require("express");
var validator = require("express-validator");
var http = require("http");
var app = express();

app.use(express.bodyParser());
app.use(validator());

app.get("/products/:productId", function(req, res, next) {
  var errors;

  req.assert("productId", "Missing product ID").notEmpty();
  req.assert("productId", "Invalid product ID").isAlpha().len(2, 10);
  errors = req.validationErrors();

  if (errors) {
    return res.send(errors);
  }

  res.send("Requested " + req.params.productId);
});

http.createServer(app).listen(8000);
```

After all assertions have been made, the validationErrors() method is used to retrieve any errors. If there are no errors, null will be returned. However, if errors are detected, an array of validation errors is returned. In this example, the array of errors is simply sent back as the response.

There are a number of other useful validation methods not shown in Listing 12-16. Some of these are isInt(), isEmail(), isNull(), is(), and contains(). The first three of these methods verify that the input is an integer, e-mail address, or null. The is() method takes a regular expression argument and verifies that the parameter matches it. contains() also takes an argument, and checks if the parameter includes it.

express-validator also attaches a sanitize() method to req, which is used to clean up input. Listing 12-17 shows several examples of sanitize(). The first two examples convert the parameter's value to a Boolean and integer, respectively. The third example removes extraneous whitespace from the beginning and end of the parameter. The final example replaces character entities (such as < and >) with their corresponding characters (< and >).

Listing 12-17. Examples of the `express-validator` `sanitize()` Method

```
req.sanitize("parameter").toBoolean()
req.sanitize("parameter").toInt()
req.sanitize("parameter").trim()
req.sanitize("parameter").entityDecode()
```

REST

Representational State Transfer, or REST, is an increasingly common software architecture for creating APIs. REST, which was introduced by Roy Fielding in 2000, is not a technology in and of itself, but a set principles used to create services. RESTful APIs are almost always implemented using HTTP, but this is not a strict requirement. The following list enumerates a number of principles behind RESTful design.

- RESTful designs should have a single base URL, and a directory-like URL structure. For example, a blog API could have a base URL of /blog. Individual blog entries for a given day could then be made accessible using a URL structure like /blog/posts/2013/03/17/.

- Hypermedia as the engine of application state (HATEOAS). Clients should be able to navigate the entire API using only hyperlinks provided by the server. For example, after accessing an API's entry point, the server should provide links that the client can use to navigate the API.

- The server should not maintain any client state, such as sessions. Instead, every client request should contain all of the information required to define the state. This principle increases scalability by simplifying the server.

- Server responses should declare whether they can be cached. This declaration can be either explicit or implicit. When possible, a response should be cacheable, as it improves performance and scalability.

- RESTful designs should utilize the underlying protocol's vocabulary as much as possible. For example, CRUD (create, read, update, and delete) operations are implemented using HTTP's POST, GET, PUT, and DELETE verbs, respectively. Additionally, servers should respond with appropriate status codes whenever possible.

An Example RESTful API

Express makes it very simple to implement RESTful applications. Over the course of the next few examples, we are going to create a RESTful API for manipulating files on the server. An API would more commonly be used to manipulate database entries, but we haven't covered databases yet. Our example application is also split into a number of files. This makes the examples more readable, but also makes the application more modular.

First, we'll start with `app.js`, shown in Listing 12-18. Much of this should look familiar. However, an additional piece of middleware has been added that defines `req.store`. This is the directory containing the files the application will work with. The route declarations have also been removed, and replaced with a call to `routes.mount()`. `mount()` is a custom function defined in the file `routes.js`, which takes the Express app as its only argument.

Listing 12-18. The Contents of `app.js`

```
var express = require("express");
var routes = require("./routes");
var http = require("http");
var path = require("path");
var app = express();
var port = process.env.PORT || 8000;
```

```
app.use(express.favicon());
app.use(express.logger("dev"));
app.use(express.bodyParser());
app.use(express.methodOverride());

// define the storage area
app.use(function(req, res, next) {
  req.store = __dirname + "/store";
  next();
});

app.use(app.router);

// development only
if ("development" === app.get("env")) {
  app.use(express.errorHandler());
}

routes.mount(app);

http.createServer(app).listen(port, function() {
  console.log("Express server listening on port " + port);
});
```

The contents of routes.js are shown in Listing 12-19. The test app accepts four routes, one for each of the CRUD operations. The middleware for each route is defined in its own file (create.js, read.js, update.js, and delete.js). One thing to point out is that delete is both a HTTP verb and a JavaScript reserved word, so in some places the delete operation is referred to as simply del.

Listing 12-19. The Contents of routes.js

```
var create = require("./create");
var read = require("./read");
var update = require("./update");
var del = require("./delete");

module.exports.mount = function(app) {
  app.post("/:fileName", create);
  app.get("/:fileName", read);
  app.put("/:fileName", update);
  app.delete("/:fileName", del);
};
```

The create operation, handled by the POST route, is found in create.js, which is shown in Listing 12-20. Because we are performing file system operations, we begin by importing the fs module. Inside of the route middleware, the file path and its contents are computed. The path is composed of the req.store value and the fileName parameter. The data to write to the file comes from a POST body parameter named data. The fs.writeFile() method is then used to create the new file. The file is created using the wx flag, which causes the operation to fail if the file already exists. Inside of the writeFile() callback, we return either a 400 status code to indicate that the request could not be satisfied, or a 201 to indicate that a new file was created.

Listing 12-20. The Contents of `create.js`

```
var fs = require("fs");

module.exports = function(req, res, next) {
  var path = req.store + "/" + req.params.fileName;
  var data = req.body.data || "";

  fs.writeFile(path, data, {
    flag: "wx"
  }, function(error) {
    if (error) {
      return res.send(400);
    }

    res.send(201);
  });
};
```

The next CRUD operation is read, which is handled by the GET route. The contents of `read.js` are shown in Listing 12-21. This time, the `fs.readFile()` method is used to retrieve the contents of the file specified in the `fileName` parameter. If the read fails for any reason, a 404 status code is returned. Otherwise, a 200 status code is returned, along with a JSON body containing the file data. It is worth pointing out that the error argument could be more thoroughly inspected when setting the response code. For example, if `error.code` equals "ENOENT" then the file truly does not exist and the status code should be 404. All other errors could then simply return a 400.

Listing 12-21. The Contents of `read.js`

```
var fs = require("fs");

module.exports = function(req, res, next) {
  var path = req.store + "/" + req.params.fileName;

  fs.readFile(path, {
    encoding: "utf8"
  }, function(error, data) {
    if (error) {
      return res.send(404);
    }

    res.send(200, {
      data: data
    });
  });
};
```

Next comes the PUT route, which implements the update operation, shown in Listing 12-22. This is very similar to the create operation, with two small differences. First, a 200 status code is returned on a successful update instead of a 201. Second, the file is opened with the r+ flag instead of wx. This causes the update operation to fail if the file does not exist.

Listing 12-22. The Contents of update.js

```
var fs = require("fs");

module.exports = function(req, res, next) {
  var path = req.store + "/" + req.params.fileName;
  var data = req.body.data || "";

  fs.writeFile(path, data, {
    flag: "r+"
  }, function(error) {
    if (error) {
      return res.send(400);
    }

    res.send(200);
  });
};
```

The final CRUD operation is delete, shown in Listing 12-23. The fs.unlink() method removes the file specified by the fileName parameter. This route returns a 400 on failure and a 200 on success.

Listing 12-23. The Contents of delete.js

```
var fs = require("fs");

module.exports = function(req, res, next) {
  var path = req.store + "/" + req.params.fileName;

  fs.unlink(path, function(error) {
    if (error) {
      return res.send(400);
    }

    res.send(200);
  });
};
```

Testing the API

We can create a simple test script, shown in Listing 12-24, for exercising the API. The script uses the request module to access all of the API routes at least once. The async module is also used to avoid callback hell. By looking at the call to async.waterfall(), you can see that the script begins by creating a file and reading back the contents. Then, the file is updated and read again. Finally, we delete the file and try to read it again. All of the requests work on the same file, foo. After each request completes, the operation name and response code are displayed. For successful GET requests, the file contents are also displayed.

Listing 12-24. A Test Script for the RESTful API

```
var async = require("async");
var request = require("request");
var base = "http://localhost:8000";
var file = "foo";

function create(callback) {
  request({
    uri: base + "/" + file,
    method: "POST",
    form: {
      data: "This is a test file!"
    }
  }, function(error, response, body) {
    console.log("create:  " + response.statusCode);
    callback(error);
  });
}

function read(callback) {
  request({
    uri: base + "/" + file,
    json: true  // get the response as a JSON object
  }, function(error, response, body) {
    console.log("read:  " + response.statusCode);

    if (response.statusCode === 200) {
      console.log(response.body.data);
    }

    callback(error);
  });
}

function update(callback) {
  request({
    uri: base + "/" + file,
    method: "PUT",
    form: {
      data: "This file has been updated!"
    }
  }, function(error, response, body) {
    console.log("update:  " + response.statusCode);
    callback(error);
  });
}

function del(callback) {
  request({
    uri: base + "/" + file,
    method: "DELETE"
```

```
  }, function(error, response, body) {
    console.log("delete:  " + response.statusCode);
    callback(error);
  });
}

async.waterfall([
  create,
  read,
  update,
  read,
  del,
  read
]);
```

The test script's output is shown in Listing 12-25. Before running the script, be sure to create the store directory. The create operation returns a 201, indicating that foo was successfully created on the server. When the file is read, a 200 is returned, and the correct contents of the file are displayed. Next, the file is updated successfully and read once more. Then, the file is successfully removed. The ensuing read operation returns a 404 because the file no longer exists.

Listing 12-25. The Output from the Test Script in Listing 12-24

```
$ node rest-test.js
create:  201
read:  200
This is a test file!
update:  200
read:  200
This file has been updated!
delete:  200
read:  404
```

Summary

This chapter introduced the basics of the Express framework. Express provides a layer on top of Connect and HTTP, which greatly simplifies web application design. At the time of writing, Express is the fifth most depended-upon module in the npm registry, and has been used to build over 26,000 web apps. This makes Express extremely important to the well rounded Node developer. And, although Express could likely be the topic of an entire book, this chapter has touched on the most important aspects of the framework and surrounding technologies. To better understand the framework, you're encouraged to explore the Express documentation at http://www.expressjs.com, as well as the source code, which is available at https://github.com/visionmedia/express.

CHAPTER 13

■ ■ ■

The Real-Time Web

As you learned in Chapter 11, HTTP is designed around a request-response model. All HTTP communications are initiated by a client making a request to a server. The server then responds to the client with the requested data. In the early days of the web, this model worked because web sites were static HTML pages that linked to other static HTML pages. However, the web has evolved, and sites are no longer just static pages.

Technologies like Ajax have made the web dynamic and data-driven, and enabled a class of web applications that rival native applications. Ajax calls still make HTTP requests, but instead of retrieving an entire document from the server, they request only a small piece of data to update an existing page. Ajax calls are faster because they transfer fewer bytes per request. They also improve the user experience by smoothly updating the current page instead of forcing a full page refresh.

For everything that Ajax brings to the table, it still leaves plenty of room for improvement. First, every Ajax request is a full-blown HTTP request. That means that if an application uses Ajax just to report information back to the server (for example, an analytics application), the server will still waste the time to send back an empty response.

The second major limitation of Ajax is that all communications must still be initiated by the client. Client-initiated communication, referred to as *pull technology*, is inefficient for applications where the client always wants the most up-to-date information available on the server. These types of applications are much better suited to *push technology*, where communication is server initiated. Examples of applications that lend themselves well to push technology are sports tickers, chat programs, stock tickers, and social media newsfeeds. Push technology can be spoofed in a variety of ways with Ajax requests, but these are inelegant hacks. For example, the client can make periodic requests to the server, but this is extremely inefficient because many of the server responses are likely to contain no updates. Another technique, known as *long polling*, involves the client making a request to the server. If there is no new data, the connection is simply left open. Once data becomes available, the server sends it back to the client and closes the connection. The client then immediately makes another request, ensuring that an open connection is always available for push data. Long polling is also inefficient because of the repeated connections made to the server.

In recent years, HTML5 has introduced several new browser technologies that better facilitate push technology. The most prominent of these technologies is *WebSockets*. WebSockets give browsers the ability to communicate with a server over a full-duplex communication channel. This means that the client and server can transmit data simultaneously. Additionally, once the connection is established, WebSockets allow the client and server to communicate directly, without sending request and response headers. Browser-based games and other real-time applications are among the biggest beneficiaries of the performance boost that WebSockets provide.

This chapter introduces the WebSockets API, and shows how WebSockets applications are built using Node.js. The popular WebSockets library, Socket.IO, is also covered. Socket.IO provides an abstraction layer on top of WebSockets, in much the same way that Connect and Express are built on Node's http module. Socket.IO also provides real-time capabilities to older browsers that don't support WebSockets, by falling back on techniques such as Ajax polling. Finally, the chapter concludes by showing how Socket.IO can be integrated with the Express server.

The WebSockets API

Although client-side development is not the focus of this book, it is necessary to explain the WebSockets API before creating any Node applications. This section explains how to use WebSockets in the browser. It is worth noting that WebSockets are a relatively new feature of HTML5. Older browsers, and even some current browsers, do not support WebSockets. To determine whether your browser supports WebSockets, consult www.caniuse.com. This site provides information about which browsers support particular features. The examples shown in this section assume that WebSockets are supported in your browser.

Opening a WebSocket

WebSockets are created via the WebSocket() constructor function shown in Listing 13-1. The constructor's first argument is the URL that the WebSocket will connect to. When a WebSocket is constructed, it immediately attempts to connect to the supplied URL. There is no way to prevent or postpone the connection attempt. After construction, the WebSocket's URL is accessible via its url property. WebSocket URLs looks like the HTTP URLs that you are accustomed to; however, WebSockets use either the ws or wss protocol. Standard WebSockets use the ws protocol, and use port 80 by default. Secure WebSockets, on the other hand, use the wss protocol, and default to port 443.

Listing 13-1. The WebSocket() Constructor

```
WebSocket(url, [protocols])
```

The constructor's second argument, protocols, is optional. If it is specified, it should either be a string or an array of strings. The string(s) are subprotocol names. Using subprotocols allow a single server to handle different protocols simultaneously.

Closing WebSockets

To close a WebSocket connection, use the close() method, whose syntax is shown in Listing 13-2. close() takes two arguments, code and reason, which are both optional. The code argument is a numeric status code, while reason is a string describing the circumstances of the close event. The supported values of close are shown in Table 13-1. Typically, close() is called with no arguments.

Listing 13-2. The WebSocket close() Method

```
socket.close([code], [reason])
```

Table 13-1. Status Codes Supported by close()

Status Code(s)	Description
0-999	Reserved.
1000	Normal close. This code is used when a WebSocket is closed under normal circumstances.
1001	Going away. Either a server failure occurred, or the browser is navigating away from the page.
1002	The connection closed due to a protocol error.
1003	The connection is terminated because data was received that the endpoint does not know how to handle. An example is receiving binary data when text is expected.
1004	The connection is closed because a data frame that is too large was received.
1005	Reserved. This code indicates that no status code was provided even though one was expected.

(continued)

Table 13-1. (*continued*)

Status Code(s)	Description
1006	Reserved. This code indicates that the connection closed abnormally.
1007-1999	Reserved for future versions of the WebSocket standard.
2000-2999	Reserved for WebSocket extensions.
3000-3999	These codes should be used by libraries and frameworks, but not applications.
4000-4999	These codes are available for use by applications.

Checking a WebSocket's State

A WebSocket's state can be checked at any time via its readyState property. During its lifetime, a WebSocket can be in one of four possible states described in Table 13-2.

Table 13-2. *The Possible Values of a WebSocket's readyState Property*

State	Description
Connecting	When a WebSocket is constructed, it attempts to connect to its URL. During this time it is considered to be in the connecting state. A WebSocket in the connecting state has a readyState value of 0.
Open	After a WebSocket successfully connects to its URL, it enters the open state. A WebSocket must be in the open state in order to send and receive data over the network. A WebSocket in the open state has a readyState value of 1.
Closing	When a WebSocket is closed, it must first communicate to the remote host that it wishes to disconnect. During this period of communication, the WebSocket is considered to be in the closing state. A WebSocket in the closing state has a readyState value of 2.
Closed	A WebSocket enters the closed state once it successfully disconnects. A WebSocket in the closed state has a readyState value of 3.

Because it is not good programming practice to hard-code constant values, the WebSocket interface defines static constants representing the possible readyState values. Listing 13-3 shows how these constants can be used to evaluate the state of a connection using a switch statement.

Listing 13-3. Determining a WebSocket's State Using the readyState Property

```
switch (socket.readyState) {
  case WebSocket.CONNECTING:
    // in connecting state
    break;
  case WebSocket.OPEN:
    // in open state
    break;
  case WebSocket.CLOSING:
    // in closing state
    break;
```

```
  case WebSocket.CLOSED:
    // in closed state
    break;
  default:
    // this never happens
    break;
}
```

The open Event

When a WebSocket transitions into the open state, its open event is fired. An example open event handler is shown in Listing 13-4. An event object is the only argument passed to the event handler.

Listing 13-4. An Example open Event Handler

```
socket.onopen = function(event) {
  // handle open event
};
```

WebSocket event handlers can also be created using the addEventListener() method. Listing 13-5 shows how the same open event handler is attached using addEventListener(). This alternative syntax is preferred to onopen because it allows multiple handlers to be attached to the same event.

Listing 13-5. Attaching an open Event Handler Using addEventListener()

```
socket.addEventListener("open", function(event) {
  // handle open event
});
```

The message Event

When a WebSocket receives new data, a message event is fired. The received data is available via the data property of the message event. An example message event handler is shown in Listing 13-6. In this example, addEventListener() is used to attach the event, but onmessage could have also been used. If binary data is being received, the WebSocket's binaryType property should be set accordingly, before the event handler is called.

Listing 13-6. An Example message Event Handler

```
socket.addEventListener("message", function(event) {
  var data = event.data;
  // process data as string, Blob, or ArrayBuffer
});
```

■ **Note**   In addition to working with string data, WebSockets support binary data of two varieties—binary large objects (Blobs) and ArrayBuffers. However, an individual WebSocket can work with only one of the two binary formats at a time. When a WebSocket is created, it is initially set up to handle Blob data. The WebSocket's binaryType property is used to select between Blob and ArrayBuffer support. In order to work with Blob data, the WebSocket's binaryType should be set to "blob" before reading data. Similarly, binaryType should be set to "arraybuffer" before attempting to read an ArrayBuffer.

The close Event

When a WebSocket is closed, a close event is fired. The event object passed to the close handler has three properties, named code, reason, and wasClean. The code and reason fields correspond to the arguments of the same names passed to close(). The wasClean field is a Boolean value thast indicates whether the connection was closed cleanly. Under normal circumstances, wasClean is true. An example close event handler is shown in Listing 13-7.

Listing 13-7. An Example close Event Handler

```
socket.addEventListener("close", function(event) {
  var code = event.code;
  var reason = event.reason;
  var wasClean = event.wasClean;
  // handle close event
});
```

The error Event

When a WebSocket encounters a problem, an error event is fired. The event passed to the handler is a standard error object, including name and message properties. An example WebSocket error event handler is shown in Listing 13-8.

Listing 13-8. An Example error Event Handler

```
socket.addEventListener("error", function(event) {
  // handle error event
});
```

Sending Data

WebSockets transmit data via the send() method, which comes in three flavors—one for sending UTF-8 string data, a second for sending an ArrayBuffer, and a third for sending Blob data. All three versions of send() take a single argument, which represents the data to be transmitted. The syntax for send() is shown in Listing 13-9.

Listing 13-9. Using the WebSocket's send() Method

```
socket.send(data)
```

WebSockets in Node

WebSockets are not supported in the Node core, but luckily there are a plethora of third-party WebSocket modules available in the npm registry. Although you are free to pick any module you want, the examples in this book use the ws module. The reasoning behind this decision is that ws is fast, popular, well-supported, and is used in the Socket.IO library that is covered later in this chapter.

To demonstrate how the ws module works, let's dive head-first into an example. The code in Listing 13-10 is a WebSocket echo server built using the ws, http, and connect modules. This server accepts HTTP and WebSocket connections on port 8000. Connect's static middleware allows arbitrary static content to be served from the public subdirectory over HTTP, whereas ws handles WebSocket connections.

Listing 13-10. A WebSocket Echo Server Built Using the ws, http, and connect Modules

```
var http = require("http");
var connect = require("connect");
var app = connect();
var WebSocketServer = require("ws").Server;
var server;
var wsServer;

app.use(connect.static("public"));
server = http.createServer(app);
wsServer = new WebSocketServer({
  server: server
});

wsServer.on("connection", function(ws) {
  ws.on("message", function(message, flags) {
    ws.send(message, flags);
  });
});

server.listen(8000);
```

To create the WebSocket component of the server, we must first import the ws module's Server() constructor. The constructor is stored in the WebSocketServer variable in Listing 13-10. Next, an instance of the WebSocket server, wsServer, is created by calling the constructor. The HTTP server, server, is passed to the constructor, allowing WebSockets and HTTP to coexist on the same port. Technically, a WebSocket-only server could be built without http and connect, by passing {port: 8000} to the WebSocketServer() constructor.

When a WebSocket connection is received, the connection event handler is invoked. The handler accepts a WebSocket instance, ws, as its only argument. The WebSocket attaches a message event handler that is used to receive data from the client. When data is received, the message and its associated flags are simply echoed back to the client using the WebSocket's send() method. The message flags are used to indicate information such as whether the message contains binary data.

A WebSocket Client

The ws module also allows for the creation of WebSockets clients. A client that works with the echo server from Listing 13-10 is shown in Listing 13-11. The client begins by importing the ws module as the variable WebSocket. On the second line of the example, a WebSocket is constructed that connects to port 8000 of the local machine. Recall that WebSocket clients immediately attempt to connect to the URL passed to the constructor. Therefore, instead of telling the WebSocket to connect, we simply set up an open event handler. Once the connection is established, the open event handler sends the string "Hello!" to the server.

Listing 13-11. A WebSocket Client that Works with the Server in Listing 13-10

```
var WebSocket = require("ws");
var ws = new WebSocket("ws://localhost:8000");

ws.on("open", function() {
  ws.send("Hello!");
});
```

```
ws.on("message", function(data, flags) {
  console.log("Server says:");
  console.log(data);
  ws.close();
});
```

Once the server receives the message, it will echo it back to the client. To handle incoming data, we also have to set up a message event handler. In Listing 13-11, the message handler displays the data to the screen and then closes the WebSocket using close().

A HTML Client

Because the example server supports HTTP and WebSockets, we can serve HTML pages with embedded WebSocket functionality. An example page that works with the echo server is shown in Listing 13-12. The HTML5 page contains buttons for connecting and disconnecting from the server, as well as a text field and button for typing and sending messages. Initially, only the Connect button is enabled. Once connected, the Connect button is disabled, and the other controls are enabled. You can then enter some text and press the Send button. Data will then be sent to the server, echoed back, and displayed on the page. To test this page, first save it as test.htm in the echo server's public subdirectory. With the server running, simply navigate to http://localhost:8000/test.htm.

Listing 13-12. A HTML Client that Works with the Server in Listing 13-10

```
<!DOCTYPE html>
<html lang="en">
<head>
  <title>WebSocket Echo Client</title>
  <meta charset="UTF-8" />
  <script>
    "use strict";
    // Initialize everything when the window finishes loading
    window.addEventListener("load", function(event) {
      var status = document.getElementById("status");
      var open = document.getElementById("open");
      var close = document.getElementById("close");
      var send = document.getElementById("send");
      var text = document.getElementById("text");
      var message = document.getElementById("message");
      var socket;

      status.textContent = "Not Connected";
      close.disabled = true;
      send.disabled = true;

      // Create a new connection when the Connect button is clicked
      open.addEventListener("click", function(event) {
        open.disabled = true;
        socket = new WebSocket("ws://localhost:8000");

        socket.addEventListener("open", function(event) {
          close.disabled = false;
          send.disabled = false;
          status.textContent = "Connected";
        });
```

```
    // Display messages received from the server
    socket.addEventListener("message", function(event) {
      message.textContent = "Server Says: " + event.data;
    });

    // Display any errors that occur
    socket.addEventListener("error", function(event) {
      message.textContent = "Error: " + event;
    });

    socket.addEventListener("close", function(event) {
      open.disabled = false;
      status.textContent = "Not Connected";
    });
  });

  // Close the connection when the Disconnect button is clicked
  close.addEventListener("click", function(event) {
    close.disabled = true;
    send.disabled = true;
    message.textContent = "";
    socket.close();
  });

  // Send text to the server when the Send button is clicked
  send.addEventListener("click", function(event) {
    socket.send(text.value);
    text.value = "";
  });
  });
</script>
</head>
<body>
  Status: <span id="status"></span><br />
  <input id="open" type="button" value="Connect" /> 
  <input id="close" type="button" value="Disconnect" /><br />
  <input id="send" type="button" value="Send" /> 
  <input id="text" /><br />
  <span id="message"></span>
</body>
</html>
```

Examining the WebSocket Connection

You may be wondering how HTTP and WebSockets can listen on the same port at the same time. The reason is that the initial WebSocket connection occurs over HTTP. Figure 13-1 shows what a WebSocket connection looks like through the eyes of Chrome's developer tools. The top portion of the image shows the actual test page from Listing 13-12. The bottom portion of the figure shows the Chrome developer tools, and displays two recorded network requests. The first request, test.htm, simply downloads the test page. The second request, labeled localhost, occurs when the Connect button is pressed on the web page. This request sends WebSocket headers and an Upgrade header, which enables future communication to occur over the WebSocket protocol. By examining the response status code and headers, you can see that the connection successfully switches from HTTP to the WebSocket protocol.

Status: Connected

Connect | **Disconnect**

Send | _____

Figure 13-1. *Examining a WebSocket connection using Chrome's developer tools*

Socket.IO

The numerous benefits of WebSockets were explained earlier in this chapter. However, their biggest drawback is probably their lack of browser support, especially in legacy browsers. Enter Socket.IO, a JavaScript library that touts itself as "the cross-browser WebSocket for real-time apps." Socket.IO adds another layer of abstraction on top of WebSockets by providing additional features such as heartbeats and timeouts. These features, which are commonly used in real-time applications, can be implemented using WebSockets, but are not part of the standard.

The real strength of Socket.IO is its ability to maintain the same API across older browsers that do not support WebSockets at all. This is accomplished by falling back on older technologies such as Adobe Flash Sockets, Ajax long polling, and JSONP polling when native WebSockets are not available. By providing fallback mechanisms, Socket.IO can work with ancient browsers such as Internet Explorer 5.5. Its flexibility has caused it to become the fifth most starred module in the npm registry, while being depended on by over 700 npm modules.

Creating a Socket.IO Server

Socket.IO, like ws, can easily be combined with the http module. Listing 13-13 shows another echo server that combines HTTP and WebSockets (via Socket.IO). The third line of Listing 13-13 imports the Socket.IO module. The Socket.IO listen() method forces Socket.IO to listen on the HTTP server, server. The value returned by listen(), io, is then used to configure the WebSockets portion of the application.

Listing 13-13. An Echo Server Using http, connect, and Socket.IO

```
var http = require("http");
var connect = require("connect");
var socketio = require("socket.io");
var app = connect();
```

```
var server;
var io;

app.use(connect.static("public"));
server = http.createServer(app);
io = socketio.listen(server);

io.on("connection", function(socket) {
  socket.on("message", function(data) {
    socket.emit("echo", data);
  });
});

server.listen(8000);
```

A connection event handler processes incoming WebSocket connections. Much like ws, the connection handler takes a WebSocket as its only argument. Next, notice the message event handler. This handler is invoked when new data arrives over the WebSocket. However, unlike standard WebSockets, Socket.IO allows for arbitrarily named events. That means that instead of listening for message events, we could have listened for, say, foo events. Regardless of the event's name, data that is received is passed to the event handler. The data is then echoed back to the client by emitting an echo event. Again, the event name is arbitrary. Also, notice that data is sent using the familiar emit() method of EventEmitter syntax.

Creating a Socket.IO Client

Socket.IO also ships with a client-side script that can be used in browser development. Listing 13-14 provides an example page that can talk to the echo server from Listing 13-13. Place this page in the echo server's public subdirectory. The first thing to note is the included Socket.IO script in the document's head. This script is handled automatically by the server-side module, and does not need to be added to the public directory.

Listing 13-14. A Socket.IO Client that Works with the Server in Listing 13-13

```
<!DOCTYPE html>
<html>
<head>
  <script src="/socket.io/socket.io.js"></script>
</head>
<body>
<body>
  <script>
    var socket = io.connect("http://localhost");

    socket.emit("message", "Hello!");
    socket.on("echo", function(data) {
      document.write(data);
    });
  </script>
</body>
</html>
```

The next thing to examine is the inline `<script>` tag. This is the Socket.IO application logic. When the page is loaded, the io.connect() method is used to establish a connection to the server. Notice that the connection is made using a HTTP URL, as opposed to the ws protocol. The emit() method is then used to send a message event to the server. Again, the choice of event name is arbitrary, but the client and server must agree on the name. Since the server will send back an echo event, the last thing we do is create an echo event handler that prints the received message to the document.

Socket.IO and Express

Integrating Socket.IO and Express is very straightforward. In fact, it's not much different than integrating Socket.IO with http and Connect. Listing 13-15 shows how this is accomplished. The only major difference is that Express is imported and used to create the app variable and attach middleware instead of Connect. Just for the sake of the example, an Express route has also been added to the existing echo server. The client page from Listing 13-14 can still be used with this example, without modification.

Listing 13-15. An Echo Server Built Using Socket.IO and Express

```
var express = require("express");
var http = require("http");
var socketio = require("socket.io");
var app = express();
var server = http.createServer(app);
var io = socketio.listen(server);

app.use(express.static("public"));

app.get("/foo", function(req, res, next) {
  res.send(200, {
    body: "Hello from foo!"
  });
});

io.on("connection", function(socket) {
  socket.on("message", function(data) {
    socket.emit("echo", data);
  });
});

server.listen(8000);
```

Summary

This chapter covered the concepts of the real-time web. The biggest player in this sphere is undoubtedly WebSockets. WebSockets provide top-notch performance by providing bidirectional communication between the client and server without the need to send HTTP headers. However, while WebSockets provide a potentially large performance boost, they are a relatively new standard, and are not supported in legacy browsers. Therefore, this chapter has also introduced Socket.IO, a cross-browser WebSocket module that supports older browsers by falling back on other less efficient data transfer mechanisms. Additionally, this chapter has shown you how to integrate Socket.IO with the other technologies that were covered in Chapters 11 and 12. In the next chapter, you learn how to access databases and integrate them with all of the Node modules you've learned about thus far.

CHAPTER 14

■ ■ ■

Databases

Nearly all web applications have some type of backing data store. Typically this data store is a database of some sort, and is used to store everything from addresses and credit card numbers to sensor readings and prescription information. Databases provide a way of accessing large amounts of data very quickly. There are generally two types of databases—relational databases and NoSQL databases. This chapter focuses on databases, and how they are accessed from Node applications. More specifically, the MySQL relational database and the MongoDB NoSQL database are explored. Please note that this chapter does not provide instructions for installing MySQL and MongoDB. Additionally, it assumes that you are already familiar with the Structured Query Language (SQL), which is used in conjunction with relational databases.

Relational Databases

A relational database is made up of a collection of tables. Each table holds a collection of records that are comprised of data. Individual records in a table are referred to as rows or *tuples*. The data types stored in these tuples are predefined using a *schema*. An example table is shown in Figure 14-1. This table holds information on individual people, including their names, gender, social security numbers (SSN), and the cities and states in which they reside (to save space, information such as address has been omitted).

SSN	LastName	FirstName	Gender	City	State
123-45-6789	Pluck	Peter	M	Pittsburgh	PA
234-56-7890	Johnson	John	M	San Diego	CA
345-67-8901	Doe	Jane	F	Las Vegas	NV
456-78-9012	Doe	John	M	Las Vegas	NV

Figure 14-1. An example table in a relational database

The SQL CREATE statement used to create the table in Figure 14-1 is shown in Listing 14-1. This SQL command defines the table's schema, which all tuples must adhere to. In this case, the person's social security number must be eleven characters long (to accommodate dashes), their gender must be a single character, and their state of residence must be two characters. The person's last name, first name, and city of residence can each be up to 50 characters long.

Listing 14-1. SQL Used to Create the Table in Figure 14-1

```
CREATE TABLE Person (
  SSN CHAR(11) NOT NULL,
  LastName VARCHAR(50) NOT NULL,
  FirstName VARCHAR(50) NOT NULL,
```

```
  Gender CHAR(1),
  City VARCHAR(50) NOT NULL,
  State CHAR(2) NOT NULL,
  PRIMARY KEY(SSN)
);
```

Also note that the social security number is used as the table's *primary key*. The primary key is one or more fields that ensure the uniqueness of an individual tuple within a table. Since every person should have a unique social security number, this makes it the ideal choice for the primary key.

The SQL INSERT statements shown in Listing 14-2 are used to populate the Person table. Notice that all of the values in each statement conform to the predefined schema. If you were to enter an invalid piece of data, or a SSN that already exists in the table, then the database management system would reject the insertion.

Listing 14-2. SQL Used to Populate the Table in Figure 14-1

```
INSERT INTO Person (SSN, LastName, FirstName, Gender, City, State)
  VALUES ('123-45-6789', 'Pluck', 'Peter', 'M', 'Pittsburgh', 'PA');
INSERT INTO Person (SSN, LastName, FirstName, Gender, City, State)
  VALUES ('234-56-7890', 'Johnson', 'John', 'M', 'San Diego', 'CA');
INSERT INTO Person (SSN, LastName, FirstName, Gender, City, State)
  VALUES ('345-67-8901', 'Doe', 'Jane', 'F', 'Las Vegas', 'NV');
INSERT INTO Person (SSN, LastName, FirstName, Gender, City, State)
  VALUES ('456-78-9012', 'Doe', 'John', 'M', 'Las Vegas', 'NV');
```

Relational databases attempt to remove redundancies by storing data in only a single place. The process of updating and deleting data is much simpler if it needs to happen in only one location. The process of removing redundancies, referred to as *normalization*, results in multiple tables that reference one another using *foreign keys*. A foreign key is one or more fields that uniquely identify a tuple in a different table.

For a concrete example, let's return to our example database. It currently has one table, Person, that stores information on individuals. What if we wanted to also track these individuals' cars? That information could be stored in the Person table by creating additional columns in the schema. However, how would that handle the case in which a single person owns more than one car? You would have to continue adding additional car fields to the table (car1, car2, and so on), many of which would be empty (most people have one or zero cars). The better alternative is to create a separate Vehicle table that contains car information and a foreign key that references the Person table. An example Vehicle table is shown in Figure 14-2.

SSN	VIN	Type	Year
123-45-6789	12345	Jeep	2014
234-56-7890	67890	Van	2010
345-67-8901	54327	Truck	2009
123-45-6789	98032	Car	2006

Figure 14-2. *A simplified Vehicle table*

The CREATE statement used to define the Vehicle table is shown in Listing 14-3, while the INSERT statements used to populate it are shown in Listing 14-4. Notice that the Vehicle. SSN field references the Person.SSN field. This is a foreign key relationship, and although the fields have the same name in both tables in this example, it is not a requirement.

Listing 14-3. SQL Used to Create the Vehicle Table

```
CREATE TABLE Vehicle (
  SSN CHAR(11) NOT NULL,
  VIN INT UNSIGNED NOT NULL,
  Type VARCHAR(50) NOT NULL,
  Year INT UNSIGNED NOT NULL,
  PRIMARY KEY(VIN),
  FOREIGN KEY(SSN)
    REFERENCES Person(SSN)
);
```

Listing 14-4. SQL Used to Populate the Vehicle Table

```
INSERT INTO Vehicle (SSN, VIN, Type, Year)
  VALUES ('123-45-6789', 12345, 'Jeep', 2014);
INSERT INTO Vehicle (SSN, VIN, Type, Year)
  VALUES ('234-56-7890', 67890, 'Van', 2010);
INSERT INTO Vehicle (SSN, VIN, Type, Year)
  VALUES ('345-67-8901', 54327, 'Truck', 2009);
INSERT INTO Vehicle (SSN, VIN, Type, Year)
  VALUES ('123-45-6789', 98032, 'Car', 2006);
```

One of the true strengths of relational databases is the ability to quickly query for information, even if that information is split up across multiple tables. This is accomplished using the JOIN operation. The SQL SELECT statement shown in Listing 14-5 uses a JOIN operation to select the name of every person who owns a vehicle in Las Vegas. In this case there are two people from Las Vegas in the People table, but only one who owns a vehicle. Therefore, this query will return the name Jane Doe.

Listing 14-5. SQL Query Involving a JOIN Operation

```
SELECT FirstName, LastName FROM Person INNER JOIN Vehicle
  WHERE Person.SSN = Vehicle.SSN AND City = 'Las Vegas';
```

MySQL

MySQL is an extremely popular relational database management system. It is also open source, making it freely available. It is so widely used that the M in LAMP stack stands for MySQL. It has been used on many high-profile projects and sites such as WordPress, Wikipedia, Google, and Twitter. The MySQL examples in this chapter access the database using the mysql third-party module, which must be installed using the command shown in Listing 14-6.

Listing 14-6. npm Command Used to Install the mysql Module

```
$ npm install mysql
```

Connecting to MySQL

In order to access a database, you must first establish a connection. The examples throughout this chapter assume that MySQL is running on your local machine. To establish a connection, you should first create a connection object using the createConnection( ) method. There are two incarnations of createConnection( ) that achieve the same end result. The first version takes an object as its sole argument. This argument contains parameters for establishing the connection. An example that creates a connection is shown in Listing 14-7. This example creates a connection to the MySQL database named dbname, which is running on localhost:3306 (MySQL defaults to port 3306, so this option can typically be omitted). The user and password options provide security by preventing the database from being accessed arbitrarily.

Listing 14-7. Creating a Connection to a MySQL Database

```
var mysql = require("mysql");
var connection = mysql.createConnection({
  "host": "localhost",
  "port": 3306,
  "user": "username",
  "password": "secret",
  "database": "dbname"
});
```

The alternative version of createConnection( ) takes a MySQL URL string as its only argument. Listing 14-8 shows how the same createConnection( ) example is rewritten to use a URL string. While this version provides a more concise syntax, it is less readable than using an object literal.

Listing 14-8. Creating a Connection to a MySQL Database Using a URL String

```
var mysql = require("mysql");
var connection =
  mysql.createConnection("mysql://username:secret@localhost:3306/dbname");
```

After a connection object has been created, the next step is to call its connect( ) method. This method takes a single argument, a callback function that is invoked after the connection has been established. If an error occurs while connecting, it is passed as the first and only argument to the callback function. Listing 14-9 illustrates the process of establishing a connection.

Listing 14-9. Using the connect( ) Method to Establish a Connection

```
var mysql = require("mysql");
var connection = mysql.createConnection({
  "host": "localhost",
  "port": 3306,
  "user": "username",
  "password": "secret",
  "database": "dbname"
});

connection.connect(function(error) {
  if (error) {
    return console.error(error);
  }

  // Connection successfully established
});
```

Connection Pooling

In the previous examples, a new connection would be established each time the application needed to access the database. However, if you know ahead of time that your application will require many frequent connections to the database, it may be more efficient to establish a pool of reusable connections. Each time a new connection is required, the application can simply ask for one from the pool. Once the connection has fulfilled its purpose, it can be returned to the pool for use on a future request. A connection pool is created using the createPool() method, shown in Listing 14-10. Notice that createPool() is very similar to createConnection(). createPool() also supports some additional options that are pool specific. These options are listed in Table 14-1.

Listing 14-10. Creating a Connection Pool Using the createPool() Method

```
var mysql = require("mysql");
var pool = mysql.createPool({
  "host": "localhost",
  "user": "username",
  "password": "secret",
  "database": "dbname"
});
```

Table 14-1. *Additional Options Supported by createPool()*

Option	Description
createConnection	The function to use when creating pool connections. This defaults to createConnection().
connectionLimit	The maximum number of connections that can be created at once. If omitted, this defaults to 10.
queueLimit	The maximum number of connection requests that can be queued by the pool. If this value is zero (the default), then there is no limit. If a limit exists and it is exceeded, then an error is returned from createConnection().
waitForConnections	If this is true (the default), then requests are added to a queue if there are no available connections. If this is false, then the pool will immediately call back with an error.

The pool's getConnection() method is used to request a connection. This method takes a callback function as its only argument. The callback function's arguments are a possible error condition and the requested connection object. If no error occurs, then the connection object will already be in the connected state, meaning that there is no need to call connect(). Listing 14-11 shows how a connection is requested from a pool.

Listing 14-11. Requesting a Connection from a Pool Using the getConnection() Method

```
var mysql = require("mysql");
var pool = mysql.createPool({
  "host": "localhost",
  "user": "username",
  "password": "secret",
  "database": "dbname"
});
```

```
pool.getConnection(function(error, connection) {
  if (error) {
    return console.error(error);
  }

  // Connection available for use
});
```

Closing a Connection

A non-pooled connection can be closed using the end( ) and destroy( ) methods. The end( ) method closes the connection gracefully, allowing any queued queries to execute. end( ) takes a callback as its only argument. Listing 14-12 shows how end( ) is used to close an opened connection.

Listing 14-12. Opening a Connection and then Closing it Using end( )

```
var mysql = require("mysql");
var connection =
  mysql.createConnection("mysql://username:secret@localhost/dbname");

connection.connect(function(error) {
  if (error) {
    return console.error(error);
  }

  connection.end(function(error) {
    if (error) {
      return console.error(error);
    }
  });
});
```

The destroy( ) method, on the other hand, immediately shuts down the underlying socket, regardless of what is going on. The usage of destroy( ) is shown in Listing 14-13.

Listing 14-13. Usage of the connection.destroy( ) Method

```
connection.destroy();
```

Pooled connections are closed using the release( ) and destroy( ) methods. release( ) does not actually terminate the connection but simply returns it to the pool for use by another request. Alternatively, the destroy( ) method is used to terminate a connection and remove it from the pool. The next time a new connection is requested, the pool will create a new one to replace the destroyed one. Listing 14-14 provides an example of the release( ) method
in action.

Listing 14-14. Releasing a Pooled Connection Using the release( ) Method

```
var mysql = require("mysql");
var pool = mysql.createPool({
  "host": "localhost",
```

```
    "user": "username",
    "password": "secret",
    "database": "dbname"
});

pool.getConnection(function(error, connection) {
  if (error) {
    return console.error(error);
  }

  connection.release();
});
```

Executing Queries

You've learned how to open connections, and you've learned how to close connections. Now it's time to learn what goes on between the opening and closing. After connecting to the database, your application will execute one or more queries. This is accomplished using the connection's query( ) method. The query( ) method takes two arguments—a SQL string to execute and a callback function. The arguments to the callback function are a possible error object and the results of the SQL command.

Listing 14-15 shows a complete example that creates a connection pool, requests a connection, executes a SQL query on the Person table, displays the results, and then releases the connection back to the pool. The resulting output is shown in Listing 14-16.

Listing 14-15. Executing a Query on the Person Table

```
var mysql = require("mysql");
var pool = mysql.createPool({
  "host": "localhost",
  "user": "username",
  "password": "secret",
  "database": "dbname"
});

pool.getConnection(function(error, connection) {
  if (error) {
    return console.error(error);
  }

  var sql = "SELECT * FROM Person";

  connection.query(sql, function(error, results) {
    if (error) {
      return console.error(error);
    }

    console.log(results);
    connection.release();
  });
});
```

Listing 14-16. The Output of the Code in Listing 14-15

```
$ node sql-query.js
[ { SSN: '123-45-6789',
    LastName: 'Pluck',
    FirstName: 'Peter',
    Gender: 'M',
    City: 'Pittsburgh',
    State: 'PA' },
  { SSN: '234-56-7890',
    LastName: 'Johnson',
    FirstName: 'John',
    Gender: 'M',
    City: 'San Diego',
    State: 'CA' },
  { SSN: '345-67-8901',
    LastName: 'Doe',
    FirstName: 'Jane',
    Gender: 'F',
    City: 'Las Vegas',
    State: 'NV' },
  { SSN: '456-78-9012',
    LastName: 'Doe',
    FirstName: 'John',
    Gender: 'M',
    City: 'Las Vegas',
    State: 'NV' } ]
```

Notice that the results displayed in Listing 14-16 are formatted as an array of objects. That is because the executed query was a SELECT operation. Had the operation been a different type (UPDATE, INSERT, DELETE, and so on) then the result would have been a single object containing information about the operation. As an example, the command in Listing 14-17 removes all of the individuals in the People table. The resulting object is shown in Listing 14-18. Notice that the affectedRows property is set to four to indicate the number of tuples that were removed.

Listing 14-17. SQL DELETE Command for Clearing the People Table

```
DELETE FROM People;
```

Listing 14-18. The Result Object from query( ) When Executing the Statement in Listing 14-17

```
{ fieldCount: 0,
  affectedRows: 4,
  insertId: 0,
  serverStatus: 34,
  warningCount: 0,
  message: '',
  protocol41: true,
  changedRows: 0 }
```

■ **Note**   The result object's insertId property is useful when inserting rows into a table that has an auto increment primary key.

NoSQL Databases

NoSQL databases represent the other major flavor of database. There are many types of NoSQL databases available, with some examples being key/value stores, object stores, and document stores. Common NoSQL characteristics are lack of schemas, simple APIs, and relaxed consistency models. The one thing that NoSQL databases have in common is that they abandon the relational data model used by systems like MySQL in the pursuit of increased performance and scalability.

The relational data model excels at keeping data consistent using atomic operations known as *transactions*. However, maintaining data consistency comes at the cost of additional overhead. Some applications such as banking require data to be absolutely correct. After all, a bank that loses track of its customers' money won't be in business very long. However, many applications can get away with the relaxed constraints that NoSQL data stores provide. For example, if an update doesn't immediately show up on a social media newsfeed, it won't be the end of the world.

MongoDB

One of the most prominent NoSQL databases used in conjunction with Node.js is MongoDB, sometimes referred to as just Mongo. Mongo is a document-oriented database that stores data in BSON (Binary JSON) formatted documents. Mongo's prominent use in Node applications has given rise to the term MEAN stack. The acronym MEAN refers to the popular software stack consisting of MongoDB, Express, AngularJS (a front-end framework used to create single-page applications), and Node.js. Mongo has been used at many popular web companies, including eBay, Foursquare, and Craigslist.

To access Mongo from within a Node application, a driver is required. There are a number of Mongo drivers available, but Mongoose is among the most popular. Listing 14-19 shows the npm command used to install the mongoose module.

Listing 14-19. Command Used to Install the mongoose Module

```
$ npm install mongoose
```

Connecting to MongoDB

The createConnection() method is used to create a new MongoDB connection. This method takes a MongoDB URL as an input argument. An example URL, which uses the same connection parameters as the previous MySQL examples, is shown in Listing 14-20. In this example, username, secret, localhost, and dbname correspond to the username, password, server host, and database name, respectively.

Listing 14-20. Connecting to MongoDB Using Mongoose

```
var mongoose = require("mongoose");
var connection =
  mongoose.createConnection("mongodb://username:secret@localhost/dbname");
```

■ **Note**   There are multiple ways to create connections in MongoDB. The method shown in this book is believed to be the most flexible as it works with an arbitrary number of database connections. The alternative technique is no simpler, yet it only works with a single database connection.

Once the connection is established, the connection object emits an open event. The open event handler does not take any arguments. An example handler is shown in Listing 14-21. Notice that the close( ) method is also used to terminate the connection.

Listing 14-21. An Example Connection open Event Handler

```
var mongoose = require("mongoose");
var connection = mongoose.createConnection("mongodb://localhost/test");

connection.on("open", function() {
  console.log("Connection established");
  connection.close();
});
```

Schemas

MongoDB does not have a predefined schema. Mongoose helps to define the structure of a Mongo document by defining schemas. A *schema* is an object that defines the structure of the data to be stored. To illustrate how schemas work, we are going to revisit our People table from the MySQL section. Listing 14-22 shows the People table refactored as a Mongoose Schema object. On the second line of the example, the Schema( ) constructor is imported. The Schema( ) constructor takes a single argument, an object containing schema definitions. In this example, all of the schema fields are of type String. Other data types supported by Schema( ) include Number, Date, Buffer, Boolean, Mixed, Objectid, and Array.

Listing 14-22. Creating a Schema Representing the Person Table

```
var mongoose = require("mongoose");
var Schema = mongoose.Schema;
var PersonSchema = new Schema({
  SSN: String,
  LastName: String,
  FirstName: String,
  Gender: String,
  City: String,
  State: String
});
```

Recall that the original Person table was referenced by a Vehicle table using a foreign key relationship. In the world of relational databases, this was a good idea. However, in the MongoDB world, the vehicle information can be added directly to the Person schema as an array. Listing 14-23 shows the schema for the Person-Vehicle hybrid. Note that this approach requires no JOIN operations.

Listing 14-23. Combining the Person and Vehicle Tables in a MongoDB Schema

```
var mongoose = require("mongoose");
var Schema = mongoose.Schema;
var PersonSchema = new Schema({
  SSN: String,
  LastName: String,
  FirstName: String,
  Gender: String,
  City: String,
```

```
  State: String,
  Vehicles: [{
    VIN: Number,
    Type: String,
    Year: Number
  }]
});
```

Models

To use our newly created Schema object, we must associate it with a database connection. In Mongoose terminology, this association is referred to as a *model*. To create a model, use the connection object's model( ) method. This method takes two arguments, a string representing the model's name, and a Schema object. Listing 14-24 shows how a Person model is created. The example defines the Person model as a module export in order to facilitate code reuse.

Listing 14-24. Defining a Person Model in a Reusable Manner

```
var mongoose = require("mongoose");
var Schema = mongoose.Schema;
var PersonSchema = new Schema({
  SSN: String,
  LastName: String,
  FirstName: String,
  Gender: String,
  City: String,
  State: String,
  Vehicles: [{
    VIN: Number,
    Type: String,
    Year: Number
  }]
});

module.exports = {
  getModel: function getModel(connection) {
    return connection.model("Person", PersonSchema);
  }
};
```

Because the Person model has been designed with reusability in mind, it can be easily imported into other files, as shown in Listing 14-25. This example assumes that the model has been saved in a file named PersonModel.js.

Listing 14-25. Importing the Person Model in Another File

```
var mongoose = require("mongoose");
var connection = mongoose.createConnection("mongodb://localhost/test");
var Person = require(__dirname + "/PersonModel").getModel(connection);
```

Inserting Data

Inserting data into MongoDB is a simple two-step process using Mongoose models. The first step is to instantiate an object using a model constructor. Based on Listing 14-25, the constructor would be Person( ). After the object is created, you can manipulate it like any other JavaScript object. To actually insert the data, call the model's save( ) method. save( ) takes a single optional argument, a callback function that takes an error argument.

The example in Listing 14-26 creates a Person object using the model defined in Listing 14-24. Next, a custom foo field is added to the module. Finally, the model's save( ) method is used to insert the data into the database. One thing to note is that when the data is saved, the foo field will not persist. The reason is that foo is not part of the model's schema. The model will prevent additional data from being added to the model, but it will not ensure that any missing fields are included. For example, if the LastName field was omitted, the insertion would still go off without a hitch.

Listing 14-26. Inserting a Person Object into MongoDB Using Mongoose

```
var mongoose = require("mongoose");
var connection = mongoose.createConnection("mongodb://localhost/test");
var Person = require(__dirname + "/PersonModel").getModel(connection);

connection.on("open", function() {
  var person = new Person({
    SSN: "123-45-6789",
    LastName: "Pluck",
    FirstName: "Peter",
    Gender: "M",
    City: "Pittsburgh",
    State: "PA",
    Vehicles: [
      {
        VIN: 12345,
        Type: "Jeep",
        Year: 2014
      },
      {
        VIN: 98032,
        Type: "Car",
        Year: 2006
      }
    ]
  });

  person.foo = "bar";
  person.save(function(error) {
    connection.close();

    if (error) {
      return console.error(error);
    } else {
      console.log("Successfully saved!");
    }
  });
});
```

Querying Data

Models have several methods for performing queries. To retrieve data from Mongo, use the model object's find( ) method. The first argument passed to find( ) is an object that defines the condition(s) of the query. This argument will be revisited momentarily. The second argument to find( ) is an optional callback function. If present, the callback function takes a possible error as its first argument, and the query results as the second argument.

The example in Listing 14-27 uses the Person model's find( ) method to select all car owners that live in Las Vegas. The condition object selects all Las Vegas citizens by specifying City: "Las Vegas". To further refine the search, we look for Vehicle arrays whose size is not equal to zero (meaning that the person owns at least one car). The results are then displayed in the callback function, provided that no errors occur. Sample output is shown in Listing 14-28.

Listing 14-27. Querying MongoDB for All Car Owners Living in Las Vegas

```
var mongoose = require("mongoose");
var connection = mongoose.createConnection("mongodb://localhost/test");
var Person = require(__dirname + "/PersonModel").getModel(connection);

connection.on("open", function() {
  Person.find({
    City: "Las Vegas",
    Vehicles: {
      $not: {$size: 0}
    }
  }, function(error, results) {
    connection.close();

    if (error) {
      return console.error(error);
    }

    console.log(results);
  });
});
```

Listing 14-28. Output from Running the Code in Listing 14-27

```
$ node mongoose-query
[ { City: 'Las Vegas',
    FirstName: 'Jane',
    Gender: 'F',
    LastName: 'Doe',
    SSN: '345-67-8901',
    State: 'NV',
    __v: 0,
    _id: 528190b19e13b00000000007,
    Vehicles:
     [ { VIN: 54327,
         Type: 'Truck',
         Year: 2009,
         _id: 528190b19e13b00000000008 } ] } ]
```

Query Builder Methods

If a callback function is not provided to find( ), then a query object is returned. This query object provides a query builder interface that allows more complex queries to be constructed by chaining together function calls using helper methods. Some of these helper functions are discussed in Table 14-2.

Table 14-2. *Various Query Builder Helper Methods*

Method	Description
where()	Creates an additional search refinement. This is analogous to the SQL WHERE clause.
limit()	Takes an integer argument specifying the maximum number of results to return.
sort()	Sorts the results by some criteria. This is analogous to the SQL ORDER BY clause.
select()	Returns a subset of the fields that have been selected.
exec()	Executes the query and invokes a callback function.

An example query builder is shown in Listing 14-29. In this example, the find( ) method is used to select all individuals from Las Vegas. The where( ) and equals( ) methods are then used to refine the search further to individuals whose last name is Doe. Next, the limit( ) method is used to ensure that a maximum of 10 individuals are selected. The sort( ) method is then used to sort the results by last name and then reverse order by first name. Next, the select( ) method is used to extract only the first name and last name fields from the results. Finally, the query is executed and the results are printed. This particular query will return John and Jane Doe from our example database.

Listing 14-29. An Example of a Query Builder

```
var mongoose = require("mongoose");
var connection = mongoose.createConnection("mongodb://localhost/test");
var Person = require(__dirname + "/PersonModel").getModel(connection);

connection.on("open", function() {
  Person.find({
    City: "Las Vegas"
  })
  .where("LastName").equals("Doe")
  .limit(10)
  .sort("LastName -FirstName")
  .select("FirstName LastName")
  .exec(function(error, results) {
    connection.close();

    if (error) {
      return console.error(error);
    }

    console.log(results);
  });
});
```

Updating Data

In Mongoose, data is updated using a model's update( ) method. update( ) takes two required arguments, followed by two optional arguments. The first argument is an object used to specify the conditions of the update. This object behaves like the object passed to find( ). The second argument to update( ) is an object that performs the actual update operation. The optional third argument is another object that is used to pass in options. The options supported by update( ) are summarized in Table 14-3. The final argument is an optional callback function that takes three arguments. These arguments are an error, the number of updated Mongo documents, and the raw response returned by Mongo.

Table 14-3. *The Options Supported by update( )*

Option	Description
safe	This is a Boolean that sets the value of safe mode. If this is not specified, it defaults to the value set in the schema (true). If this is true, then any errors that occur are passed to the callback function.
upsert	If this is true, the document will be created if it doesn't exist. This defaults to false.
multi	If true, multiple documents can be updated with a single operation. This defaults to false.
strict	This is a Boolean that sets the strict option for the update. If strict is true, then non-schema data will not written to the document. This defaults to false, meaning that extraneous data will not persist.

The example in Listing 14-30 performs an update operation on all people whose city of residence is Las Vegas. The second argument updates their city of residence to be New York. The third argument sets the multi option to true, meaning that multiple documents can be updated using a single operation. The callback function checks for errors and then displays the number of affected documents and the response received from Mongo.

Listing 14-30. An Update that Moves All Las Vegas Citizens to New York

```
var mongoose = require("mongoose");
var connection = mongoose.createConnection("mongodb://localhost/test");
var Person = require(__dirname + "/PersonModel").getModel(connection);

connection.on("open", function() {
  Person.update({
    City: "Las Vegas"
  }, {
    City: "New York"
  }, {
    multi: true
  }, function(error, numberAffected, rawResponse) {
    connection.close();

    if (error) {
      return console.error(error);
    }

    console.log(numberAffected + " documents affected");
    console.log(rawResponse);
  });
});
```

Deleting Data

To delete data using a model, use the model's remove( ) method. remove( ) takes two arguments. The first argument is an object that specifies the removal criteria. This object works like the object passed to find( ). The second argument is an optional callback function that is invoked after the removal is executed. An example that removes people who live in San Diego is shown in Listing 14-31. When this code is executed, it will display the number 1, corresponding to the number of items removed.

Listing 14-31. Removing Data Using a MongoDB Model

```
var mongoose = require("mongoose");
var connection = mongoose.createConnection("mongodb://localhost/test");
var Person = require(__dirname + "/PersonModel").getModel(connection);

connection.on("open", function() {
  Person.remove({
    City: "San Diego"
  }, function(error, response) {
    connection.close();

    if (error) {
      return console.error(error);
    }

    console.log(response);
  });
});
```

Summary

This chapter showed you how to work with databases in Node.js. The chapter began with a look at the more traditional relational data model. After a very brief overview of relational databases, we moved on to the MySQL database. By introducing the mysql module, you learned how to interact with one of the most popular relational databases in existence. Next, the chapter turned its focus to the NoSQL class of data stores. These databases have become increasingly popular in recent years as they tend to be less complex and more performant than their relational counterparts. Out of all of the NoSQL databases available, this chapter chose to focus on MongoDB, as it is a part of the increasingly popular MEAN stack. To work with Mongo, we turned to the mongoose module. Of course we couldn't possibly cover every database (or even every detail of MySQL and Mongo) in a single chapter, but by understanding the core concepts, you should be able to apply what you've learned here to other systems.

■ ■ ■

## CHAPTER 15

Logging, Debugging, and Testing

Production code, in any language, must have a certain polish that is lacking in toy or academic programs. This chapter explores the topics of logging, debugging, and testing, which will increase code quality while reducing the time required to diagnose and fix bugs. By logging useful information and errors, you can more easily fix bugs once they appear. A debugger is a critical tool in any programmer's toolbelt, as it allows code to be explored with a fine-toothed comb, inspecting variables and finding bugs. Finally, testing is the process of systematically identifying bugs in computer programs. This chapter looks at several prominent modules and frameworks used for logging, debugging, and testing.

Logging

In Chapter 5, you learned about logging at its most basic level via the console.log() and console.error() methods. The first thing to notice is that there are different logging methods for different types of messages. For example, in Listing 15-1, the fs module is used to open a file named foo.txt. If the file is successfully opened, then a message is printed to stdout using console.log(). However, if an error occurs, it is logged to stderr using console.error().

Listing 15-1. An Example Including Error and Success Logs

```
var fs = require("fs");
var path = "foo.txt";

fs.open(path, "r", function(error, fd) {
  if (error) {
    console.error("open error:  " + error.message);
  } else {
    console.log("Successfully opened " + path);
  }
});
```

The drawback to this approach is that someone must be watching the console to detect errors. Typically though, production applications are deployed to one or more servers that are separate from the machine(s) that the application was originally developed on. These production servers also typically sit in a server room, data center, or on the cloud, and do not have a person monitoring a terminal window for errors. Even if someone were monitoring the console, the errors could easily scroll off the screen and be lost forever. For these reasons, printing to the console is generally discouraged in production environments.

Logging to a file is preferred to console logging in production environments. Unfortunately, the fs module does not lend itself well to logging. Ideally, logging code should blend in with the application code like a console.log() call would. However, the asynchronous nature of file operations leads to code blocks that include callback functions and error handling. Recall that the fs module also provides synchronous equivalents for many of its methods. These should be avoided, as they can create a major bottleneck in your application.

The winston Module

Node's core modules do not provide an ideal logging solution. Luckily, the developer community has created a number of useful third-party logging modules. Among the best is winston, an asynchronous logging library that maintains the simplistic interface of console.log(). Listing 15-2 shows how winston is imported and used in a trivial application. Of course, you must first npm install winston in order to use the module. Listing 15-2 demonstrates how the winston.log() method is used. The first argument passed to log() is the logging level. By default, winston provides the log levels info, warn, and error. The second argument to log() is the message being logged.

Listing 15-2. Logging Different Level Messages Using winston

```
var winston = require("winston");

winston.log("info", "Hello winston!");
winston.log("warn", "Something not so good happened");
winston.log("error", "Something really bad happened");
```

The output from Listing 15-2 is shown in Listing 15-3. Notice that winston displays the log level before outputting the message.

Listing 15-3. The Output from Listing 15-2

```
$ node winston-basics.js
info: Hello winston!
warn: Something not so good happened
error: Something really bad happened
```

winston also provides convenience methods for the various log levels. These methods (info(), warn(), and error()) are shown in Listing 15-4. The output for this code is identical to that shown in Listing 15-3.

Listing 15-4. Rewriting Listing 15-2 Using the Log Level Methods

```
var winston = require("winston");

winston.info("Hello winston!");
winston.warn("Something not so good happened");
winston.error("Something really bad happened");
```

All of the logging methods described thus far support string formatting using util.format() placeholders. For a refresher on util.format(), see Chapter 5. An optional callback function can be provided as the final argument to the logging methods. Additionally, metadata can be attached to a log message by providing an argument after any formatting placeholders. Listing 15-5 shows these features in action. In this example, if an error occurs, winston logs a message that contains the value of the path variable. Additionally, the actual error is passed to winston as metadata. Example output when the file foo.txt does not exist is shown in Listing 15-6.

Listing 15-5. An Example of a Log Containing Formatting and Metadata

```
var winston = require("winston");
var fs = require("fs");
var path = "foo.txt";
```

```
fs.open(path, "r", function(error, fd) {
  if (error) {
    winston.error("An error occurred while opening %s.", path, error);
  } else {
    winston.info("Successfully opened %s.", path);
  }
});
```

Listing 15-6 *The Resulting Output of Listing 15-5 When the File Does Not Exist*

```
$ node winston-formatting.js
error: An error occurred while opening foo.txt. errno=34, code=ENOENT, path=foo.txt
```

Transports

winston makes extensive use of *transports*. Transports are essentially storage devices for logs. The core transport types supported by winston are Console, File, and Http. As the name implies, the Console transport is used for logging information to the console. The File transport is used for logging to an output file or any other writable stream. The Http transport is used to log data to an arbitrary HTTP (or HTTPS) endpoint. By default, the winston logger uses only the Console transport, but that can be changed. A logger can have multiple transports, or no transports at all.

Additional transports can be attached to a logger using the add() method. add() takes two arguments, a transport type and an options object. The supported options are listed in Table 15-1. It is worth noting that the supported options vary by transport type. Similarly, an existing transport is removed using the remove() method. The remove() method accepts the transport type as its only argument.

Table 15-1. *The Options Supported by the winston Core Transports*

Option	Description
level	The log level used by the transport.
silent	A Boolean used to suppress output. Defaults to false.
colorize	A Boolean flag used to make the output colorful. Defaults to false.
timestamp	A Boolean flag that causes timestamps to be included in the output. Defaults to false.
filename	The name of the file to log output to.
maxsize	The maximum size (in bytes) of the log file. If the size is exceeded, a new file is created.
maxFiles	The maximum number of log files to ceate when the size of the log file is exceeded.
stream	The writable stream to log output to.
json	A Boolean flag that, when enabled, causes data to be logged as JSON. Defaults to true.
host	The remote host used for HTTP logging. Defaults to localhost.
port	The remote port used for HTTP logging. Defaults to 80 or 443, depending on whether HTTP or HTTPS is used.
path	The remote URI used for HTTP logging. Defaults to /.
auth	An object that, if included, should contain a username and password field. This is used for HTTP Basic Authentication.
ssl	A Boolean flag that, if enabled, causes HTTPS to be used. Defaults to false.

Listing 15-7 shows how transports can be removed and added to the winston logger. In this example, the default Console transport is removed. A new Console transport, which responds only to error messages, is then added. The new transport also turns on colorization and timestamping. Note that the remove() and add() methods can be chained together. After winston is configured, the new settings are tested with calls to info() and error(). The output will display a timestamped, colorized message for the call to error(), but the call to info() will not display anything, as there is no transport for info level logging.

Listing 15-7. Adding and Removing Transports Using winston

```
var winston = require("winston");

winston
  .remove(winston.transports.Console)
  .add(winston.transports.Console, {
    level: "error",
    colorize: true,
    timestamp: true
  });

winston.info("test info");
winston.error("test error");
```

Creating New Loggers

The default logger uses the winston object, as demonstrated in previous examples. It is also possible to create new logger objects using the winston.Logger() constructor. The example in Listing 15-8 creates a new logger with two transports. The first transport prints colorized output to the console. The second transport dumps errors to the file output.log. To test the new logger, one call is made to info() and another is made to error(). Both logging calls will be printed to the console; however, only the error is printed to the output file.

Listing 15-8. Creating a New Logger Using winston

```
var winston = require("winston");
var logger = new winston.Logger({
  transports: [
    new winston.transports.Console({
      colorize: true
    }),
    new winston.transports.File({
      level: "error",
      filename: "output.log"
    })
  ]
});

logger.info("foo");
logger.error("bar");
```

Debugging

Debugging is the process of locating and fixing software bugs. A debugger is a program that helps accelerate this process. Among other things, debuggers allow developers to step through instructions one-by-one, inspecting the value of variables along the way. Debuggers are extremely useful for diagnosing program crashes and unexpected values. V8 comes with a built-in debugger that can be accessed over TCP. This allows a Node application to be debugged over a network. Unfortunately, the built-in debugger has a less than friendly command-line interface.

To access the debugger, Node must be invoked with the debug argument. Therefore, if your application were stored in app.js, you would need to execute the command shown in Listing 15-9.

Listing 15-9. Enabling Node's Debugger When Running an Application

```
node debug app.js
```

■ **Note**   Providing the debug argument causes Node to launch with an interactive debugger. However, you can also provide a --debug (notice the hyphens) option, which causes the debugger to listen for connections on port 5858. A third option, --debug-brk, causes the debugger to listen on port 5858 while also setting a breakpoint on the first line.

You can then step through the code as you would in any other debugger. The commands used to step through code are shown in Table 15-2.

Table 15-2. *Instruction Stepping Commands Supported by the Node Debugger*

Command	Description
cont or c	Continues execution.
next or n	Steps to the next instruction.
step or s	Steps in to a function call.
out or o	Steps out of a function call.
pause	Pauses running code.

You likely will not want to step through your entire application. Therefore, you should also set breakpoints. The simplest way to add breakpoints is by adding debugger statements to the source code. These statements will cause a debugger to halt execution, but will be ignored if a debugger is not in use. The example shown in Listing 15-10 will cause the debugger to pause before the second assignment to foo.

Listing 15-10. An Example Application that Includes a debugger Statement

```
var foo = 2;
var bar = 3;

debugger;
foo = foo + bar;
```

After attaching the debugger, issue the cont or c command to continue to the debugger statement. At this point, the value of foo is 2, and the value of bar is 3. You can confirm this by entering the repl command, which will invoke the REPL that was covered in Chapter 1. Within the REPL, type foo or bar to inspect the variable value. Next, exit the REPL by pressing Control+C. Issue the next (or n) command twice, to step past the second assignment statement. By launching the REPL again, you can verify that the value has been updated to 5.

The previous example has laid out the general flow for using Node's debugger. As previously mentioned, the debugger isn't exactly user friendly. Luckily, there is a third-party module called node-inspector that allows Node's debugger to interface with Google Chrome's developer tools in a user-friendly way. Before diving into node-inspector, take a moment to review some of the other commands supported by Node's debugger, which are shown in Table 15-3.

Table 15-3. *Additional Commands Supported by the Node Debugger*

Command	Description
setBreakpoint() or sb()	Sets a breakpoint on the current line. As these are functions, you can also pass an argument to specify the line number on which to set the breakpoint. A breakpoint can be set on a line number in a specific file using the syntax sb("script.js", line).
clearBreakpoint() or cb()	Clears a breakpoint on the current line. As when using sb(), you can pass arguments in to clear breakpoints on specific lines.
backtrace or bt	Prints the backtrace of the current execution frame.
watch(expr)	Adds the expression specified by expr to the watch list.
unwatch(expr)	Removes the expression specified by expr from the watch list.
watchers	Lists all watchers and their values.
run	Runs the script.
restart	Restarts the script.
kill	Kills the script.
list(n)	Displays source code with n line context (n lines before and n lines after the current line).
scripts	Lists all loaded scripts.
version	Displays the version of v8.

The node-inspector Module

This section does not provide a tutorial on using Chrome's developer tools. Luckily, they are fairly self-explanatory, and there is an abundance of content available online. This section steps you through the process of getting node-inspector set up and running on your machine . You need to have a recent version of Chrome on your machine. You also need to install node-inspector globally using the command shown in Listing 15-11.

Listing 15-11. Globally Installing the node-inspector Module

```
npm install node-inspector -g
```

Next, start the application (saved in `app.js`) from Listing 15-10 using the command shown in Listing 15-12. Notice that the `--debug-brk` flag has been used. This is because we do not want to use the interactive debugger's command-line interface.

Listing 15-12. Launching an Application Using the `--debug-brk` Flag

```
$ node --debug-brk app.js
```

Next, in a separate terminal window, launch `node-inspector` using the command shown in Listing 15-13.

Listing 15-13. Launching the `node-inspector` Application

```
$ node-inspector
```

After starting `node-inspector`, you should see some terminal output. This output will include directions to visit a URL. The URL will most likely be the one shown in Listing 15-14. Visit this URL in Chrome. The page should look like Figure 15-1.

Listing 15-14. The URL to Visit While `node-inspector` Is Running

```
http://127.0.0.1:8080/debug?port=5858
```

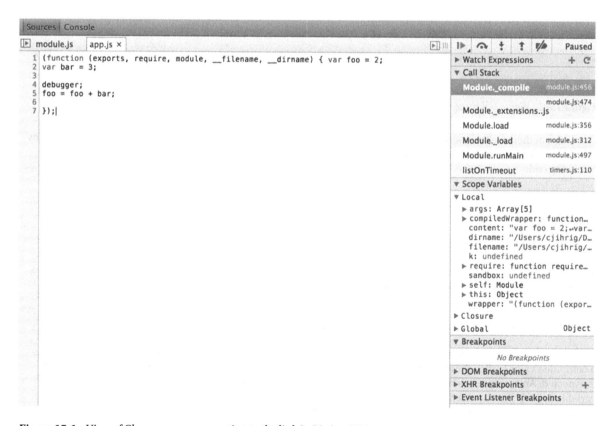

Figure 15-1. *View of Chrome upon connecting to the link in Listing 15-14*

Upon opening Chrome, execution is halted at a breakpoint. Resume execution by pressing the small Play button in the panel on the right side of the window. This will cause the application to execute until the next breakpoint is reached, at which point Chrome will look like Figure 15-2. Notice the Scope Variables section on the right side of the image. This section allows you to view the variables that are currently in scope, as well as their values. In Figure 15-2, you can see that foo is equal to 2 and bar is equal to 3.

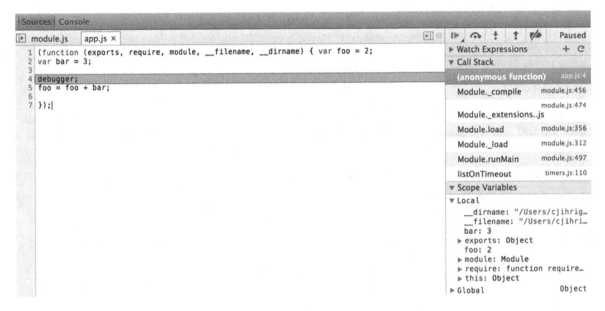

Figure 15-2. *View of Chrome stopped at a debugger statement*

You can then use the controls to step in, over, and out of instructions and functions while watching the variables update. Additionally, you can click on the Console tab to bring up an interactive console for inspecting values and executing code.

Testing

Testing is a crucial part of the software development process. It is so important that software companies have entire departments dedicated to testing. The goal of this section is not to provide comprehensive coverage of software testing. There are many books dedicated to the various software testing methodologies. Instead, this section teaches you how to write unit tests using the core assert module as well as Mocha, a flexible JavaScript testing framework.

The assert Module

assert is a core module that is used to write simple unit tests. assert provides convenience methods that compare a computed value (called the actual value) to an expected value, and throw an exception if the results are not what is expected. An example assertion is shown in Listing 15-15. In this example, a value is computed and stored in the variable actual. The expected value is also stored in the expected variable. The actual and expected values are then passed as the first and second arguments to the assert.strictEqual() method. As the method name implies, the two values are compared using strict equality (the === operator). In this case, the assertion test is passed, so nothing happens.

Listing 15-15. An Example Test Using a Strict Equals Assertion

```
var assert = require("assert");
var actual = 2 + 3;
var expected = 5;

assert.strictEqual(actual, expected);
```

Listing 15-16 examines the case where the assertion fails. In this example, the actual value is the sum of the floating point numbers 0.1 and 0.2, while the expected value is 0.3. Basic math would lead you to believe that the assertion will be passed. However, because of the way that floating point math works, the sum is not exactly 0.3. This causes the assertion to fail, and the exception shown in Listing 15-17 is thrown.

Listing 15-16. An Example of a Failed Assertion

```
var assert = require("assert");
var actual = 0.1 + 0.2;
var expected = 0.3;

assert.strictEqual(actual, expected);
```

By examining the error message in Listing 15-17, you can see that the actual value contains an extremely small amount of error. This is something that must be accounted for any time math is performed in JavaScript.

Listing 15-17. The Exception that Results from the Code in Listing 15-16

```
AssertionError: 0.30000000000000004 === 0.3
```

The basic assertion methods also take an optional third argument that is used to specify a custom error message. Listing 15-16 has been rewritten in Listing 15-18 to include a custom message. When this code is run, you will see the error message "AssertionError: JavaScript math is quirky".

Listing 15-18. Creating an Assertion with a Custom Error Message

```
var assert = require("assert");
var actual = 0.1 + 0.2;
var expected = 0.3;

assert.strictEqual(actual, expected, "JavaScript math is quirky");
```

In addition to strictEqual(), the assert module possesses a number of other methods that are used to create various types of assertions. These methods, which are used like strictEqual(), are summarized in Table 15-4.

Table 15-4. *Additional Assertion Methods*

Method	Description
equal()	Performs a shallow check for equality using the == comparison operator. Using a shallow check, two objects will not evaluate as equal unless they are, in fact, the same object.
notEqual()	Performs a shallow check for non-equality using the != comparison operator.
deepEqual()	Performs a deep check for equality. By using a deep check, equality is determined by comparing the keys and values stored in an object.
notDeepEqual()	Performs a deep check for inequality.
notStrictEqual()	Performs a check for strict inequality using the !== comparison operator.
ok()	ok()takes only two arguments—value and an optional message. This method works as shorthand for assert.equal(true, !!value, message). In other words, this method tests if the provided value is truthy.
assert()	This function is used exactly like ok(). However, this is not a method of the assert module, but rather the assert module itself. This function is the value returned by require("assert").

The throws() Method

The assert module also provides the throws() method to verify whether a given function throws an exception as expected. An example of throws() is shown in Listing 15-19. The block argument is the function under test, and is expected to throw an exception. If an exception is not thrown by block, the assertion will fail. The error argument will be revisited in a moment. The optional message argument behaves in the same fashion as it does for the previously discussed assertion methods.

Listing 15-19. Using assert.throws()

```
assert.throws(block, [error], [message])
```

The optional error argument is used to verify that the correct exception was thrown. This argument can be a constructor function, a regular expression object, or a user-defined validation function. If error is a constructor function, then the exception object is validated using the instanceof operator. If error is a regular expression, then validation is performed by testing for a match. If error is a non-constructor function, then the function should return true if error is validated.

As an example, assume that you are trying to test a function that performs division. If division by zero occurs, then the function under test should throw an exception. Otherwise, the function should return the quotient of the division operation. Listing 15-20 shows the definition of this division function, as well as several successful assertion tests using throws(). The bind() method creates copies of the divide() method whose numerator and denominator arguments are bound to specific values. In each of the example test cases, the denominator is bound to zero to ensure that an exception is thrown.

Listing 15-20. Testing a Division Function Using assert.throws()

```
var assert = require("assert");

function divide(numerator, denominator) {
  if (!denominator) {
    throw new RangeError("Division by zero");
  }
```

```
  return numerator / denominator;
}

assert.throws(divide.bind(null, 1, 0));
assert.throws(divide.bind(null, 2, 0), RangeError);
assert.throws(divide.bind(null, 3, 0), Error);
assert.throws(divide.bind(null, 4, 0), /Division by zero/);
assert.throws(divide.bind(null, 5, 0), function(error) {
  return error instanceof Error && /zero/.test(error.message);
});
```

In Listing 15-20, all of the assertions were successful. Listing 15-21 includes a number of example assertions that would throw exceptions. The first assertion fails because the denominator is not zero, so an exception is not thrown. The second assertion fails because a RangeError is thrown, but the TypeError constructor is provided. The third assertion fails because the regular expression /foo/ does not match the thrown exception. The fourth assertion fails because the validation function returns false.

Listing 15-21. Invalid Assertions Using the assert.throws() Method

```
var assert = require("assert");

function divide(numerator, denominator) {
  if (!denominator) {
    throw new RangeError("Division by zero");
  }

  return numerator / denominator;
}

assert.throws(divide.bind(null, 1, 1));
assert.throws(divide.bind(null, 2, 0), TypeError);
assert.throws(divide.bind(null, 3, 0), /foo/);
assert.throws(divide.bind(null, 4, 0), function(error) {
  return false;
});
```

The doesNotThrow() Method

The inverse function of throws() is doesNotThrow(), which expects a function to not throw an exception. The doesNotThrow() function is shown in Listing 15-22. The block argument is the function under test. If block throws an exception then the assertion fails. The optional message argument behaves as it does in the previously discussed assertion methods.

Listing 15-22. Using assert.doesNotThrow()

```
assert.doesNotThrow(block, [message])
```

The ifError() Method

The ifError() method is useful for testing the first argument of callback functions that is conventionally used for passing error conditions. Since error arguments are normally null or undefined, the ifError() method checks for falsy values. If a truthy value is detected then the assertion fails. For example, the assertion shown in Listing 15-23 passes, while the assertion shown in Listing 15-24 fails.

Listing 15-23. Successful Assertion Using `assert.ifError()`

```
var assert = require("assert");

assert.ifError(null);
```

Listing 15-24. Failed Assertion Using `assert.ifError()`

```
var assert = require("assert");

assert.ifError(new Error("error"));
```

The Mocha Testing Framework

The `assert` module is useful for writing small, simple unit tests. However, programs of serious complexity typically have large test suites for validating every feature of an application. Running comprehensive test suites also aids in *regression testing*—the testing of existing features to ensure that the addition of new code doesn't break existing code. Furthermore, as new bugs are found a unit test can be created for it and added to the test suite. In order to manage and run a large test suite, you should turn to a testing framework. There are many testing frameworks available, but this section focuses on Mocha. Mocha was created by TJ Holowaychuk, the creator of Express, and touts itself as a "simple, flexible, fun JavaScript test framework for Node.js and the browser."

Running Mocha

Mocha must be installed before it can be used. Although Mocha can be installed on a project-by-project basis, it is simpler to install it globally using the command shown in Listing 15-25.

Listing 15-25. Globally Installing the Mocha Framework

```
$ npm install -g mocha
```

By installing Mocha globally, you can launch it directly from the command line using the `mocha` command. By default, `mocha` will attempt to execute JavaScript source files in the `test` subdirectory. If the `test` subdirectory does not exist, it will look for a file named `test.js` in the current directory. Alternatively, you can specify a test file by simply providing the file name on the command line. Listing 15-26 shows example output from running `mocha` in an empty directory. The output shows the number of tests that successfully ran, and the amount of time that they took. In this case, no tests were run, and there was one millisecond of overhead from running `mocha`.

Listing 15-26. Example Output from Running `mocha` with no Tests

```
$ mocha

  0 passing (1ms)
```

Creating Tests

Mocha allows multiple tests to be defined in a single JavaScript source file. Theoretically, a project's entire test suite could be included in a single file. However, for the sake of clarity and simplicity, only related tests should be placed in the same file. Individual tests are created using the `it()` function. `it()` takes two arguments, a string that describes what the test does, and a function that implements the test's logic. Listing 15-27 shows the simplest test possible. The test doesn't actually do anything, yet when it is run with mocha, it will be reported as a passed test. The reason that this test passes is because it doesn't throw an exception. In Mocha, a test is considered to have failed if it throws an exception.

Listing 15-27. A Trivial Mocha Test

```
it("An example test", function() {
});
```

Another thing worth noting about the test case in Listing 15-27 is that Mocha was never imported, yet the it() function is available. If you were to execute this test directly in Node, you would see an error because it() is not defined. However, by running the test through mocha, it() and other Mocha functions are brought into scope.

Creating Test Suites

Mocha groups tests together into suites using the describe() method. describe() takes two arguments. The first is a string that provides a description of the test suite. The second argument is a function containing zero or more tests. An example of a test suite containing two tests is shown in Listing 15-28.

Listing 15-28. A Simple Test Suite Containing Two Tests

```
describe("Test Suite 1", function() {
  it("Test 1", function() {
  });

  it("Test 2", function() {
  });
});
```

■ **Note** Although test suites are useful for grouping related tests together, they are not essential. If no test suites are specified, all tests will be placed in Mocha's preexisting, nameless global test suite.

Mocha also supports the nesting of test suites. For example, assume that you are creating tests for multiple classes in a framework. Each class is worthy of its own test suite. However, if a class is complex enough, then you might want to create test suites for individual pieces of functionality, such as methods. Listing 15-29 provides an example of how you might go about structuring your test suites. Notice that the example makes use of nested suites.

Listing 15-29. An Example of Nested Test Suites

```
describe("Class Test Suite", function() {
  describe("Method Test Suite", function() {
    it("Method Test 1", function() {
    });

    it("Method Test 2", function() {
    });
  });
});
```

Testing Asynchronous Code

Mocha also makes it extremely easy to test asynchronous code, which is absolutely necessary in order to work with Node. To create an asynchronous test, simply pass a callback function to it(). Conventionally, this callback function is named done(), and it is passed as an argument to the function passed to it(). When the test is finished, simply invoke done(), as shown in Listing 15-30.

Listing 15-30. The Mocha Test from Listing 15-27 Rewritten to be Asynchronous

```
it("An example asynchronous test", function(done) {
  done();
});
```

Defining a Failure

If a test does not yield the expected results, it is considered a failure. Mocha defines a failure as any test that throws an exception. This makes Mocha compatible with the assert module discussed earlier in this chapter. Listing 15-31 shows an example test that exercises the string indexOf() method. This simple test verifies that indexOf() returns -1 when the searched string is not found. Since the strings "World" and "Goodbye" are not found in the string "Hello Mocha!", both assertions will pass. However, if the value of str were changed to "Hello World!", then the first assertion would throw an exception, causing the test to fail.

Listing 15-31. An Example Test with Assertions

```
var assert = require("assert");

it("Should return -1 if not found", function() {
  var str = "Hello Mocha!";

  assert.strictEqual(str.indexOf("World"), -1);
  assert.strictEqual(str.indexOf("Goodbye"), -1);
});
```

An example of an asynchronous test that includes an assertion is shown in Listing 15-32. In this example, the fs.exists() method determines if a file exists. In this case, we are assuming that the file does exist, so the test will pass.

Listing 15-32. An Asynchronous Test Including an Assertion

```
var assert = require("assert");
var fs = require("fs");

it("Should return true if file exists", function(done) {
  var filename = "foo.txt";

  fs.exists(filename, function(exists) {
    assert(exists);
    done();
  });
});
```

■ **Note**   Error objects can be passed directly to done() in asynchronous tests. Doing so causes the test to fail as if an exception had been thrown.

Test Hooks

Mocha supports optional hooks that are called before and after tests are executed. These hooks are used to set up test data before a test runs, and clean up data after the test finishes. These before/after hooks come in two flavors. The first executes before, and the second executes after the entire test suite is run. These hooks are implemented using the before() and after() functions. The second variety of hooks are run before and after each individual test. To implement this type of hook, use the beforeEach() and afterEach() functions. All four of these functions take a hook function as their only argument. If the hook executes asynchronous code, then a done() callback should be supplied in the same manner as it would for the it() function.

Listing 15-33 demonstrates how hooks are used in Mocha test suites. This example includes all four types of hooks. To illustrate the flow of execution, the output from running this test suite is shown in Listing 15-34. Notice that the first and last things to execute are the hooks provided via before() and after(). Also notice that the after() hook has been implemented using asynchronous style, even though the hook function is synchronous. Next, notice that each individual test is run between calls to the beforeEach() and afterEach() hooks.

Listing 15-33. A Test Suite Containing Test Hooks and Two Tests

```
describe("Test Suite", function() {
  before(function() {
    console.log("Setting up the test suite");
  });

  beforeEach(function() {
    console.log("Setting up an individual test");
  });

  afterEach(function() {
    console.log("Tearing down an individual test");
  });

  after(function(done) {
    console.log("Tearing down the test suite");
    done();
  });

  it("Test 1", function() {
    console.log("Running Test 1");
  });

  it("Test 2", function() {
    console.log("Running Test 2");
  });
});
```

Listing 15-34. Console Output from Running the Test Suite in Listing 15-33

```
$ mocha

  Setting up the test suite
Setting up an individual test
Running Test 1
 Tearing down an individual test
```

```
Setting up an individual test
Running Test 2
 Tearing down an individual test
Tearing down the test suite

  2 passing (5ms)
```

Disabling Tests

Individual tests or test suites can be disabled using the skip() method. Listing 15-35 shows how individual tests are disabled. Notice that skip() has been applied to the second test. If this collection of tests is executed using mocha, only the first test will run. Similarly, entire test suites can be skipped using describe.skip().

Listing 15-35. Disabling a Test Using the skip() Method

```
it("Test 1", function() {
  console.log("Test 1");
});

it.skip("Test 2", function() {
  console.log("Test 2");
});
```

Running a Single Test Suite

The only() method is used to run a single suite or test. This eliminates the need to comment out large groups of tests when you want to run only one. Using only() is identical to using skip(), although the semantics are different. When the example shown in Listing 15-36 is run, only the second test will be executed.

Listing 15-36. Running a Single Test Using only()

```
it("Test 1", function() {
  console.log("Test 1");
});

it.only("Test 2", function() {
  console.log("Test 2");
});
```

Summary

This chapter introduced the topics of logging, debugging, and testing as they pertain to Node.js. All three of these topics are critical in diagnosing and resolving bugs. Debugging and testing are important parts of the development process because they help prevent bugs from making it into production code. Logging, on the other hand, helps track down bugs that slip through the cracks and make it into production. By implementing logging, debugging, and testing, you ensure that your code will have the polish necessary to move into production. The next chapter explores how production code can be deployed and scaled.

## CHAPTER 16

Application Scaling

Scaling Node.js applications can be a challenge. JavaScript's single threaded nature prevents Node from taking advantage of modern multi-core hardware. In order to scale effectively, Node applications must find a way to take advantage of all of the resources at their disposal. The `cluster` core module serves this purpose, allowing a single application to launch a collection of Node processes that share resources while distributing the load.

Another way to scale a Node application is to reduce the amount of work the application must complete. A perfect example of this is a web server that serves both static and dynamic content. Because static content does not change (or changes infrequently), a separate server, or even a *content delivery network* (CDN), can be used to handle static requests, leaving Node to handle dynamic content only. The upside of this approach is twofold. First, the load on Node's single thread is lightened significantly. Second, static content can be funneled through a CDN or server that is specifically optimized for static data. A common way to distribute load among multiple servers is to employ a reverse proxy server.

Perhaps the best example of application scaling in modern computing is the *cloud*. Cloud computing provides on demand application scaling, while distributing an application to multiple locations around the world. Two of the more popular Node.js cloud-computing platforms are Heroku and Nodejitsu. Both of these platforms allow you to deploy Node applications to the cloud, while specifying the number of processes used to handle the traffic.

This chapter explores various techniques for scaling Node applications. The chapter begins by examining the `cluster` module for scaling on a single machine. From there, the chapter moves on to scaling via the use of a reverse proxy server. Finally, the chapter concludes by showing how applications can be deployed to the cloud using Heroku and Nodejitsu.

The `cluster` Module

The core `cluster` module allows a single application to be forked as multiple processes. These processes run independently of one another, but can share ports in order to balance the load of incoming connections. To demonstrate how `cluster` works, let's begin by looking at a trivial HTTP server, shown in Listing 16-1. For any request, the server displays its process ID and the requested URL before returning a 200 status code and the message `"Hello World!"`.

Listing 16-1. A Very Simple Hello World HTTP Server

```
var http = require("http");

http.createServer(function(request, response) {
  console.log(process.pid + ":  request for " + request.url);
  response.writeHead(200);
  response.end("Hello World!");
}).listen(8000);
```

The server in Listing 16-1 will always run in a single process on a single processor core, no matter what. Given that most modern machines have at least two processors, it would be nice if one instance of the server could run on each available core. Note that we don't want to run multiple instances on a single core, as doing so can adversely affect performance by requiring constant context switching. Listing 16-2 shows exactly how this is accomplished using the cluster module.

Listing 16-2. The Server from Listing 16-1 Implemented Using the cluster Module

```
var http = require("http");
var cluster = require("cluster");
var numCPUs = require("os").cpus().length;

if (cluster.isMaster) {
  for (var i = 0; i < numCPUs; i++) {
    console.log("Forking child");
    cluster.fork();
  }
} else {
  http.createServer(function(request, response) {
    console.log(process.pid + ":  request for " + request.url);
    response.writeHead(200);
    response.end("Hello World!");
  }).listen(8000);
}
```

Listing 16-2 imports the cluster and os core modules, as well as the http module used in the original server. The os module's cpus() method returns an array containing the details of each core on the current machine. This array's length property determines the number of cores available to the application.

The subsequent if statement, which checks the value of cluster.isMaster, is the most important thing to understand when working with the cluster module. The master process is used to fork child processes, also referred to as *workers*. The child processes are then used to implement the application's real functionality. However, each forked child process executes the same code as the original master process. Without this if statement, the child processes would attempt to fork additional processes. By adding the if statement, the master process can fork a child process for each core, while the forked processes (which execute the else branch) implement the HTTP server on the shared port 8000.

■ **Note**   Just as cluster.isMaster identifies the master process, cluster.isWorker identifies a child process.

The fork() Method

The actual process forking is done using the cluster module's fork() method. Under the hood, the child_process.fork() method from Chapter 9 is called. This means that the master and worker processes can communicate via the built-in IPC channel. The cluster.fork() method can be called only from the master process. Although not shown in Listing 16-2, fork() takes an optional object as its only argument; that object represents the child process' environment. fork() also returns a cluster.Worker object, which can be used to interact with the child process.

When the master process attempts to fork a new worker, a fork event is emitted. Once the worker is successfully forked, it sends an online message to the master process. After receiving this message, the master emits an online event. The example in Listing 16-3 shows how the fork and online events are handled in a cluster application. Notice that the event handlers have been added to the master process only. Although the handlers could have been added to the worker processes as well, it would have been redundant as the events are emitted only in the master. You learn how to listen for similar events in the worker processes later in the chapter.

Listing 16-3. A cluster Example Including a fork Event Handler

```
var http = require("http");
var cluster = require("cluster");
var numCPUs = require("os").cpus().length;

if (cluster.isMaster) {
  cluster.on("fork", function(worker) {
    console.log("Attempting to fork worker");
  });

  cluster.on("online", function(worker) {
    console.log("Successfully forked worker");
  });

  for (var i = 0; i < numCPUs; i++) {
    cluster.fork();
  }
} else {
  // implement worker code
}
```

Changing the Default `fork()` Behavior

By default, calling fork() causes the current application to be forked. However, this behavior can be altered using the cluster.setupMaster() method. setupMaster() accepts a settings object as its only argument. The possible settings are described in Table 16-1. An example of setupMaster() is shown in Listing 16-4. In this example, the values passed to setupMaster() are the default values, and so the default behavior is still observed.

Table 16-1. The Various Settings Supported by setupMaster()

Setting	Description
exec	A string representing the worker file to fork. Defaults to __filename.
args	An array of string arguments passed to the worker. Defaults to the current process.argv variable, minus the first two arguments (the node application and the script).
silent	A Boolean value that defaults to false. When false, the worker's output is sent to the master's standard streams. When true, the worker's output is silenced.

Listing 16-4. A cluster Example that Uses setupMaster() to Set the Default Values

```
var http = require("http");
var cluster = require("cluster");
var numCPUs = require("os").cpus().length;

if (cluster.isMaster) {
  cluster.setupMaster({
    exec: __filename,
    args: process.argv.slice(2),
    silent: false
  });
```

```
  for (var i = 0; i < numCPUs; i++) {
    cluster.fork();
  }
} else {
  // implement worker code
}
```

The disconnect() Method

The disconnect() method causes all worker processes to gracefully terminate themselves. Once all of the workers have terminated, the master process can also terminate if no other events are in the event loop. disconnect() accepts an optional callback function as its only argument. It is called after all of the workers have died. An example that forks and then immediately terminates workers using disconnect() is shown in Listing 16-5.

Listing 16-5. A cluster Example that Terminates All Workers Using disconnect()

```
var http = require("http");
var cluster = require("cluster");
var numCPUs = require("os").cpus().length;

if (cluster.isMaster) {
  for (var i = 0; i < numCPUs; i++) {
    cluster.fork();
  }

  cluster.disconnect(function() {
    console.log("All workers have disconnected");
  });
} else {
  // implement worker code
}
```

When a child process terminates itself, it will close its IPC channel. This causes a disconnect event to be emitted in the master process. Once the child completely terminates, an exit event is emitted in the master. Listing 16-6 shows how these events are handled in the master process. Both event handlers take the worker in question as arguments. Notice that the exit handler also accepts code and signal arguments. These are the exit code and the name of the signal that killed the process. However, these might not be set if the worker exited abnormally. Therefore, the worker's exit code has been obtained from the worker object itself.

Listing 16-6. An Example that Handles disconnect and exit Events

```
var http = require("http");
var cluster = require("cluster");
var numCPUs = require("os").cpus().length;

if (cluster.isMaster) {
  cluster.on("disconnect", function(worker) {
    console.log("Worker " + worker.id + " disconnected");
  });
```

```
  cluster.on("exit", function(worker, code, signal) {
    var exitCode = worker.process.exitCode;

    console.log("Worker " + worker.id + " exited with code " + exitCode);
  });

  for (var i = 0; i < numCPUs; i++) {
    cluster.fork();
  }

  cluster.disconnect();
} else {
  // implement worker code
}
```

The exit event is extremely useful for restarting a worker following a crash. For example, in Listing 16-7 when an exit event is emitted, the master tries to determine if a crash occurred. In this example, we assume that all worker exits are crashes. When a crash is detected, fork() is called again to replace the crashed worker.

Listing 16-7. An Example that Restarts Crashed Worker Processes

```
var http = require("http");
var cluster = require("cluster");
var numCPUs = require("os").cpus().length;

if (cluster.isMaster) {
  cluster.on("exit", function(worker, code, signal) {
    // determine that a crash occurred
    var crash = true;

    if (crash) {
      console.log("Restarting worker");
      cluster.fork();
    }
  });

  for (var i = 0; i < numCPUs; i++) {
    cluster.fork();
  }
} else {
  // implement worker code
}
```

The workers Object

The master process can loop over all of its workers by iterating through the workers object, a property of the cluster module. Listing 16-8 shows how all of the forked workers are looped over using a for...in loop and the cluster. workers object. In this example, the forked workers are immediately terminated by calling each worker's kill() method.

Listing 16-8. An Example that Loops Over and Kills All Forked Workers

```
var http = require("http");
var cluster = require("cluster");
var numCPUs = require("os").cpus().length;

if (cluster.isMaster) {
  for (var i = 0; i < numCPUs; i++) {
    cluster.fork();
  }

  for (var id in cluster.workers) {
    console.log("Killing " + id);
    cluster.workers[id].kill();
  }
}
```

■ **Note**   `cluster.workers` is available only in the master process. However, each worker process can reference its own `worker` object via the `cluster.worker` property.

The Worker Class

The Worker class is used to interact with forked processes. In the master process, individual workers can be accessed via `cluster.workers`. From individual workers, the Worker class can be referenced via `cluster.worker`. Each worker process is assigned a unique ID (different from its process ID), which is available via the Worker's `id` property. The `ChildProcess` object created by `child_process.fork()` is also available via the Worker's `process` property. For more information on the ChildProcess class, see Chapter 9. The Worker class also contains a `send()` method, used for interprocess communication, which is identical to `ChildProcess.send()` (`process.send()` can also be used from within the worker process). As you've already seen in Listing 16-8, the Worker class also contains a `kill()` method, which is used to send signals to a worker process. By default the signal name is set to the string SIGTERM, but any other signal name can be passed in as an argument.

The Worker class also contains some of the same methods and events as the `cluster` module. For example, the `disconnect()` method and several events are shown in Listing 16-9. This example attaches event listeners for each individual worker, and then calls the Worker's `disconnect()` method. It is worth pointing out that there are some slight differences with these features at the Worker level. For example, the `disconnect()` method disconnects only the current worker instead of all workers. Also, the event handlers do not take a Worker as an argument, as they do at the cluster level.

Listing 16-9. Worker-Level Events and the `disconnect()` Method

```
var http = require("http");
var cluster = require("cluster");
var numCPUs = require("os").cpus().length;
var worker;

if (cluster.isMaster) {
  for (var i = 0; i < numCPUs; i++) {
    worker = cluster.fork();
```

```
  worker.on("online", function() {
    console.log("Worker " + worker.id + " is online");
  });

  worker.on("disconnect", function() {
    console.log("Worker " + worker.id + " disconnected");
  });

  worker.on("exit", function(code, signal) {
    console.log("Worker " + worker.id + " exited");
  });

  worker.disconnect();
  }
} else {
  // implement worker code
}
```

Scaling Across Machines

Using the cluster module, you can more effectively take advantage of modern hardware. However, you are still limited by the resources of a single machine. If your application receives significant traffic, eventually you will need to scale out to multiple machines. This can be done using a reverse proxy server that load balances the incoming requests among multiple servers. A reverse proxy retrieves resources from one or more servers on behalf of the client. By employing a reverse proxy and multiple application servers, the amount of traffic that an application can handle is increased. There are many reverse proxies available, but this section focuses on two specifically—http-proxy and nginx.

http-proxy

Nodejitsu, which we will discuss later, developed http-proxy, an open source module for implementing proxy servers and reverse proxy servers in Node applications. http-proxy supports WebSockets and HTTPS, among other things, and is thoroughly tested through production deployment at nodejitsu.com. Choosing http-proxy also allows you to keep your entire server stack written in JavaScript, if you so choose.

To demonstrate a solution involving a load balancing reverse proxy, we must first create the application servers, which are shown in Listing 16-10. The application servers are responsible for serving the content requested by the reverse proxy. This is the same basic HTTP server from Listing 16-1, adapted to read a port number from the command line.

Listing 16-10. A Simple Hello World Web Server that Reads a Port from the Command Line

```
var http = require("http");
var port = ~~process.argv[2];

http.createServer(function(request, response) {
  console.log(process.pid + ":  request for " + request.url);
  response.writeHead(200);
  response.end("Hello World!");
}).listen(port);
```

Run two separate instances of the HTTP server, with one listening on port 8001 and the other listening on port 8002. Next, create the reverse proxy, shown in Listing 16-11. Begin by installing the http-proxy module. The first line of Listing 16-11 imports the http-proxy module. The second line defines an array of servers that requests can be proxied to. In a real application, this information would likely come from a configuration file, and not be hard-coded. Next, the createServer() method, which should be familiar from working with HTTP, is used to define the behavior of the reverse proxy. The example server proxies requests in a round-robin fashion by maintaining an array of servers. As requests come in, they are proxied to the first server in the array. That server is then pushed to the end of the array to allow the next server to handle a request.

Listing 16-11. A Reverse Proxy Server Based on the http-proxy Module

```
var proxyServer = require("http-proxy");
var servers = [
  {
    host: "localhost",
    port: 8001
  },
  {
    host: "localhost",
    port: 8002
  }
];

proxyServer.createServer(function (req, res, proxy) {
  var target = servers.shift();

  console.log("proxying to " + JSON.stringify(target));
  proxy.proxyRequest(req, res, target);
  servers.push(target);
}).listen(8000);
```

Of course, the previous example uses only one machine. However, if you have access to multiple machines, you can run the reverse proxy on one machine, while one or more other machines run the HTTP server(s). You might also want to add code that handles static resources, such as images and stylesheets, in the proxy server, or even add another server all together.

nginx

Using a Node reverse proxy is nice because it keeps your software stack in the same technology. However, in production systems, it is more common to use nginx to handle load balancing and static content. nginx is an open source HTTP server and reverse proxy that is extremely good at serving static data. Therefore, nginx can be used to handle tasks such as caching and serving static files, while forwarding requests for dynamic content to the Node server(s).

To implement load balancing, you simply need to install nginx, then add the Node servers as upstream resources in the server configuration file. The configuration file is located at {nginx-root}/conf/nginx.conf, where {nginx-root} is the nginx root installation directory. The entire configuration file is shown in Listing 16-12; however, we are interested in only a few key pieces.

Listing 16-12. An nginx Configuration File with Node Servers Listed as Upstream Resources

```
#user   nobody;
worker_processes  1;

#error_log  logs/error.log;
#error_log  logs/error.log  notice;
#error_log  logs/error.log  info;

#pid        logs/nginx.pid;

events {
    worker_connections  1024;
}

http {
    include       mime.types;
    default_type  application/octet-stream;

    #log_format   main  '$remote_addr - $remote_user [$time_local] "$request" '
    #                     '$status $body_bytes_sent "$http_referer" '
    #                     '"$http_user_agent" "$http_x_forwarded_for"';

    #access_log  logs/access.log  main;

    sendfile        on;
    #tcp_nopush     on;

    #keepalive_timeout  0;
    keepalive_timeout  65;

    #gzip  on;

    upstream node_app {
      server 127.0.0.1:8001;
      server 127.0.0.1:8002;
    }

    server {
        listen       80;
        server_name  localhost;

        #charset koi8-r;

        #access_log  logs/host.access.log  main;

        location / {
            root   html;
            index  index.html index.htm;
        }
```

```
    location /foo {
      proxy_redirect off;
      proxy_set_header   X-Real-IP            $remote_addr;
      proxy_set_header   X-Forwarded-For $proxy_add_x_forwarded_for;
      proxy_set_header   X-Forwarded-Proto $scheme;
      proxy_set_header   Host                $http_host;
      proxy_set_header   X-NginX-Proxy      true;
      proxy_set_header   Connection "";
      proxy_http_version 1.1;
      proxy_pass         http://node_app;
    }

    #error_page  404              /404.html;

    # redirect server error pages to the static page /50x.html
    #
    error_page   500 502 503 504  /50x.html;
    location = /50x.html {
        root    html;
    }

    # proxy the PHP scripts to Apache listening on 127.0.0.1:80
    #
    #location ~ \.php$ {
    #    proxy_pass   http://127.0.0.1;
    #}

    # pass the PHP scripts to FastCGI server listening on 127.0.0.1:9000
    #
    #location ~ \.php$ {
    #    root           html;
    #    fastcgi_pass   127.0.0.1:9000;
    #    fastcgi_index  index.php;
    #    fastcgi_param  SCRIPT_FILENAME  /scripts$fastcgi_script_name;
    #    include        fastcgi_params;
    #}

    # deny access to .htaccess files, if Apache's document root
    # concurs with nginx's one
    #
    #location ~ /\.ht {
    #    deny  all;
    #}
}

# another virtual host using mix of IP-, name-, and port-based configuration
#
#server {
#    listen        8000;
#    listen        somename:8080;
#    server_name   somename  alias  another.alias;
```

```
#    location / {
#        root   html;
#        index  index.html index.htm;
#    }
#}

# HTTPS server
#
#server {
#    listen       443;
#    server_name  localhost;

#    ssl                  on;
#    ssl_certificate      cert.pem;
#    ssl_certificate_key  cert.key;

#    ssl_session_timeout  5m;

#    ssl_protocols  SSLv2 SSLv3 TLSv1;
#    ssl_ciphers  HIGH:!aNULL:!MD5;
#    ssl_prefer_server_ciphers   on;

#    location / {
#        root   html;
#        index  index.html index.htm;
#    }
#}

}
```

As previously mentioned, we are interested in only a few portions of the configuration file. The first interesting piece, which you must add to your configuration file, is shown in Listing 16-13 and defines an upstream server named node_app, which is balanced between two IP addresses. Of course, these IP addresses will vary based on the location of your servers.

Listing 16-13. An Upstream Resource Named node_app that Is Balanced Between Two Servers

```
upstream node_app {
  server 127.0.0.1:8001;
  server 127.0.0.1:8002;
}
```

Simply defining the upstream server does not tell nginx how to use the resource. Therefore, we must define a route using the directives shown in Listing 16-14. Using this route, any requests to /foo are proxied upstream to one of the Node servers.

Listing 16-14. Defining a Route that Is Reverse Proxied to Upstream Servers

```
location /foo {
  proxy_redirect off;
  proxy_set_header    X-Real-IP            $remote_addr;
  proxy_set_header    X-Forwarded-For  $proxy_add_x_forwarded_for;
```

```
proxy_set_header    X-Forwarded-Proto $scheme;
proxy_set_header    Host                    $http_host;
proxy_set_header    X-NginX-Proxy     true;
proxy_set_header    Connection "";
proxy_http_version 1.1;
proxy_pass          http://node_app;
}
```

Installing and configuring nginx is well beyond the scope of this book. In fact, there are entire books dedicated to nginx. This extremely brief introduction is just meant to get you pointed in the right direction. You can find more information about nginx on the project's home page at www.nginx.org.

Scaling in the Cloud

Computing resources are increasingly thought of as commodities. Cloud computing providers allow servers to be spun up and torn down in seconds in order to accommodate spikes in traffic. These servers can be geographically distributed throughout the world, and best of all, you typically pay only for the computing time you actually use. There are a number of public cloud providers to choose from, but this section focuses specifically on Nodejitsu and Heroku. This section introduces the basics of getting a Node application deployed using each of these platforms.

Nodejitsu

Nodejitsu, founded in April 2010, is a platform as a service (PaaS) company based out of New York City. Nodejitsu provides a set of command-line tools that are used to deploy applications to their cloud. To begin using Nodejitsu, you must first register for an account at www.nodejitsu.com. Although signing up is free, deploying your application is not. Nodejitsu will provide you with a free 30-day trial, but after that you have to pay a minimum of $9 per month (at the time of this writing) to host your application.

After signing up, you'll need to install Nodejitsu's command-line tool, jitsu. jitsu can be installed using the command npm install -g jitsu. During account creation, you will receive an e-mail with instructions on creating a jitsu account. The instructions include a command similar to the one shown in Listing 16-15. After entering the command e-mailed to you, your account will be created, and you will be prompted to create an account password.

Listing 16-15. Generic Command that Confirms a jitsu Account

```
$ jitsu users confirm username confirmation_code
```

Next, create a Node application as you normally would. For the purposes of this example, simply use the HTTP server from Listing 16-1. To deploy your project to Nodejitsu, it must contain a package.json file. If you need a refresher on the package.json file, see Chapter 2. Next, issue the command shown in Listing 16-16 from within your application's directory.

Listing 16-16. Deploying a Project Using jitsu

```
$ jitsu deploy
```

If your project does not contain a package.json file, jitsu will create one for you by stepping you through a short wizard. The package.json file should include the name, version, scripts, engines, and subdomain fields. The engines field should contain a node field to specify the required version of Node. Similarly, the scripts field should contain a start script so that Nodejitsu knows how to initialize your application. The subdomain will be used in your application's URL, and must be unique. An example package.json file suitable for jitsu deployment is shown in Listing 16-17. Notice that the subdomain shown in this example includes a username (cjihrig) to help ensure that the string is unique.

Listing 16-17. An Example `package.json` File Suitable for Nodejitsu Deployment

```
{
  "name": "simple-server",
  "subdomain": "simpleserver.cjihrig",
  "scripts": {
    "start": "simple-server.js"
  },
  "version": "0.0.1",
  "engines": {
    "node": "0.10.x"
  }
}
```

If everything is configured properly and your desired subdomain is available, your application will be deployed to Nodejitsu's cloud. To access your application, visit `http://subdomain.jit.su`, where `subdomain` is the value found in the `package.json` file.

Heroku

Heroku is a PaaS company founded in 2007 and acquired by `Salesforce.com` in 2010. Unlike Nodejitsu, Heroku is not strictly dedicated to Node. It supports Ruby, Java, Scala, and Python, among other languages. In order to deploy a Node application to Heroku, you need a Heroku user account. Signing up for Heroku is free, and unlike Nodejitsu, Heroku offers free hosting for small, single-core applications.

Begin by installing the Heroku Toolbelt on your local machine. You can download the Toolbelt from Heroku's site at `www.heroku.com`. Once the Toolbelt is installed, log in to Heroku using the command shown in Listing 16-18. After entering the login command, you will be prompted for your Heroku credentials, as well as an SSH key.

Listing 16-18. Logging in to Heroku from the Command Line

```
$ heroku login
```

Next, write your application as you normally would. As with Nodejitsu, your application will need a `package.json` file, as Heroku will use it to install your app. One point to note is that Heroku will assign a single port number to your application, regardless of what you specify in your code. The port number will be passed in from the command line, and you must account for this. Listing 16-19 shows how this is accomplished. Notice that the || operator is used to select a port if one is not specified in the environment. This allows the code to run locally as well as on Heroku.

Listing 16-19. Selecting a Port Number via an Environment Variable

```
var port = process.env.PORT || 8000;
```

Next, create a `Procfile`. The `Procfile` is a text file located in an application's root directory that includes the command used to start the program. Assuming that your program is stored in a file named `app.js`, Listing 16-20 shows an example `Procfile`. The `web` part of the `Procfile` denotes that the application will be attached to Heroku's HTTP routing stack and receive web traffic.

Listing 16-20. An Example Heroku `Procfile`

```
web: node app.js
```

Next, add your application files, `package.json`, `Procfile`, and anything other required files to a git repository. This is required, as Heroku uses `git` for deployment. A new `git` repository can be created using the commands shown in Listing 16-21. This assumes that you have `git` installed locally.

Listing 16-21. Commands to Create a `git` Repository for Your Application

```
$ git init
$ git add .
$ git commit -m "init"
```

The next step is to create the Heroku application. This is done using the command shown in Listing 16-22. You will want to replace app_name with your desired application name.

Listing 16-22. The Command Used to Create a Heroku Application

```
$ heroku apps:create app_name
```

The final step is to deploy your application using the `git` command shown in Listing 16-23. This command pushes your code to Heroku for deployment. Once your code is deployed, you can access your application at http://app_name.herokuapp.com, where app_name is your application's name.

Listing 16-23. The Command Used to Deploy a Heroku Application

```
$ git push heroku master
```

Summary

This chapter introduced a variety of techniques for scaling Node.js applications. We began by exploring the `cluster` module, which allows an application to take advantage of all of the cores that modern machines have to offer, despite JavaScript's single threaded nature. Next, we moved on to reverse proxy servers, which allow an application to be scaled across multiple machines. The reverse proxies discussed in this chapter can be combined with the `cluster` module to take advantage of multiple cores as well as multiple machines. Finally, the chapter concluded by exploring Node.js in the cloud. We examined two popular PaaS providers—Nodejitsu and Heroku.

This chapter concludes our exploration of the Node.js ecosystem. We sincerely hope that you have learned a lot by reading this book. We know that we have learned a lot by writing it. The book isn't *quite* finished, though. Please read on for a primer/refresher on JavaScript Object Notation (JSON).

APPENDIX A

■ ■ ■

JavaScript Object Notation

JavaScript Object Notation, or JSON, is a plain-text, data-interchange format based on a subset of the third edition of the ECMA-262 standard. JSON is used as a mechanism for serializing data structures into strings. These strings are often sent across networks, written to output files, or used for debugging. JSON is often touted as a "fat-free alternative to XML" because it provides the same functionality as XML, but typically requires fewer characters to do so. JSON is also much easier to parse compared to XML. Many developers have forgone XML in favor of JSON due to its simplicity and low overhead.

Syntactically, JSON is very similar to JavaScript's object literal syntax. JSON objects begin with an opening curly brace, {, and end with a closing curly brace, }. Between the curly braces are zero or more key/value pairs, known as *members*. Members are delimited by commas, while colons are used to separate a member's key from its corresponding value. The key must be a string enclosed in double quotes. This is the biggest difference from object literal syntax, which allows double quotes, single quotes, or no quotes at all. The format of the value depends on its data type. Listing A-1 shows a generic JSON string.

Listing A-1. A Generic Example of a JSON Object

```
{"key1": value1, "key2": value2, ..., "keyN": valueN}
```

■ **Note** The root of a piece of JSON is almost always an object. However, this is not an absolute requirement. The top level can also be an array.

Supported Data Types

JSON supports many of JavaScript's native data types. Specifically, JSON supports numbers, strings, Booleans, arrays, objects, and null. This section covers the details associated with each of the supported data types.

Numbers

JSON numbers must not have leading zeros, and must have at least one digit following a decimal point if one is present. Due to the restriction on leading zeros, JSON supports base-10 numbers only (octal and hexadecimal literals both require a leading zero). If you want to include numbers in other radixes, they must be converted to base-10 first. In Listing A-2, four different JSON strings are created. All of the JSON strings define a field named foo holding the decimal value 100. In the first string, the value of foo comes from the integer constant 100. In the second string, foo takes its value from the base-10 variable decimal. The third string, json3, takes its value from the base-8 variable octal, while json4 gets its value from the base-16 variable hex. All of the strings result in the same JSON string, despite the fact that some of the variables have a different radix. This is possible because the variables octal and hex are implicitly converted to base-10 numbers during string concatenation.

Listing A-2. An Example of Numbers Used in JSON Strings

```
var decimal = 100;
var octal = 0144; // JavaScript octals have a leading zero
var hex = 0x64;    // JavaScript hex numbers begin with 0x
var json1 = "{\"foo\":100}";
var json2 = "{\"foo\":" + decimal + "}";
var json3 = "{\"foo\":" + octal + "}";
var json4 = "{\"foo\":" + hex + "}";

// all JSON strings are {"foo":100}
```

The strings shown in Listing A-3 are not valid JSON because the non-decimal numbers are built directly into the string. In this example, there is no chance for the octal and hex literals to be converted to their decimal equivalents.

Listing A-3. An Example of Invalid Numeric Values in JSON Strings

```
var json1 = "{\"foo\":0144}";
var json2 = "{\"foo\":0x64}";
```

Strings

JSON strings are very similar to normal JavaScript strings. However, JSON requires strings to be enclosed in double quotes. Attempting to use single quotes will result in an error. In Listing A-4, a JSON string is created with a field named foo whose string value is bar.

Listing A-4. An Example of a JSON String Containing String Data

```
var json = "{\"foo\":\"bar\"}";

// json is {"foo":"bar"}
```

Booleans

JSON Booleans are identical to normal JavaScript Booleans, and can only hold the values true and false. The example in Listing A-5 creates a JSON string with two fields, foo and bar, which hold the Boolean values true and false, respectively.

Listing A-5. An Example of a JSON String Containing Boolean Data

```
var json = "{\"foo\":true, \"bar\":false}";

// json is {"foo":true, "bar":false}
```

Arrays

An *array* is an ordered sequence of values. JSON arrays begin with an opening square bracket, [, and end with a closing square bracket,]. Between the brackets are zero or more values, separated by commas. All of the values do not have to be of the same data type. Arrays can contain any of the data types supported by JSON, including nested arrays. Several JSON strings containing arrays are shown in Listing A-6. The foo array defined in json1 is empty, while the one defined in json2 holds two strings. The foo array defined in json3 is more complex—it holds a number, a Boolean, a nested array of strings, and an empty object.

Listing A-6. Examples of Arrays Within JSON Strings

```
var json1 = "{\"foo\":[]}";
var json2 = "{\"foo\":[\"bar\", \"baz\"]}";
var json3 = "{\"foo\":[100, true, [\"bar\", \"baz\"], {}]}";

// json1 is {"foo":[]}
// json2 is {"foo":["bar", "baz"]}
// json3 is {"foo":[100, true, ["bar", "baz"], {}]}
```

Objects

An *object* is an unordered collection of key/value pairs. As with arrays, objects can be composed of any of the data types supported by JSON. The example in Listing A-7 shows how JSON objects can be nested within each other.

Listing A-7. An Example of Nested Objects in JSON

```
var json = "{\"foo\":{\"bar\":{\"baz\":true}}}";

// json is {"foo":{"bar":{"baz":true}}}
```

null

JavaScript's null data type is also supported in JSON. Listing A-8 creates a JSON string with a null-valued field named foo.

Listing A-8. Using the null Data Type in a JSON String

```
var json = "{\"foo\":null}";

// json is {"foo":null}
```

Unsupported Data Types

A number of JavaScript's built-in data types are not supported by JSON. These types are undefined and the built-in objects Function, Date, RegExp, Error, and Math. undefined values simply cannot be represented in JSON, but the other unsupported types can be represented, if you use a little creativity. In order to serialize an unsupported data type, it must first be converted into some other representation that is JSON compliant. Although there is no standardized way of doing this, many of these data types can simply be converted to a string using the toString() method.

Functions for Working with JSON

Working with raw JSON strings can be tedious and error prone considering all of the braces and brackets that must be accounted for. In order to avoid this tedium, JavaScript provides a global JSON object for working with JSON data. The JSON object contains two methods—`stringify()` and `parse()`—which are used to serialize objects into JSON strings and deserialize JSON strings into objects. This section explains how these methods work in detail.

JSON.stringify()

`JSON.stringify()` is the recommended way to serialize JavaScript objects into JSON strings. The syntax for `stringify()` is shown in Listing A-9. The first argument, `value`, is the JavaScript object being stringified. The other two arguments, `replacer` and `space`, are optional and can be used to customize the stringification process. These arguments will be revisited shortly.

Listing A-9. Usage of the `JSON.stringify()` Method

```
JSON.stringify(value[, replacer[, space]])
```

The toJSON() Method

It is possible to customize the stringification process in several ways. One example of this is using the `toJSON()` method. During serialization, JSON checks the objects for a method named `toJSON()`. If this method exists then it is called by `stringify()`. Instead of processing the original object, `stringify()` will serialize whatever value is returned by `toJSON()`. This is how JavaScript's Date objects are serialized. Since JSON does not support the Date type, Date objects come equipped with a `toJSON()` method.

Listing A-10 shows `toJSON()` in action. In the example, an object named obj is created with the fields foo, bar, and baz. When obj is stringified, its `toJSON()` method is called. In this example, `toJSON()` returns a copy of obj, minus the foo field. The copy of obj is serialized, resulting in a JSON string containing only the bar and baz fields.

Listing A-10. An Example Using a Custom `toJSON()` Method

```javascript
var obj = {foo: 0, bar: 1, baz: 2};

obj.toJSON = function() {
  var copy = {};

  for (var key in this) {
    if (key === "foo") {
      continue;
    } else {
      copy[key] = this[key];
    }
  }

  return copy;
};

var json = JSON.stringify(obj);

console.log(json);

//json is {"bar":1,"baz":2}
```

The `replacer` Argument

The `replacer` argument to `JSON.stringify()` can be used as a function that takes two arguments representing a key/value pair. First, the function is called with an empty key, and the object being serialized as the value. The `replacer()` function must check for the empty string as the key in order to handle this case. Next, each of the object's properties and corresponding value are passed to the `replacer()`, one by one. The value returned by `replacer()` is used in the stringification process. An example `replacer()` function, with no customized behavior, is shown in Listing A-11.

Listing A-11. An Example `replacer()` Function with no Custom Behavior

```
function(key, value) {
  // check for the top level object
  if (key === "") {
    return value;
  } else {
    return value;
  }
}
```

It is important to handle the top-level object properly. Typically, it is best to simply return the object's value. In the example in Listing A-12, the top-level object returns the string foo. Therefore, no matter how the object's properties are handled, `stringify()` will always just return foo.

Listing A-12. A `replacer()` Function that Serializes Any Object as the String foo

```
function(key, value) {
  if (key === "") {
    return "foo";
  } else {
    // this is now irrelevant
    return value;
  }
}
```

In Listing A-13, an object is serialized using a custom `replacer()` function named `filter()`. The job of the `filter()` function is to serialize numeric values only. All non-numeric fields will return an `undefined` value. Fields that return undefined are automatically removed from the stringified object. In this example, the `replacer()` function causes baz to be dropped because it holds a string.

Listing A-13. An Example `replacer()` Function that Only Serializes Numbers

```
function filter(key, value) {
  // check for the top level object
  if (key === "") {
    return value;
  } else if (typeof value === "number") {
    return value;
  }
}
```

```
var obj = {foo: 0, bar: 1, baz: "x"};
var json = JSON.stringify(obj, filter);

console.log(json);
// json is {"foo":0,"bar":1}
```

The Array Form of `replacer`

The `replacer` argument can also hold an array of strings. Each string represents the name of a field that should be serialized. Any field that is not included in the `replacer` array will not be included in the JSON string. In the example in Listing A-14, an object is defined with fields named `foo` and `bar`. An array is also defined, containing the strings `foo` and `baz`. During stringification, the `bar` field is dropped because it is not part of the `replacer` array. Note that a `baz` field is not created because, although it is defined in the `replacer` array, it is not defined in the original object. This leaves `foo` as the only field in the stringified object.

Listing A-14. An Example of the `replacer` Argument as an Array

```
var obj = {foo: 0, bar: 1};
var arr = ["foo", "baz"];
var json = JSON.stringify(obj, arr);

console.log(json);
// json is {"foo":0}
```

The `space` Argument

JSON strings are commonly viewed for logging and debugging purposes. In order to aid readability, the `stringify()` function supports a third argument named `space`, which allows the developer to format whitespace in the resulting JSON string. This argument can be a number or a string. If `space` is a number then up to 10 space characters can be used as whitespace. If the value is less than one then no spaces are used. If the value exceeds 10 then the maximum value of 10 is used. If `space` is a string then that string is used as whitespace. If the string length is greater than 10, then only the first 10 characters are used. If `space` is omitted or `null`, then no whitespace is used. Listing A-15 shows how the space argument is used.

Listing A-15. An Example of Stringification Using the `space` Argument

```
var obj = {
  foo: 0,
  bar: [null, true, false],
  baz: {
    bizz: "boff"
  }
};
var json1 = JSON.stringify(obj, null, "  ");
var json2 = JSON.stringify(obj, null, 2);

console.log(json1);
console.log(json2);
```

In Listing A-15, the JSON strings in `json1` and `json2` end up being identical. The resulting JSON is shown in Listing A-16. Notice that the string now spans multiple lines and the properties are indented by an additional two spaces as nesting increases. For non-trivial objects, this formatting greatly improves readability.

Listing A-16. The Formatted JSON String Generated in Listing A-15

```
{
  "foo": 0,
  "bar": [
    null,
    true,
    false
  ],
  "baz": {
    "bizz": "boff"
  }
}
```

JSON.parse()

To build a JavaScript object from a JSON-formatted string, you use the JSON.parse() method. parse() provides the inverse functionality of stringify(). It is used as a safer alternative to eval(), because, while eval() will execute arbitrary JavaScript code, parse() was designed to only handle valid JSON strings.

The syntax of the parse() method is shown in Listing A-17. The first argument, text, is a JSON-formatted string. If text is not a valid JSON string, a SyntaxError exception will be thrown. This exception will be thrown synchronously, meaning that try...catch...finally statements can be used with parse(). If no problems are encountered, parse() returns a JavaScript object corresponding to the JSON string. parse() also takes an optional second argument named reviver, which will be covered shortly.

Listing A-17. Usage of the JSON.parse() Method

```
JSON.parse(text[, reviver])
```

In Listing A-18, the parse() method is used to construct an object from a JSON string. The resulting object, stored in obj, has two properties—foo and bar—which hold the numeric values 10 and 20.

Listing A-18. An Example of Using JSON.parse() to Deserialize a JSON String

```
var string = "{\"foo\":10, \"bar\":20}";
var obj = JSON.parse(string);

console.log(obj.foo);
console.log(obj.bar);
// obj.foo is equal to 10
// obj.bar is equal to 20
```

The reviver() Argument

The second argument to parse(), reviver(), is a function that allows an object to be transformed during parsing. As each property is parsed from the JSON string it is run through the reviver() function. The value returned by reviver() is used as the property's value in the constructed object. If an undefined value is returned by reviver() then the property is removed from the object.

The reviver() function takes two arguments, the property name (key) and its parsed value (value). reviver() should always check the key argument for the empty string. The reason is, after reviver() is called on each individual property, it is called on the constructed object. On the last call to reviver(), the empty string is passed as the key argument, and the constructed object is passed as value. After taking this case into consideration, an example reviver() function with no customization is shown in Listing A-19.

Listing A-19. An Example reviver() Function

```javascript
function(key, value) {
  // check for the top level object
  if (key === "") {
    // be sure to return the top level object
    // otherwise the constructed object will be undefined
    return value;
  } else {
    // return the original untransformed value
    return value;
  }
}
```

In Listing A-20, an object is constructed from a JSON string using a custom reviver() function named square(). As the name implies, square() squares the value of each property encountered during parsing. This causes the values of the foo and bar properties to become 100 and 400 after parsing.

Listing A-20. An Example Using JSON.parse() and a Custom reviver() Function

```javascript
function square(key, value) {
  if (key === "") {
    return value;
  } else {
    return value * value;
  }
}

var string = "{\"foo\":10, \"bar\":20}";
var obj = JSON.parse(string, square);

console.log(obj.foo);
console.log(obj.bar);
// obj.foo is 100
// obj.bar is 400
```

■ **Note** Both JSON.parse() and JSON.stringify() are synchronous methods that can throw exceptions. Therefore, any use of these methods should be wrapped in a try...catch statement.

Summary

JSON is used extensively in the Node ecosystem, as you've undoubtedly seen by now. For example, any package worth using will contain a package.json file. In fact, a package.json is required in order for a module to be used with npm. Nearly every data API is built using JSON as well, as the Node community has a strong preference toward JSON, as opposed to XML. Therefore, understanding JSON is critical to using Node effectively. Luckily, JSON is simple to read, write, and understand. After reading this chapter, you should understand JSON well enough to use it in your own applications, or interface with other applications that do (for example, RESTful web services).

Index